Making All Th...gs New

Making All Things New

*Women's Ordination – A Catalyst for Change
in the Roman Catholic Church*

Dorothea McEwan and Myra Poole

With an Afterword by
John Wijngaards

CANTERBURY
PRESS
Norwich

© Dorothea McEwan and Myra Poole 2003

First published in 2003 by the Canterbury Press Norwich
(a publishing imprint of Hymns Ancient & Modern Limited,
a registered charity)
St Mary's Works, St Mary's Plain,
Norwich, Norfolk, NR3 3BH

www.scm-canterburypress.co.uk

British Library Cataloguing in Publication data

A catalogue record for this book is available
from the British Library

ISBN 1-85311-528-2

Typeset by Rowland Phototypesetting Ltd,
Bury St Edmunds, Suffolk
Printed in Great Britain by
St Edmundsbury Press Ltd, Bury St Edmunds, Suffolk

Contents

Acknowledgements   vii

Preface   ix

Part One   How Did We Get Here?

1   The State We Are In   3

2   Lifting the Stained Glass Ceiling – Who and
What is Church?   21

3   Tools for Change – Equality and Difference   42

Part Two   Steps Towards Change

4   Bringing Women in From the Cold   61

5   The No Chat Show – Silencing Women   65

6   Women's Experiences – a Source for Change   82

7   Ludmila Javorova's Call to Priesthood   118

8   Christine Mayr-Lumetzberger and the
Ordinations on the Danube   129

9   Public Action   152

Part Three   A Vision for the Future

10   Making All Things New   173

Afterword by John Wijngaards
  Autonomy Versus Authority?   180

Notes   207
Bibliography   233

Acknowledgements

This book grew out of the generosity of many women and men concerned about 'church' at present. While people hunger for spiritual, religious or theological nourishment, they feel that their church does not understand their needs. As authors we attempted to present a picture of people's hopes and fears, their visions of church and their practical steps towards realizing that vision. We approached and were approached by many people while researching this book. We made a deliberate decision to present views from what can loosely be termed the Western world, wishing to follow up this book with a similar study of the hopes and experiences of people in Asia and Africa.

Our thanks go to all those who gave us their time and were willing to share their stories of inspiration, frustration and even despair. In particular we wish to thank Marie Bouclin, Anne Martin, Andrea Johnson, Judith McKloskey, Mary Ann Rossi, Sue Williamson, Ruth Schäfer, Petronella Phillips-Devaney and Barry Phillips-Devaney for their insights summarized in Chapter 6, Christine Mayr-Lumetzberger in Chapter 8, Janice Sèvre-Duszynska, Mary Hunt and Diann Neu in Chapter 9, and John Wijngaards for his Afterword.

Scores of chats and phone conversations informed us of many group actions, organisations and campaigns. The writing of the text, multiple re-writings and discussions were sometimes hard work, sometimes exhilarating and fun. Our thanks go especially to Pat Pinsent for very kindly reading the first draft and offering important comments, to our editor at the Canterbury Press, and to our friends and families for putting up with us with patience and forbearance during a time of intense writing.

Although this book has been written from a Roman Catholic perspective, it has also been written for all in search of new ways of approaching theology, being 'church', and simply getting on with a living spirituality in our midst.

Dorothea McEwan and Myra Poole SND
Easter 2003

Preface

The trigger for this book was preparing for and attending the First International Conference of Women's Ordination Worldwide (WOW) in Dublin, Ireland, 2001. WOW was founded at the First European Women's Synod in Gmunden, Austria, 1996. Although its origin was ecumenical, and this still remains the vision of WOW, at this moment in time it is mainly working towards the ordination of women in the Roman Catholic tradition. The authors come from that tradition and bring with them long experience of its many facets. As the book concentrates on this tradition only, the Church referred to is the Roman Catholic Church.

The authors were interested in listening not only to the stories of those who have a call to ordained ministry but also to their ideas for the transformation of Church in attitudes and structures. For this reason, the book is divided into three parts, using the pastoral model of reflection in Part One, of action in Part Two and of reflection in Part Three. It became very clear to the authors in writing the book that the question of women's ordination is wrongly placed in systematic theology. Its real place lies in the evolving social teaching of the Church, since the non-ordination of women is not a part of revelation but a part of the inherited general, historical understanding of women as inferior beings to men.

Part One is a mainly theoretical introduction to the problems facing the Church today. It includes a brief survey of the history of the over-centralization of the Church, accompanied by an introduction to the official church documents that clearly limit women's role. These documents form the backdrop to the book. Other topics discussed in this part are the re-imaging of some inherited models of Church, the dangers of co-dependency and addiction within the present system, and the importance of the feminist debate of equality and difference mirrored in feminist philosophy, psychology and scripture.

The case stories in Part Two exemplify the variety of theories expressed in Part One. Each of the eight women and one man who speak has a long history of living and serving within the Church, and most of them still do so. Some of them attended the WOW Conference in Dublin. While relating their personal stories of being silenced and side-lined by the Church, they also reflect on the urgent need for new ways of being Church. Separate chapters are devoted to different forms of public action, including the ordinations of Ludmila Javorova, in the underground Church of Czechoslovakia, and Christine Mayr-Lumetzberger, spokeswoman for the ordinations in Austria in June 2002. Whether or not readers agree with the various responses in this book, they reflect a growing awareness that the 'People of God' are crying out for change. The people whose stories are told here see telling the truth of their own experience as prophecy.

The title of the book and of the final chapter, in Part Three, *Making All Things New*, reflects the authors' desire to place the call for the ordination of women within a vision of an inclusive ecclesiology that accepts rather than rejects the long neglected experiences and viewpoints of women. Although the authors concentrate on change, particularly in the RC Church, they understand that change will only bear fruit in an ecumenical setting that includes the Orthodox. Throughout the book, the emphasis is on building up the local Church as the centre and core of a life shared by an inclusive international Church, where love, compassion and hope have a home.

Autonomy versus authority is the major theme developed by John Wijngaards in the Afterword. He names those who cling to traditional certainties as the 'security seekers', juxtaposing them with the generation of people of all ages who are progressively becoming 'fulfilment seekers'. The consequence of the change from being a security seeker to a fulfilment seeker is a growing resistance to religious creeds and organizations that impose restrictions on personal views and behaviour.

The experiences narrated in this book demonstrate how friction is often a trigger for change. The case stories of the people in this book are an inspiration and provide a model to others on how to deal creatively and positively with a Church that does not have the will to embrace the discipline of real dialogue with its members. The authors' aim throughout has been to take a long loving look at the Church – not to destroy it, but rather, by loyal critique, to help it reflect more profoundly the mind of Christ, the 'cornerstone' of any Christian Church.

Dorothea McEwan and Myra Poole SND

Part One

How Did We Get Here?

I

The State We Are In

This book is written from the viewpoint of women and their present position in the Roman Catholic Church. Adrian B. Smith in his book *A Reason for Living and Hoping*[1] concentrates on the sweeping changes we are faced with and the new, emerging era of what he calls 'metaphysical consciousness'. His and many other books are part of the reflection that follows the example of Alvin Toffler's ground-breaking book *Future Shock*, first published in 1970.[2] 'Future shock' is a term used by Toffler to diagnose the inability of individuals and communities to cope with change as a problem, naming those concerned as 'museum pieces'.

The debate continues on how to prevent this disease spreading further in the RC Church, already seen by many as becoming an interesting but irrelevant museum piece of a dying 'patriarchal' age. To this end is shown the importance of women's insights and their possibility of transforming all areas of church life. Each chapter points the way towards a new approach to becoming Church, and the experiences narrated in Part Two illustrate that approaches vary according to local and personal circumstances. What arises from these stories are various processes crucial to any changing of the horizon of who and what is Church, the underlying question throughout the book.

The subject matter is the RC tradition, from which all the contributors come, and which is numerically one of the largest, still holding sway over many people's religious, emotional and psychological lives. But there are now clear signs that this firm hold is beginning to change rapidly. Some contributors were born into this tradition but found it wanting as they grew up, in both the intellectual and spiritual spheres. Some chose to stay and change the Church from within, others chose to leave but still feel a bond and responsibility towards it. The people who have written for this book, mainly women, are a small but significant section affected by the malaise that has struck deeply into the RC tradition.

The opening up and developing of all forms of ministry, as well as ordained ministry and leadership roles for women, is a question deeply embedded in the need for a radical revisioning of Church, 'to make and unmake again where much unmaking reigns', to use the well-known words of the poet Adrienne Rich.[3] Therefore, it is not just about enlarging the horizons of Church, for example 'include women and stir', but about changing the very horizon of who and what is Church.

The latter is a much greater task, and will take more time and many small clearly defined steps of which keeping the discussion of women's ordination to the fore is a crucial aspect. It is a reminder that women's ordination is only the beginning for serious church reform. It is pointless unless all work for deeper change in creating a less hierarchical and a more democratic and inclusive Church. A part of this process will be the breaking up of fossilized liturgies and developing new modes of liturgical expression that will include not only new metaphors for God but liturgies that reflect the life experiences of women and men.[4]

The present unrest manifests itself in unresolved moral and theological questions such as sexual orientation, contraception, abortion, women's ordination and genuine dialogue within Christian denominations, between denominations and with other faiths. But there can be no satisfying solutions to these issues until the over-arching problem of what has become known as 'high papalism' is tackled. This is an ecclesiology that gives too much emphasis to Rome at the expense of the importance

of local Church. The resulting over-centralization has deep historical roots, which have given too much power to the body of
people known as the Curia, which presides in Rome, to carry
out the daily business of the Church. An example of the negative
effect of over-centralization is the paedophilia scandal and the
crisis it has brought in its wake:

> The abuse has nothing to do with contraception, the ordina-
> tion of women, homosexuality or any other issue ... It has
> everything to do with centuries' old clerical culture and the
> attempt to maintain the fiction of a body of men who are not
> as other men and are beyond criticism. The cure goes beyond
> the departure of Cardinal Law and others who should join
> him. The whole system, which can now only be called as
> corrupt, needs a reformation as radical as that introduced by
> the Council of Trent.[5]

High Papalism

'High papalism' is a term frequently used as the effects of centralization of power in Rome become more evident. The papacy
has become the supreme authority within the Church, with no
checks or balances built into the system, whereas the original
idea of papacy was that of a bridge-builder. The importance of
the local Church is almost in abeyance, which results in a distorted idea of Church that leaves behind the spirit and teaching
of Vatican II, exemplified in *Lumen Gentium* and *Gaudium et
Spes*.

In order to correct this imbalance it is necessary to have some
understanding of the meaning of *primacy* and *infallibility* within
the Church. But the present understanding of the role of the
papacy is so deeply rooted in the Catholic psyche that any open
discussion on these subjects is often met with shock, horror and
total disbelief. It does seem that high papalism has reached its
apogee in the pontificate of John Paul II. Fundamentally the
present question among a growing majority in all churches is

not only 'what is Church?', but above all 'who is Church?', placing the emphasis on the relational rather than institutional aspect of Church. In this ecumenical age this is the most fundamental question to which many are searching an answer.[6]

Historically there are two ways of understanding *primacy*. The present interpretation is that the Pope has primacy in all spiritual, theological and moral questions, accountable to no one but God, leading many to question whether the Pope is himself outside the Church. The other interpretation of *primacy* is that the Pope is *primus inter pares*, one among equals. This has equal historical roots but is less well known to many. The revival of this lost dimension of shared authority between people, theologians, bishops and pope needs urgent historical recovery for institutional and personal transformation. Summed up in the words of Alvin Toffler: 'The illiterate of the future will not be those who cannot read and write, but those who cannot learn, unlearn and relearn.'[7]

The second concept embedded in high papalism is the exaggerated notion of *infallibility*. With the unification of Italy at the end of the nineteenth century, the Church lost much of its temporal power and was reduced to a small papal state. It was at this moment of crisis for the Church that the First Vatican Council was held and witnessed the passing of one of the most controversial and complicated decrees in church history – *Pastor Aeternus* (1870). In this decree the papacy, not the Pope, was declared 'infallible' in all matters of spiritual and moral doctrine. The Council also spoke of the 'infallibility' of the magisterium and the 'reception' by the People of God of any pronouncement. In fact infallibility has only been exercised once since that time, for the declaration of the Assumption of Our Lady in 1950, by Pius XII. The real sense of infallibility was understood in a much more restricted sense than it is understood by the present papacy and Curia. Pius XII (1939–58) followed the understanding of infallibility as laid down in *Pastor Aeternus* and consulted all the world's bishops before the dogma was declared. It is only in the papacy of John Paul II that this consultation has not been adhered to and applied to secondary matters of faith, for example women's ordination.

History used as a critical tool enables us to understand present-day reality. It is salutary to remember that there are three aspects to Church, the institutional, the critical and the mystical. Today the institutional is grossly overdeveloped, and so we are experiencing, as at other times of institutional crisis, the rise and rise of the critical and mystical Church within the People of God.[8]

A Brief History of an Over-Centralized Church

In the first millennium the Church was highly decentralized and characterized by service, *diakonia*. The second millennium was characterized by power over others, *potestas*. There is hope that the third millennium will be characterized by participation and balance.

At this time it is the aspect of power over others that is enjoying a prolonged if increasingly battered life. This form of high papalism has been developing since the beginning of the second millennium with the growth of towns and universities, especially in Northern Italy, and above all with the pervading medieval conflict of power between the Emperor of the Holy Roman Empire[9] and the papacy. This destructive struggle ended in a victory for the papacy[10] and the Pope's retention of supreme authority in both temporal and spiritual affairs throughout the known world. From the time of Gregory VII (1073–85) the emphasis shifted from the Pope as Bishop of Rome providing a service of leadership in the Church and a focus for unity, to an increasing emphasis on the secular as well as the spiritual leadership of the papacy.

With the rise of universities and the development of Canon Law a legalistic approach began to permeate church life and the medieval debate about Church centred 'on the origin and legal scope of papal power'.[11] Throughout the struggle with the Empire, and in the period following, canonical theories of power continued to develop as expressed by the introduction of clerical celibacy at the Fourth Lateran Council in 1215, presided over by Pope Innocent III (1198–1216). He claimed for himself and his successors *plenitudo potestatis*, the fullness of power, which in canonical thought became synonymous with primacy. So, in practice, sovereignty and primacy came to denote the same thing. The papacy could claim it was the source of all power, spiritual and temporal, as expressed in the bull *Unam Sanctam*, The One, Holy Catholic Church, by Boniface VIII in 1302. *Primacy* was defined in legal terms only and was split off from any theological definition of Church. This concept of papal supremacy, *plenitudo potestatis*, was severely attacked in its own time, but it has remained an underlying, unorthodox tradition ready to be used at will.

The Conciliarist Tradition of the Church – Where does Supreme Authority Lie?

The essence of the conciliarist tradition is the belief that the Pope is one among equals, *primus inter pares*, and that the supreme authority in the Church lies in the Church in Council, of which the Pope is the leading member. This principle was upheld at the Council of Constance (1414–18), called to heal the schism in the Church, to eradicate heresies and to reform the corrupt morals of the Church. Two important decrees were issued, *Haec Sancta* (1415) and *Frequens* (1417).[12] In brief, *Haec Sancta* stated that the Pope is bound to obey the Council[13] and this was consolidated by the decree *Frequens*, which formalized the calling of councils at least every ten years. The Council of Constance had a lot in common with the inspirations of Vatican II (1962–65) and as such deserves to be better known and re-embraced as a part of the tradition of the Church.

In the wake of the Reformation in the sixteenth century, the Council of Trent (between 1545 and 1563) reclaimed the high medieval tradition of *plenitudo potestatis*, reinstating the Pope as the supreme authority in the Church. The Council aimed to reform the inner life of the Church by establishing seminaries for a renewed priesthood. From these reforms the Church developed into a highly centralized, clericalized, sacramental Church, and this remained the dominant model of Church until the calling of the Second Vatican Council by John XXIII in the 1960s. Although this model of Church flourished, it was severely weakened almost to the point of extinction in France in the early years of the French Revolution in the eighteenth century.

The First Vatican Council of 1870 has already been mentioned in connection with the question of *primacy* and *infallibility*. The outcome of this Council precipitated a watershed in church history – an escalation in the centralization of the Church under the papacy. This is reflected in the first full code of Canon Law in 1917 and in the further erosion of the rights of the local bishops and hence the local Church. The bishops had to ask for more and more permissions, known as 'exceptions', from Rome, even in minor things, such as asking for permission for nuns to wash altar cloths! This concept of a uniform Church, down to the smallest detail, was also reflected in the Constitutions of Religious Congregations and led to a stifling of the full understanding of their charisms.[14]

Strengths and Weaknesses of Vatican II

For those who lived through and experienced the excitement of the possibility for radical change in a Church they loved, the 1960s were truly 'heady' days. In many ways it was the halcyon time of the RC tradition when everything was possible. The Council was led by one of the greatest popes in history, John XXIII (1958–63). The election of a man of eighty years of age was a surprise to the world. Many were to experience a Church where Pope, bishops and the People of God worked together to allow the Holy Spirit to move freely in their midst. It is important to note that the teachings of Vatican II were founded more directly on the Bible than any other previous ecumenical council.

The pastoral, theological and scriptural insights of this Council owe much to the great theologians, mostly French and German, who attended this as the *periti* (experts) of the Council, who had been burrowing away at a renewed theology and who now came into their own: Yves Congar on ecclesiology and ecumenism, Henri de Lubac on the supernatural, Marie-Dominique Chenu on the 'world' and work, and the all-round contribution of Karl Rahner SJ and Hans Küng. Abbot Bishop Christopher Butler was the outstanding British theologian at this Council. A man greatly influenced by Cardinal Newman's *Essay on the Development of Doctrine* and by Friedrich von Hugel's perception of the three elements necessary for any church, the mystical, prophetic/critical and institutional. All these elements are reflected in the leading role he played at the Council, but especially in the drafting of the Constitution on Divine Revelation.[15]

The Council produced sixteen documents but the centre-piece of the whole Council was the 'Dogmatic Constitution on the Church', *Lumen Gentium*, whose spirit summarized the major achievements of the Council. It began with a view of Church as Mystery, a communion of women and men called together to participate in the life of the Trinity, using the scriptural terminology of the People of God as the Temple of the Holy Spirit. This was a significant departure from the dominant understanding of Church prevalent since 1870. The scriptural emphasis on the People of God was marked by a specific shift towards a renewed ecclesiology of local Church and the collegiality of the bishops, although the word collegiality was never mentioned. Here as elsewhere the Council placed great stress on the theology of the local Church, thus emphasizing the community aspect of Church in dioceses, parishes, etc.

This perspective is also evident in the Decree on the 'Church's Missionary Activity', *Ad Gentes*, and in the Constitution of the Church in the Modern World, '*The Joys and Hopes*', *Gaudium et Spes*. It presents the Church as sharing in the joys, hopes, grief and anguish of the modern world. In these documents was enshrined the most important principle of all, that of *primacy of conscience* beyond any institutional interpretation: 'In the depths of his [her] conscience . . . is the most sacred core and sanctuary of a man (and of a woman) . . .' (no. 16, *Gaudium et Spes*).[16] This wonderful spiritual freedom is further extended to all religions in the document on 'The Declaration on Religious Freedom' (*Dignitatis humanae*). In these three documents the Church proposed a far more open attitude to the individual conscience and the modern world than had been characteristic in the preceding 150 years. John XXIII followed this up in 1963 with his encyclical entitled *Pacem in Terris*, which contains the famous statement: 'Those who know they have rights must claim them' (*Pacem in Terris*, paragraph 36:17).

However, before leaving this section it is important to point out a major weakness of the Council. Although the diversity of views expressed at the Council were a welcome change, no bias towards one view or another was expressed in the documents that followed. They were held in equal balance. This resulted in ambivalence and compromises built into all the Council's documents, including *Lumen Gentium*.[17] In the aftermath of the Council the results of this have become clear and are mirrored in the tensions within the Church of our time.

After the Council

The immediate response to the spirit of the Council was a feeling of great creativity. It was this spirit that lay the foundations for the burgeoning of women's theology and spirituality. First in the field was Mary Daly, who was led to reflect on the rights of women in the Church, inspired by the words and spirit of John XXIII. In her first book *The Church and the Second Sex* (1971), she began to expose the defects in women's role in the Church, followed swiftly by a development in her thought in her second book *Beyond God the Father* (1973). Daly's spiritual journey has led her out of the RC tradition into what she calls her 'Be-Dazzling Voyage' in *Outercourse* and 'galactic space' (1993).[18]

The two other firsts in the field were Elisabeth Schüssler Fiorenza (scripture) and Rosemary Radford Ruether (theology). Although the stance of these women was radical they did not follow the same course as Daly but remained as prophets within the Church – as academics and activists. The growth of women's theology was one of the most positive and freeing outcomes of the Council, although a totally unforeseen one. Meanwhile during the pontificate of Paul VI it became clear that the application of the spirit of the Council and the Decrees were proving hard to apply in life.

The ambivalence in the Vatican documents prepared the ground for the gradual erosion of the spirit of Vatican II during the papacies of both Paul VI (1963–78) and John Paul II (1978–). In fact a renewed understanding of primacy as well as infallibility is at the heart of the present unrest in the Church. The struggle for the right relationship between the present understanding of hierarchical authority and that of the believing people is illustrated in the issuing of *Humanae Vitae* on 25 July 1968, the document that stated that contraception was inherently evil, and which led later to the silencing of some of the best moral theologians, such as Charles Curran, on this and other issues. But it was Hans Küng, a prominent theologian at the Council, who was the first to be challenged. To the surprise of all, after an eight-year sometimes bitter struggle with the Vatican, the *missio canonica* issued against him in December 1979 was the mildest of rebukes from the Vatican. The Vatican did not take away his right to teach except on the disputed point of infallibility.

As more and more theologians began to assert their authority to write and speak freely, the Vatican issued on 24 May 1990 the *Instruction on the Ecclesial Vocation of the Theologian*, signed by Cardinal Ratzinger, the head of the Congregation for the Doctrine of the Faith (CDF). Initially it seemed the Instruction had much to recommend it, but the freedom of the theologian was immediately eroded as it clearly stated that the papal magisterium was the only source of accuracy, and any speculative deviation from this teaching was not acceptable. Moreover, when the magisterium speaks in a 'definitive' way the theologian must submit his 'will and intellect' to it. The concept of the theologian as prophet, a marked feature of the Council, was brought under fire.

This Instruction was followed up by the Apostolic Letter *Ad Tuendam Fidem* (1998), which now demanded a profession of faith, even in secondary matters, to the teaching magisterium of the Church by all teaching theologians. It aimed to protect the Christian faith against errors arising from some members. During the very latter part of the twentieth century women, including Religious women, also began to come under scrutiny from the same authority as authentic witnesses to how far they have grown in stature as thinkers within the Catholic tradition.

The irony is that many of these people who Rome has tried to silence have not left the Church but remained with their former authority stripped from them, but not their power to influence. Peter Hebblethwaite says of these people in his book *The Runaway Church* (1978) that 'They can no more leave the Church than they can leave humanity. To do so would be a form of spiritual suicide' (p. 236). Many, however, now ply their trade outside Catholic institutions, including Catholic publishers, to enable them to work according to the principles of religious freedom laid down in Vatican II.

Women and High Papalism – the Charade at the Vatican

It was during the early 1970s, thanks to the leadership of the Canadian bishops, that the question of women's role in the Church began to be discussed, particularly the question of the ordination of women. It was a topic that was discussed with some urgency and as a real possibility. Paul VI struggled to hold the opposing views of bishops together, but in the end the views of the *status quo* prevailed and Paul VI issued the now infamous document *Inter Insigniores* in 1976.

It is important to note that *Inter Insigniores* was a major shift in the argument of the non-ordination of women into a different area of theology, away from the male headship of St Paul and into the symbolic area of theology, declaring women could never be priests, because priests had to be male to be 'icons' of Christ. In shorthand this means biological males, irrespective of gifts and calling of the Holy Spirit. It is this argument that still prevails at the beginning of the third millennium and it was the Decree that first sparked off movements for the ordination of women and eventually a general flurry of books for and against the ordination of women.

There is no doubt this document remains one of the most controversial of his pontificate and the cause of much of the major unease in the Church. *Humanae Vitae* has long been disregarded by the majority of Catholics and relegated to the footnotes of history, whereas the controversy over women's role and place in the Church is one of the major issues to be faced if the Church is to have any relevance in the twenty-first century. It is an issue that has not been and will not be swept under the carpet. The more it is, the stronger it grows. *Inter Insigniores* was followed in 1988 with *Mulieris Dignitatem*, purported to be on the *Dignity of Women*. The key argument in this document is that women are 'equal but special' but their specialness does not spread to a place of equality in the Church on earth, only in heaven. In theological terms it is 'eschatological equality'. It is a clear statement of the outmoded anthropology on women in the Church that underpins the supposed 'icon' argument of why women cannot be priests. These points are more fully explained in Chapter 2.

Following the thought laid down in these two documents, John Paul II issued an Apostolic Letter in 1994 entitled *On Reserving Priestly Ordination to Men Alone, Ordinatio Sacerdotalis*, making the non-ordination of women as close to a definition of infallibility as possible. In theological terms it was called 'definitive', in the light of the 1990 *Instruction*, despite the fact there was no consultation with bishops before the Letter was issued, neither has there been 'reception' on this question by the faithful. A request for clarification called *Dubium* was followed by a *Responsum* by Cardinal Ratzinger, of the CDF, underlining even further the impossibility of ordaining women and claiming that it belongs to the deposit of faith. Women, it seems, were becoming such a danger to the Church that a single papal announcement was no longer enough. It even demanded a Curia response. Was the Vatican panicking?

An outcry in the press and in personal writings followed. The irrepressible Joan Chittister OSB spoke of this last Letter as a 'Dubious Dubium' challenging the whole 'definitive' basis of these Letters and questioning why basic beliefs such as the presence of Jesus in the Eucharist had not been declared infallible as well as the number of sacraments in the Church. She also reflected on the shift to the 'gender' argument in these last three documents away from the former Pauline theology of male headship. Chittister concluded her talk in the following words:

> This document has brought us to the end of 'ordinary time'. It is the catalyst for change, for it brings the pinnacles of insight, of what the Church should not be, as well as to what the Church should be. A Church at last truly in the image of God: 'In our own image let us make them male and female.' Only when this Church images God, will we know that God is in this Church.[19]

United Nations and High Papalism

The infiltration of high papalism into international organizations like the League of Nations and the United Nations goes back to the early part of the twentieth century. After the annexation of the Papal States by Italy in 1870, the territory of the Holy See was reduced to a small area, known as the Vatican City. As the Holy See still had some territorial basis, it requested membership of the League of Nations in the 1920s. This request was turned down because its status was unlike that of any other constituent state in the League of Nations. However, the Vatican

City was admitted to the World Telegraph Union and the Universal Postal Union in 1929 and little by little sought observer status in a number of specialized agencies of the UN, from 1948 onwards. It was under the leadership of the Secretary General U Thant that the Holy See was accepted as a permanent observer in the New York headquarters, the Geneva Office, the Office of the UN High Commissioner for Refugees, the World Health Organization, the International Labour Organization, the UN Conference on Trade and Development, the United Nations Industrial Development Organization, and the World Trade Organization.

The Papal State, Vatican City, is a state in name but not in reality: it is not composed of a self-perpetuating population and has none of the elements of a truly modern democratic state. Except for a tiny minority of female administrative staff and cleaners it is composed of men, gathered together from many countries, who elect to live in Rome. It is a tiny non-representative geographical enclave in the midst of another state, Italy. This 'state', however, behaves as though it were a normal state, making laws and stating values without due dialogue and representation from all segments of society around the globe. Moreover, these attitudes and laws are considered binding on all Roman Catholics. Membership of the United Nations is an attempted extension of this power and the Holy See exercises unaccountable influence through its membership in these international bodies. Although some aspects of the work of the Vatican at the UN are fruitful, especially on world peace and helping developing nations, the voting behaviour of the Vatican representatives has become notorious when it comes to resolutions on women's equality. The United Nations Conference on Women at Beijing in 1994 is an example of this influence. This led, in the latter part of the twentieth century, to the development of a strong movement, originating in the USA, called 'See Change'. This movement is working towards the removal of the special status that has been granted to the Holy See at the UN.

High Papalism and the Growth of Fundamentalism

Fundamentalism is not a new concept, it has always been around and always will be. It is the one-sided expression of opinion, the pick and choose of doctrine, where concepts of autonomy are shown the red card of theonomy, the rule of God, where professionalism counts less than the simple fact of pastors having been anointed to expound moral views, where the roles of philosophy, logics and ethics have to be made subservient to a narrow interpretation of faith: dogmatism versus pragmatism. Today, dogmatism has become largely discredited as it leads to an impasse, to a scenario where unthinking obedience can be forced upon everybody. Cultural contexts are not allowed to determine theological practice, and a spirit of enquiry or experimentation is actively discouraged. And yet, enquiry – the emergence and re-emergence of an enquiring, sceptical and analytical mind – is important to achieve the moral and mental health of the Church.

Findings from the social sciences are also not applied, temporary alliances are entered into with Evangelical Christians or Muslims when it suits the Vatican to push through a United Nations resolution.[20] Fundamentalists do not respect the totality of a belief system, they stress a limited view of scriptures because it is enough for them simply to *believe*. No longer can one talk of a monolithic Church and its relations with states, rather of an institution called Church which often has very little semblance to Catholic practice at the grassroots level. What is also difficult to accept is the fact that no part of Church as institution is accountable financially, in any way, to the mass of members of the Church. Pastors are given open-ended appointments and are not appointed from local communities but catapulted in from elsewhere. Training follows the 'seedbed' or 'seminary' model with its pre-established teaching programme. In effect, the Church has become far more fundamentalist than ever before when seen against the prevailing situation in the secular sphere. Fundamentalism is a selection process of ever-diminishing returns. Its building blocks are 'belief' and 'obedience' in a very narrow band of biblical interpretation. These are often espoused by those who are affluent and full of certainties of their own merits of unearned righteousness, with their sensibilities and anxieties dedicated to 'weekend lawn maintenance',[21] or the poor, often rootless immigrant populations or migrants from rural backwaters to towns, moving from poor continent to rich continent and living outside their language in a foreign culture.

Ideologies inevitably produce relationships of powers. Ideologies of obedience and doctrinal one-sidedness no longer satisfy the need for moral and ethical guidelines. We as individuals create institutions to help us live and make life decisions. We have to become very suspicious when institutions become so strong that they dictate to us how to live and what to do and what not to do. These institutions with their rigid hierarchies can no longer demonstrate that they 'serve' us, that they love us, that they wish the best for us in their self-appointed importance or pomposity, because they are not open to change, not in tune with people's problems and desires. What results is not orthopraxis, but orthodoxy profaned by its patriarchal nature.

The effects of fundamentalism on the Christian tradition are grave. First, tradition is understood as 'handed down' rather than as a creative concept of tradition as 'handed over' to be transformed by the new generation. Second, it results in a lack of spirit dynamism, which manifests itself in a 'distorted tradition' where past content has more importance than process and 'hierarchies of truth' are overturned.

Conclusion

It is clear that under the leadership of John Paul II the papacy has reached a crossroads. This chapter has pointed to the causes and the many facets of change that are required at this time of crisis. The following chapters contain positive suggestions for a way forward out of high papalism to a more life-giving form of adult Christianity and Church for women and men. Part Two of this book, based on the experiences of different people, clearly illustrates that the system no longer fulfils the need of the people of this time. The mounting vocal opposition to high papalism is increasing, especially in the USA. Mary's Pence has been in existence in the USA for nearly twenty years: women and men give money towards women's projects rather than support the present system. Now, as a result of the paedophilia crisis in the USA, a group that is growing daily, 'The Voice of the People', is not only voicing its protests about the scandals but is withdrawing its money from the Church. It is clear that high papalism with its devastating consequences no longer works. This is not the time for putting our heads in the sand and hoping it will go away, but for increasing the pressure for change in the Church, in whatever ways are required; a Church that has the possibility within its very critical/mystical nature for vibrant change.

When researching this book the authors repeatedly heard statements like 'I have left patriarchy behind and I found myself', 'I am out of it – religion is a control thing', 'To insist on Canon Law to uphold one rule or another is spiritual impoverishment', 'I no longer want to channel religion into Canon Law, but into a moral dimension' and 'Never presume that an institution's morality is a better morality than your own'. These statements reveal the growing alienation from organized religion, from a world full of exhortations on how things are supposed to be. There is no talk of an 'apt time', *kairos*, there is always talk of *mañana*, tomorrow. The reformers, however, stress the opposite, they sense the *kairos* and are convinced that one day the institutional Church will follow. Meanwhile, all they want is to be left alone in pursuit of their goals and methods, to gain experience and to participate in life-giving orthopraxis. For women it means that they will have to enter a process of discernment: are they willing to continue to play the role of assistant in the Church when that Church does not want to accept the skills of women for full priestly ministry? The pastoral needs of the Church, as a community of all believers, are no longer met by a celibate male leadership. Their judgements are inadequate to the point that a number of women no longer want ordination into a male system, but a new understanding of ministry which does not simply shore up an institution, but liberates and unlocks the potential of individuals.

For some, this is akin to a call for reform, not by creating a break-away Church, but a co-equal and co-responsible Church. The pursuit of women's ordination is a part of this process of lifting 'the stained glass ceiling' in this search for shared leadership and responsibility.

2

Lifting the Stained Glass Ceiling –
Who and What is Church?

The question of who and what is Church, raised by Mary Jo Weaver in her book *New Catholic Women* (1985),[1] is the underlying focus to any renewed form of priesthood. The renewal of priestly ministry is closely tied to the notion of Church as a discipleship of equals. However, the question Weaver raised precedes any re-imaging of priesthood. This chapter explores the well-established models and images of Church, from scripture and history, and considers some of the barriers that impede present growth for change, with suggestions for the way forward.

The vision of a discipleship of equals is central to any renewed vision of who and what is Church. It is a vision that has remained dormant for so long, after an initial attempt in the very early years of Christianity to live out the often-quoted baptismal formula attributed to St Paul but probably originating in the community at Corinth: 'There are neither Jew nor Greek, slave or free, male or female but all are one in Christ' (Gal. 3:26–27).[2] It is foolhardy to look for a clear descriptive blueprint for women's equality in the New Testament as it has been handed down to us. Scripture scholars today talk of the reconstruction of scripture rather than a purely descriptive explanation of scriptures. However, what is clear is that there was a nascent form of equality in Jesus' time when ministries were dependent on different gifts or charisms and not defined by institutional control. And women participated fully in the development of these ministries. As Christ's life and teaching gradually receded into the background and depended for its transmission on a second, then third generation of Christians, the tradition became influenced by secular forces in society and it began to be shaped according to the culture in which it became embedded. Among these changes was a hierarchical reordering of Christian society, and women's gifts were gradually submerged, except for those of a few very strong women. Later history shows that not only were women's gifts not recognized but they were actively discouraged and suppressed. This is the formidable 'stained glass ceiling' to be broken through in shaping a Church of partnership.[3]

Ecclesiology – What is It?

Ecclesiology is the study of what and who is Church, the community of believers, the entity or body we have grown used to call 'mystical' as it includes human experiences and more than that, a connection to the divine. It proclaims the fourth-century Council of Chalcedon understanding of the incarnation of Christ in different times and cultures: that Christ was and remains forever both divine and human. Although the modern understanding of Church can be helped by sociology, psychology, Canon Law and even theology, it always remains more than any of these scholarly disciplines.

The concept – and word – of Church, stemming from the Greek word *ekklesia*, community,[4] in the Gospels, has gone through many vicissitudes. The foundation of the Christ community is mystical and critical, that is prophetic. It was these essential aspects of the resurrected Christ that were infused into the first house churches of scripture, often led by women such as Priscilla (Acts 18:1-4, 18–28), Phoebe (1 Thess. 5:12, Rom. 16:26) and Junia, whose name was changed, for posterity, into the male version of Junias (Rom. 16:7). Later, as house churches began to spread and it became less dangerous to be a Christian, the early Christians met in Roman temples and public buildings, basilicas, and the term 'church' was applied increasingly to church buildings. Here they would share insights, meditate and reflect on the meaning of Christ's life, which in the early days many had intimately shared and witnessed, and re-enact the Last Supper in various ways. 'Did not our hearts burn within us' must have been on many lips.

It was only as Christianity spread in the first and second centuries of what became known as the 'Christian Era', in the time of Ignatius of Antioch about 109, that the adjective *catholic* was added. The concept of something bigger than the local community began to grow. The belief in the death and resurrection of Christ was their strong, yet by its nature, invisible connection. The modern concept of an institution with its offices and paid employees, real estate and banks, having power over the lives of many, would not only have been totally out of character with their expectations and alien to their experience and understanding of Church, but also totally unacceptable to believers who had accepted an ethos of sharing. In fact, many Christians today share the same values when they reclaim the original connectedness between believers, when they have a strong desire to reach back, retrieve and drink again from the real source of Church – the life and death of Christ.

A very slight knowledge of the scriptures and church history soon reveals that it is unwise for any one Church to claim that it possesses the whole truth or that it is indistinguishable from the kingdom of God.[5] What we need today is for individual members and groups in churches to have the courage to discern what is really of God in their Church and what is literally a man-made interpretation that has distorted Christian truth. It is a painful and long process. There is no easy way. In church language it is called *ecclesia semper reformanda*, a permanently self-reforming or adapting Church. But recent events in the Church reveal that change only comes about as a result of considerable outside and inside pressure. The idea of a self-regulatory mechanism no longer works – if it ever has. When looking back over church history the shifts in understanding and practice have always meant that some people moved with the times and some stayed behind. A more thorough-going process than self-regulation is required, a transformation, which is, however, radically resisted at present.

Scriptural Images of Church

The images of the *mustard seed, leaven, hidden treasure, a field of wheat* and *its sowing, a fish-net* or *boat, a flock of sheep, a sheep-fold*, etc., have often been applied as images of Church. The question is how far is that correct, as these images were primarily about the kingdom of God, summed up in the famous phrase of Alfred Loisy that Jesus came to proclaim the kingdom of God, and what resulted was the Church.[6] It is important to note that in republican cultures, as well as in feminist ecclesiology, the concept of kingdom becomes an extremely difficult metaphor.[7] Besides the difference of political experiences, the subjugation of unvoiced experiences of the economic and culturally poor, generally women, is central to the development of any understanding of the 'kingdom of God'. When only word and reason dominate, other creative, emotional and intuitive ways of knowing are neglected. Ways of knowing mainly attributed to women in Western culture and generally unacknowledged.[8]

Among other biblical images included in the New Testament are *the Church as the temple of Christ* and the most controversial of all, *the Church as the bride of Christ*.[9] This bridal image of Church was incorporated into the language of the marriage ritual, at a time when a woman's womb was understood, even in medical terms, as a mere receptacle of the male seed. With the growth of medical knowledge, especially of menstruation, in the twentieth century, and the importance of the woman's eggs in procreation, this former understanding has been cast out into the archives of history. However, the continuation of the former understanding of reproduction and women as receptacles has lived on in the idea of a male-only priesthood. So if we take this bridal image of Church as interpreted within the tradition seriously, it becomes one of the strongest symbols of why women, and not men, should be ordained.

Other Models and Metaphors for Church

Various models of Church have long been discussed. These are neatly summed up in Avery Dulles' book *Models of Church* (1978) into five main models of Church: Church as Institution; Church as Mystical Communion; Church as Servant; Church as Sacrament;[10] and Church as Herald.[11] Although the two latter models help much with our perception of Church, it is the first three that will be given major consideration. Unfortunately, however, as discussed in Chapter 1, it is the hierarchical, institutional model of Church that has dominated our modern understanding of Church since the sixteenth century.

Robert Bellarmine is credited with having popularized this model of Church during the Reformation. This *political society model* of Church was rooted in the political culture of its time and soon acquired the epithet of *perfect society*.[12] It is not surprising, therefore, that an institution that believes it is a perfect society will resist rather than embrace change. Resistance brings with it a mentality that seduces the institution to become self-serving and inward looking with horrific results, as exposed by the paedophilia crisis of the twenty-first century. Scandals that were forced into the open by the victims themselves and met initially with disbelief and a half-hearted response. Although the Church has been shamed into sharpening up its procedures in this area, there is still no recognition or even any sign of a thorough investigation into the religious, male, clerical culture that spawned this sickness as the seed-bed for these crimes. Furthermore, there is no indication of a shift to a return to an informed biblical understanding of the plurality of officially recognized and publicly sanctioned ministries of leadership, prophecy, preaching and teaching, regardless of gender, that were recognized in the early stages of Church, before most ministries were consumed into the all-embracing concept of male priesthood.[13]

The ancient model of Church of the *Mystical Body of Christ* was reinstated by Pope Pius XII in his encyclical *Mystici Corporis* in 1943. For this scriptural image of Church the Pope drew on the work of M. J. Sheeban, the nineteenth-century scholar of the Tübingen school of theology, and Emile Mersch, the twentieth-century Belgian Jesuit, who devoted his life to restoring the notion of the Mystical Body of Christ. This encyclical, however, stated that the Mystical Body of Christ was identical with the Church, in its attempts to harmonize it with Bellarmine's societal concept. It points to the Pope and bishops as being the joints and ligaments of the body and that those who 'exercise power are its chief members' and the laity only as those who 'assist the ecclesiastical hierarchy in spreading the Kingdom'.[14] Vatican II, in *Lumen Gentium*, attempted to rescind this interpretation of *Mystici Corporis* by distinguishing between Church as hierarchical society and Church as the Body of Christ, and by claiming that the two are related to each other in the same way as that of the divine and human life in Christ. At the same time the Council acknowledged, in all humility, that the Church is both holy and sinful, and in continual need of reform and repentance. The problem with this model as it stands is that the 'Body of Christ' has to be 'a male body which becomes the place of salvation'.[15]

However, the two chief paradigms of Church that emerged from Vatican II were the *Church as the People of God* and the *Church as Servant*, returning again to the most ancient and scriptural traditions of Church. Both metaphors are much more acceptable to Protestant theology and pick up some of its favourite themes. The concept of the *People of God* and the *Body of Christ* need to be merged into a model of Church as the *Mystical Body of Christ*. It develops a meaning of Church beyond that of a civil society and a male hierarchical body.

The *Church as Servant* derives from the very nature of Christ's earthly life and from the understanding of the incarnation. Hence, Christ came to serve and any Church that declared itself to be a follower would try to live this out to the full. This model of *servanthood* has also been problematic, especially for women, as their socialization has always been that of fulfilling the needs, desires, whims and fancies of others before their own. Thus the patriarchal interpretation of Christian servanthood has led to a form of slavery and even depersonalization for many women.[16]

The organization that claims to be Church must listen to and be in continual dialogue with all groups within the society it professes to serve. No Church can be just one of cultic celebration, empty ritual or of condemnation of others, as exemplified in the words of Christ's, 'woe to you Scribes and Pharisees'. Humility, truth, dialogue and above all mutual care of all must be its virtues and primary mark.

The present deficiencies within these models and images of Church have been touched on. It is clear that no matter how attractive these are they are all crippled by the dominant, sexist, cultural theology that continues to permeate the RC tradition. The development of consciousness on the prevalence of sexism in all areas of life places a double imperative on all churches, which have not been catalysts for change but have been dragged screaming and shouting into the realities of this socially developing human consciousness.

The ecclesiologist Richard O'Brien from the Chicago Theological Union had this to say at the Women in the Church Conference, held in Washington DC in 1986, concerning the way forward in developing an inclusive ecclesiology for women and men:

The use and abuse of power in the Church is not simply a political or a sociological question. It is a theological question, more precisely an ecclesiological question because of the nature of the community in which that power is exercised. If the power conflicts today are simply between the haves and have-nots, such conflicts are unworthy of the Church ... On the other hand, if our power conflicts in the Church do reflect fundamental differences about the meaning and purpose of the Church itself, then the conflicts are actually much more serious than they might at first appear. To some extent this is the case. And that is why it is so important to get our ecclesiological principles straight.[17]

What the Church is and what it is sent to do are not a matter for Canon Law. Canon Law is the second not the first stage of theological development. What the Church is and what the Church has been sent to do are ecclesiological questions.

In the end we have no words to encapsulate entirely what is Church. It is in essence a mystery, as was and is the life of Christ both in his historical manifestation and in the life of his Spirit in all generations. The two together are a much stronger sense of who and what is Church. The Church is also much more than just a collection of people. It is a people who help to make up and complete the work of Christ's Body here on earth.

Addiction and Co-dependency in the Church

Contributions to a deeper understanding of Church and the damage done and influenced by the present hierarchical model of Church come from many perspectives. Two of the most interesting books written on this subject recently are Michael H. Crosby's *The Dysfunctional Church: Addiction and Codependency in the Family of Catholicism* (1991)[18] and Desmond Murphy's *A Return to Spirit: After the Mythic Church* (1997).[19]

Crosby takes the twelve steps undergone by alcoholics in order to be cured and applies them to the Church. He claims that the problem in a hierarchical Church, where power is understood as 'power over others', results in a Church where co-dependency is a major addiction. The ultimate test of loyalty for office holders becomes a blind unthinking obedience. It is an abuse that translates into a misinterpretation of 'infallibility' in all things that come from this form of authority. At the same time church members are reduced to a state of disempowerment and co-dependency. This manifests itself in continually seeking verification of ideas – the 'ask Father' or 'what the Pope has said' syndrome. People do not learn to stand on their own feet; they have to assure themselves constantly that they are still on the right track, that they have not strayed from the narrow path of what is permissible to think and what is not.

This culture of co-dependency keeps office holders, as well as members of the Church in religious matters, in a state of infantilism – in many cases for all of their adult lives. Each feeds on the other and needs the other in order to perpetuate the *status quo*. This leads to a tragic dichotomy in so many lives. Many people are well educated in secular spheres of their lives, but childish in their obdurate refusal to grow up in the demanding Christian tradition. There are others, less formally educated, who are less dependent on this model of Church. And at the heart of this thinking is a dualism: either/or rather than both/and.

It is impossible to talk about real dialogue in a Church stuck in this dualistic model. Monologues are built into its very nature, and when pronouncements come from a man whose honorific title is not only Father, but Holy Father, it is clear what is happening: a further ratching up of authority that nobody else can match or check. Students of the history of the papacy know that many popes led far from blameless lives and that the many errors propounded by those in high ecclesiastical offices were only grudgingly retracted by their successors.

Yet public conflict with the authorities of his time, both secular and religious, was the bedrock of Christ's life. In Matthew 23 Jesus unleashed an unparalleled litany of abuse. Addressing the crowds and his disciples he said:

> The scribes and the Pharisees occupy the chair of Moses . . .
> Do not be guided by what they do, since they do not practise

what they preach. Every paragraph in this chapter opens with
the word 'Alas for you scribes and Pharisees . . . you are like
white-washed tombs (verse 27) . . . you build the sepulchres
of the prophets and decorate the tombs of the upright
(verse 29) . . . you serpents, you brood of vipers . . . I am
sending you prophets and wise men and scribes; some you
will slaughter and crucify, some you will scourge in your
synagogues and hunt from town to town; and so you will
draw upon yourself the blood of every upright person that
has been shed on earth (verse 33).

Unfortunately, it is the Church of Matthew 16, 'The Yeast of
the Pharisees and Sadducees', rather than the Church of
Matthew 18, 'The Discourse on the Church', that has dominated. The discourse that begins 'Who is the greatest in the
kingdom of Heaven' goes on to the promissory words of the
kingdom of Heaven: 'so he called a little child to him who he
sat amongst them . . . In truth I tell you unless you change and
become like little children you will never enter the kingdom of
Heaven. And so the one who makes himself as little as this little
child is the greatest in the kingdom of Heaven' (Matt. 18:1–4).
It ends with the Parable of the unforgiving debtor.

The leaders' addiction to power shown in Matthew's Gospel
reveals how they destroyed themselves and their institutions.
For the Christian tradition, to deny that tradition by consistently
refusing to live by its source has deep tensions built into its very
being. If they remain unresolved, these very powers will destroy
the institution itself, in a way analogous to alcoholics who refuse
to acknowledge their illness. In other words, it will self-destruct.
Christ did not promise to stay with any one form of Church,
which anyway did not exist in his time. He promised only to
be with us as a person through the Holy Spirit 'until the end of
time'. What Matthew said in Chapter 23 is as pertinent today
as it was in biblical times. None of us is without blame in the
perpetuation of addiction and co-dependency in the Church.
Even the ecumenical movement is in danger of this by its over-

desire to be in union with Rome at this time in its troubled history. Numbers maketh not a Church?

One of the first needs in working towards healing the Church from the 'sin of sexism' is to find a way to awaken its members to the insidious harm to the Christian tradition of co-dependency, which has a long history. Addictive behaviour of any kind is disordered behaviour, fed by fear and anxiety, named in spiritual language as 'disordered desires'. Christ continually stresses love as the opposite to this human fear and anxiety, illustrated in his reference to the lilies of the field that neither sow nor reap: 'will he not much more clothe you – you of little faith?'

Those in authority fear losing control over their members and this shows itself in forbidding discussion on certain topics coupled with the final threat of excommunication. It is not surprising that the initial response of co-dependants is fearfulness at offending or displeasing this all present father figure. For Roman Catholics this is personified in the power structure of authority in the RC Church.

It does appear that many people find the development of this critical faculty much more difficult to develop in their religious life than in the secular sphere of life. And the way that the Christian message has been constructed has caused a psychological block to the development of a deeper understanding of the life and message of Christ. People who have been able to develop and become liberated from this blockage tend to have a mystical inclination, they 'hear the Word of God and keep it'. Temperamentally it is easier for some to stand outside the accepted parameters, more comfortable and more desirable. But to challenge directly an authority that has been garlanded with epithets such as 'divine' authority is not an easy calling.

Desmond Murphy (1997) illustrates the way forward by using the tool of transrational psychology as a way to begin to explain both the causes of the illness and the process of healing. To look outside, to look for scapegoats, to blame all others, modern society, women's changing role, etc., is a continuation of the co-dependency or the syndrome of shifting the responsibility elsewhere. This in itself further propagates the concept of a Church that is mythic, that is an unchangeable concept of Church, something that has to be.

The first stage of recovery lies in the recognition of the cause or causes of the crisis. As in all addictive behaviour, there can be no cure without first a recognition of the disease within us all to a greater or lesser extent. This must be followed by a step-by-step approach towards transforming the prevalent culture of tradition, from monologue to open dialogue and shared authority. The mustard seed will then have the space to thrive and grow into a great tree. With the death of the old will come the burgeoning of the new structures pulsating with new life. Like change everywhere, which is not purely superficial, this will take time, understanding, forgiveness on all sides, and the willingness to let go and take prudent risks. To trust is to let go.

Not all that is new will work, and a desire to flee back to the old will become very attractive. The new will probably be lived by a faithful new remnant[20] similar to that within the Jewish tradition before the birth of Christ, of which Mary and Joseph were a part, to differentiate them from the Pharisees and the Scribes, and then grow into a blazing bush for all to see. This can only be achieved by letting go of much that is perceived as defining Church; it will require considerable personal and institutional maturity. Desmond Murphy names these people, in psychological terms, 'trans-law' people. He takes his framework from the transpersonal psychology of Kenneth Wilber and divides humankind into three types. For some scholars it is an over-simplified typology, but it will suffice here to make a point: people can be said to tend towards being pre-law, counter-law or trans-law. Most of us possess all three tendencies in some areas of our life at different stages but one eventually begins to dominate our thoughts and feelings.

Pre-law people are, in the words of Virginia Woolf, 'the angel of the house' people, who find their identity in conforming to the wishes of others and being praised accordingly. They are people who generally lack a clear sense of self and look to others and institutions for their self-definition. Unfortunately many churches have reinforced this kind of behaviour because it is the form that is transmitted by those addicted to power within a hierarchical structure. To change behaviour of this nature takes time, and the people themselves, women and men, have to be given space, free from fear of reprisals, to find their voice and begin to articulate their needs.

Counter-law people tend to react rather than to respond reflectively to situations, often with over-anxiety or over-aggression. They, too, have reduced self-identity. 'Counter-law behaviour is a flight from the anxiety provoked by the call to transformation and results in surface structure change. For all its external promise, it is destructive. Kind but firm confrontation is called for, so that this inappropriate behaviour is not reinforced.'[21] People who easily abandon the past and uncritically embrace the new could be exhibiting either pre-law or counter-law behaviour.

The danger is that they can be confused with the third type of people. Trans-law people are not your paradigms of virtue, but they have the essential qualities for leading others towards deep and lasting change. In church situations they have generally stayed within but refused to compromise on issues they consider are not Gospel-based values. Sometimes counter-law people are confused with trans-law people, but there are distinct differences: 'The former will often go contrary to the law out of frustration. The latter will work within the law and only go outside where higher values are at stake. The former will easily lose heart, give up and go on to other things, but not the latter.'[22] Counter-law behaviour de-energizes, trans-law inspires. Trans-law people learn to respect the views of others, according to their understanding, but will try to open their minds on their journey towards God. The former will court martyrdom, the latter will accept it only as the price of being true to Gospel imperative. Finally, the person with trans-law qualities is more likely to be found on the periphery of the established authority structure in the present Church. These people are generally the prophetic people or group of people within a community:

> The call to transformation enunciated by the prophet arouses anxiety in the listener since it evokes leaving the security of the present of adaptation. The core construct is threatened. Such anxiety leads some in-laws to indulge in outright persecution of the unwelcome messenger ... rather than persecuting individuals ... the true role of church leaders is to help discern individuals with trans-law qualities and orchestrate initiatives.[23]

Murphy names these trans-law people the 'seed crystals' of the future. They are people who hold the key to present dilemmas and have the ability to lead people towards the 'promised land'. They bring the continuity between the old and the new coupled with an ongoing openness to the deeper unknown. They have demythologized their belief systems, and have turned the light of reason on its patriarchal and regressive elements. They are independent thinkers who see the good in the inheritance from the past and discern the sickness within with greater clarity than others. The trans-law people are the mystics of all ages. People like Edwina Gateley, a British woman who founded the Voluntary Missionary Movement in Britain (1969) and the Genesis House for prostitutes in Chicago (1982), who understand that their 'God is the God of the backdoor', as Gateley so graphically states in many of her talks.

Exposing and Healing Violence Against Women in the Churches

For many women in the Church the pinnacle of abuse against women was encapsulated in the papal statement *Inter Insigniores* in 1976 – the argument that only men can be priests because only they have the biological form to represent Christ, the so-called 'icon of Christ' argument.

The image of women in Christianity has oscillated between the obedient woman, the chaste virgin and married wife, bearing children, raising them and running the household for the husband, to the women called wild, untamed, the whore, the witch, the paradigm for disobedience. Topics touch on the good Christian iconic woman, Monica, mother of St Augustine, who suffered from two violent husbands and considered this was the woman's role, or on early Christian canonical texts that wrote out references that conceived God, among other images, as both male and female. God language is important, permanent omission of female images of God opens the one-sided interpretation of exclusively male images of God. This interpretation was easily translated into the domination of men over women and instituted by law into the proper 'God-given' order for the human race and the Christian Church. God is male, therefore the male is God.[24] Augustine locates the cause of sin in the male erection and women the cause of it. Thus Augustine was the inventor of what the Germans call the 'three Ks, Kinder, Küche, Kirche: that is children, kitchen and church'.[25]

Woman's fate was well summed up in the words of Tertullian, 'Do you not know that each of you women is an Eve? . . . You are the gateway to Hell, you are a temptress of the forbidden tree. You are the first deserter of divine law.' Words that are echoed in writings of other Church Fathers and later by Thomas Aquinas, who followed the Augustinian tradition and adopted the Aristotelian definition of woman as a 'misbegotten male', and reiterated the prejudice.

The sayings and writings of the Church Fathers flowed into a corpus of laws that mirrored a culture in which the female sex was undervalued, despised and rated second best. The result was law-sanctioned battering (it was perfectly correct to beat a wife as long as the wooden stick was no thicker than one's little finger), raping (judges famously or infamously argued that women 'asked for it') and poverty (laws on women owning property, employment rights, inheritance rights, pension rights worldwide had to be argued and argued again to be changed on the statute books in line with rights enjoyed by men). Examples from around the globe and from history fill large volumes of women's anthologies.[26] These stereotypical images of women have been carried from generation to generation, because the Church did not challenge the cultural context of their time and we are inheritors of a sexist theology.

Biological and physiological knowledge was extremely limited. What is more, these ideas were clearly culturally defined. To us they seem absurd. The tragedy is that the Church has obviously moved on from these ideas but has not been able to shift from the underlying message that is conveyed in this thought, that women are inferior to men. It has been transmitted to the present day, in a more hidden and sophisticated symbolic form in the theology of the 'icon' argument for the non-ordination of women, and further underwritten within the Code of Canon Law of 1983.[27]

The undervaluing of and disregard for women's humanity was manifest by linguistic use as masculine nouns were employed when speaking of God. All that was female became gradually debased.[28]

Research by women theologians of all nationalities – Carter Heyward, Rosemary Radford Ruether, Catherine Halkes, Mary Grey, Ursula King, Graze Jantzen, Mercy Oduyoye, Elsa Tamez and Chung Hyun Kyung, to name but a few in the past decade – has helped to make the radical connection between inherited theology and all forms of abuse against women. This has been underpinned by biblical narratives that have been used to support the so-called sinful deviousness and sexual licentiousness of women, illustrated by the popular historical interpretation of Mary Magdalene as a prostitute, an interpretation that modern scholarship has disproved.[29]

The total rule of one group over another, in pursuance of narrow aims, historically male on a public scale – and men as well suffered in their own way, if they stepped out of the narrow prescriptions on how to lead their lives – continues its way in so many lives even today. This second class, or non-status of women, is vividly reflected in the continuing economic poverty of women, the reality of prostitution and in traditional attitudes towards illegitimacy and even towards one-parent families in the twenty-first century. For example, throughout much of history it was women not men who were blamed for illegitimacy. The latter were considered as unwilling victims. This helped to cement the image of women as 'whores' in society and for churches was personified in the misunderstood written and artistic tradition of Mary Magdalene.

This connection is vividly illustrated by the words of women from West Somoa, Pacific, recorded by Aruna Gnanadason during the Decade on Women (1988–98) commissioned by the World Council of Churches:

> we shared the stories of violence against women . . . the lack of support of governments, churches and the society as a whole . . . We acknowledge that the kind of theology taught by the Church not only perpetuates violence against women but often condones it.[30]

Less severe, but nonetheless disabling, are the many daily acts of oppression and forms of exclusion, still accepted in societies and Churches as a God-given division of labour, that re-enforce the message of superiority of one group and the inferiority of the other. There are daily occurrences of this in women's lives – less wages for comparable work, denial of employment rights and diminished career prospects as a result of maternity leave. Women who break their career to look after children are often believed to be incapable of filling managerial positions and then they experience the glass-ceiling reality of daily life. This is reflected, in like manner, by the horror expressed at the thought of a pregnant woman presiding at the Eucharist. These daily realities are damaging, particularly to women with children, because they are insidious and infect attitudes in society and Churches at a very deep level. A sickness so deeply embedded in the general mindset that it appears the 'norm'.[31] As already stated in Chapter 1 the question of women's role in the Church is a sociological rather than a theological issue and its rightful place lies within the developing social theology of the Church.[32]

Counteracting the falsehoods, wrong assumptions, even heresies inflicted on women almost sounds like a heresy in itself. It is daunting, especially when speaking to parish groups, having to speak almost continually in opposition to many of the basic tenets the members of these groups have been taught and have believed in from youth. The gospel message of inclusion and equality has strayed far from the Church throughout church history. The fact that fewer people are willing to stay within the old patriarchal traditions is a severe warning. People leaving abusive structures may indeed be prophetic in their actions to help this model of Church to die.

People have made different choices in the face of the present patriarchal construct of Church. Many have chosen to leave the Church altogether, but not Christianity or at least some form of spirituality. This phenomenon is more prevalent in the Western world, a cultural and educational situation very different to the lives of those in extreme poverty. Where there is acute poverty the magic element of religion appeals, there is no other help. In affluent countries, medicine and education have removed this necessity and a magical concept of religion has to be replaced with a reason- and justice-filled religion otherwise it rings hollow. Sandra Schneiders in her book *Beyond Patching* wonders whether the present institutional form of Church is beyond redemption.[33] Others have chosen to stay publicly within the present patriarchal tradition and try to change it from within, because it holds so many poor people in thrall who do not have the luxury to choose anything else. They also believe that the inherited and still-lived mystical, prophetic tradition has nurtured them through the institutional aspect of Church, which has severely wounded them.

There is nothing wrong with an institution *per se* that serves the needs of its time, but not when the human rather than the divine element dominates and inhibits the full understanding of the incarnation. It is clear from the many groups voicing dissent in the Church – there are hundreds of websites on the internet – that the patriarchal form of the present institutional Church clashes profoundly with the call of the prophetic and mystical aspects of Church. The reactionary actions of the present Church in silencing people and forbidding discussion on topics of urgent interest are a sign of a group that knows but will not recognize that it is in total denial.

The Christian Church and its institutions became co-terminous with the secular institutions of the Roman Empire from the time of Emperor Constantine's conversion in 312. The community units of parishes became administrative units, useful to serve the state. Church law was by and large administered to everybody for hundreds of years. It took a raft of developments in the Western Church, which we would term with a modern concept 'civil disobedience', to shake church law free from state law. Residual traces are still with us today; the fact that the Church of England is called a 'State Church' is one example, or that training to the priesthood in a whole range of denominations and religions is exempt from the equal opportunity legislation of the state. This neatly sanctions the exclusion of women from employment in the Church – otherwise women could take the Church to court for failing to provide equal opportunities for them.

But generally church laws no longer inform secular laws, or not to such a degree as to disable women's lives. The Enlightenment, philosophical considerations on equality, natural law and a whole host of other ideas, notably the abolition of slavery, brought a different understanding of everybody's worth and value. The non-ordination of women in the Church, a very highly visible disability put on women for all the wrong reasons, is a topic that has not been resolved in the light of the modern understanding of the value of each individual.

Although in itself the ordination of women might appear a minor question, it is clearly the lynch-pin for fundamental change in the fight against female poverty, not only in the

Churches but also in secular life. If women cannot image God at the altar then they must be less valuable than men and can be treated as second-class citizens, or even as less than human. Economic, cultural and religious poverty is the ultimate outcome. The accusations against theology in Churches that still maintain the *status quo* on women are extremely serious and devastating in their effects as clearly shown in the already mentioned research of Aruna Gnanadason of the World Council of Churches.[34]

Conclusion

This chapter has looked at traditionally inherited models as well as metaphors and similes for Church in the New Testament. What has not been discussed are the important developments in Christology from a feminist perspective or the perspective of non-white races. A renewed Christology will be an essential part in the development of a Church of partnership. In particular the challenging question of Rosemary Radford Ruether, 'Can A Male Saviour Save Women?', has to be faced and answered, given that the maleness of Jesus has been used to exclude the gifts of women from the Church. What is required is the development of a theology of the common humanity that Jesus shares with women and men.[35]

However, suggestions have been made towards the healing of co-dependency and the sin of sexism. Past symbols and models can be purified, enlarged and transformed into a renewed inclusive understanding of the Mystical Body of Christ, the People of God, Temple of the Holy Spirit, the mustard seed, etc., that goes beyond the confines of one Church, one sex and one race. The Gospel, rightly understood, is the seed-bed of radical change, including that of racism. The shared common humanity of Jesus has to be lived in the Mystical Body of Christ, including not only the very poor, of all races and colours, but those marginalized by their sexuality and often labelled as deviant.[36]

The addiction to co-dependency can be transformed by a theology of 'right relations' into that of co-interdependency where respect of difference is the new norm. The concept of equality based on difference as well as equality based on similarities between the sexes is the major topic of discussion in Chapter 3.

3

Tools for Change –
Equality and Difference

It is not necessary to abandon all inherited models of Church for the inherent weakness of sexism to be discussed and gradually eradicated. True partnership where women are not in permanent inequality has the possibilities of transforming the Body of Christ into a discipleship of equals, an idea as old as Christian history, but formulated and brought to prominence by the biblical scholarship of Elisabeth Schüssler Fiorenza in the USA. In this respect, scriptural scholarship has been greatly influenced by the secular field of Feminist Theory, the evolving understanding of how women and men relate and contribute to society. These insights, numerous in the confusingly diverse space of post-modern society, have made and are making a major contribution to a new vision for society and Church.

Groups called Women or Woman Church have also emerged in different parts of the world. The aim of these groups is not to set up new Churches but transitional spiritual communities working towards the non-sexist transformation of Church. Some groups are women only, others according to local circumstances include men. Their primary concern is to provide the spiritual, theological and liturgical nourishment that many find lacking in the present Churches. Rosemary Radford Ruether aptly calls it the 'eucharistic famine' of modern times.[1] This indicates the need to develop a sacramental theology of social justice as the key to the celebration of the Eucharist as a celebration of the humanity of Christ, not his maleness.

The key question emerging from women's experience and now from a developing male experience, is how the present Churches with their cumbersome structures and past records can rise to the challenge of the enormous change, equivalent to a metamorphosis, which is required of its members and structures.

Women activists and academics, in the secular field as well as those of religion and spirituality, have a very important part to play in the transformation of attitudes and understandings of what it means to be human. From a religious perspective the subjects of particular importance are history, philosophy, psychology and ontology.[2] In general terms, the debate in all of these subjects is the equality/difference debate. Equality based on equal rights with men is the easiest to understand. The debate is whether there are inherent differences between the sexes, besides the obvious biological ones, and if so, what they are. This is the on-going, complex and sophisticated argument that Feminist Theory has introduced. Differences are understood as not only between the sexes but within the same sex, as well as race, class and cultural circumstances.

Within the movement for the ordination of women, all aspects of the debate are present. This is why the equality/difference debate impacts on the ordination issue and is central to any renewed understanding of Church. This chapter provides a brief introduction to some of the many facets of this debate. Different understandings that are mirrored in the experiences are related in the following chapters.

Equal to Whom – the Man of Reason!

The public debate on quality can be traced back to classical antiquity, and entered the religious realm via the philosophy of Aristotle, the father of Western philosophy. Equality became coterminous with the idea of friendship. Aristotle considered that equality, and hence friendship, was only possible between free males, who were citizens of Athens, as only the free adult male had a 'fully functioning and authoritative rational capacity'.[3] It was this rational capacity that made free men alone capable of both attributes. He explicitly and repeatedly writes that to be born female is the most common kind of deformity, basing his whole philosophy on the *dualism* he believed existed between the sexes, the either/or approach, male/female, animal/human, subject/object, inferior/superior, black/white. This dualism has infected all secular, theological and philosophical thinking to the present day.[4] In the Church, dualism has been translated into a so-called God-given division of labour – the 'equal but special' mentality of *Mulieris Dignitatem* – that underpins the message of the superiority of one group over another. It is an inherited, ingrained habit of thinking that has been called by the sociologist Elise Boulding 'a pathological twist of social memory'.[5]

In order to expose the depth of the colonization of our minds by much of our inherited system, women philosophers and others often use very dramatic, startling terms and metaphors to shock us out of our present complacency. One of the most radical feminist philosophers, Rosi Braidotti, in the early twenty-first century talks of the 'tragic phallic solemnity'[6] and the male colonization of space in all its facets. Others have used psychological terms such as a loving disrespect of the 'oedipalizing master', to use the well-known Freudian term, or the Alice in Wonderland approach that proclaims that all is a pack of cards, or the Andersen story that reveals that the emperor is naked.

Equality and Difference in Feminist Theory

Many women scholars have devoted their intellectual lives to researching an area that might be termed a new consciousness for women, its roots, and its power to effect social change. One thing that all the various forms of feminism have in common is the desire not just for some form of equality between women and men but for a deep transformation of the present norms of society, which include class, colour, race and relationship to the earth. And all feminist scholars emphasize the centrality of feminist consciousness in this process of change.[7]

Throughout history, individuals and groups have realized the malign nature of dualism and its effects embedded within society. In the last two centuries there have been profound changes that would not have been possible without the store of accumulated, if hidden, thought. This accumulated thought has formed the basis of the modern academic discipline of Feminist Theory. One much earlier example is the work of the writer Christine de Pisan (1364–1430?),[8] which sparked off the debate known as the '*querrele des femmes*', strong arguments about equality and difference among women. De Pisan and those who followed her thinking were defenders and advocates of women and made it their task to highlight misogynist tendencies in society. She was followed by women such as the seventeenth-century dramatist Aphra Behn, the first Englishwoman to support herself by writing, and Mary Astell, who under the anonymity of a 'Lover of her Sex' published in 1694 *A Serious Proposal to the Ladies*. These were followed in the eighteenth, nineteenth and twentieth centuries by such well-known names as Mary Wollstonecraft and the Pankhursts.[9]

Despite the importance of the declaration of liberty, equality and fraternity of the French Revolution, it never applied to women. However, they gained one very important thing, an increased awareness of the position of women. In the words of Olwen Hufton, a social historian of the French Revolution, it was for women a 'consciousness raising' event.[10] This consciousness of women's position in society was deepened further during the anti-slavery movement of the 1840s in women such as Susan B. Anthony and Elizabeth Cady Stanton. Women who made a clear connection between black slavery and women's position in society resolved to work for women's suffrage – the right to a political vote.

So was born what is now termed 'liberal' or 'equal rights feminism', summed up in the words: 'men, their rights and nothing more; women, their rights and nothing less'.[11] Since then many other forms of feminism have developed that fall in a very generalized way under the headings Marxist, socialist, reproduction and mothering, gender and sexuality, psychoanalytic, existentialist[12] and post-modern. For the purpose of this chapter a brief, simplified mention is made of only a few of these feminisms, in order to indicate the depth to which the ordination debate, especially within the Church, will have to reach for any form of solution to the present situation.

The causes of women's oppression have been long debated. Socialist, and more so Marxist, theory has claimed that poverty was caused by the class system. This was challenged and critiqued by Shulamith Firestone in her book *The Dialectic of Sex*.[13] She challenged the Marxist premise and replaced the class system as the cause of poverty with that of the 'biological family' as the root cause of 'an inherently unequal power distribution' of goods.[14] Firestone, in her turn, was criticized by Juliet Mitchell in *Woman's Estate* for omitting the historical perspective when speaking of women's oppression and the failure to understand the complex relationship between women and economic production. Mitchell also emphasized that laws alone would never free women.

As the higher education of more women became possible, a more radical agenda began to appear in the twentieth century. What came to light through sharing experiences and action to improve conditions proved a minefield of controversy. Books such as *Of Woman Born: Motherhood as Experience and Institution* by Adrienne Rich,[15] and Germaine Greer's *The Female Eunuch*,[16] raised the question of abuse of and control over women's bodies by state and religious misogynist institutions. The questions of sexual orientation, contraception, abortion and other unresolved moral issues began to surface. Gender differences became widely debated across historical and cultural boundaries of classes, races and gender. The belief that sexuality was the root cause of women's oppression by men meant that it became the starting point for any woman seeking to understand her personal and political position in society.[17]

French women scholars entered the debate via Freudian theories and psychoanalysis, and post-modern philosophers such as Jacques Derrida, with his use of the term *différance*, and Jacques Lacan's research on the 'symbolic order'.[18] The three best-known women scholars are Luce Irigaray, Helene Cixous and Julia Kristeva.[19] There are substantial differences between them, but Julia Kristeva differs from Irigaray and Cixous in several respects. Whereas Irigaray and Cixous tend to identify the 'feminine' with biological women, and the 'masculine' with biological men, Kristeva resists any such identification. She pinpoints what is called the *semiotic*, that is the early stage of a child's life, a time of unconscious learning that takes place in the child through a growing knowledge of its own body. This knowledge is stored in what is referred to as the *chora*.[20] It is the innocent, untouched state of being and knowing before the sensitivities of a person are dulled by the male language and culture. We call this the unconscious, a way of knowing beyond the rational, that is an intuitive way of knowing. Hence, when females enter the next phase, the *symbolic* order of the language system of symbols, their early experiences marginalize them. Femaleness in a male symbolic system is defined as marginal to the system. This means that women always remain in some ways outsiders, but it does enable them to develop other ways of knowing and insights that become dangerous to established society. Kristeva modifies this general view. For her the development of maleness or femaleness, irrespective of biological gender, depends on which parent is the main influence on the child's life. Kristeva emphasizes that femaleness is non-biological, as the 'identification of these categories with biological maleness and femaleness is a trick'.[21]

Cixous's primary concern is with language. She challenges women into what she calls *feminine écriture*, female language, as an attempt to run free from a male-controlled symbolic order. There is great joy and freedom in her thought.

Irigaray claims that we only know the 'masculine feminine',

the woman formed by man. In her study of Western philosophy and psychoanalysis she sees *sameness* everywhere. Irigaray, to overcome this sameness, takes the female body as a symbol for difference. She encourages women to understand their bodies.[22] It is through reflection on these bodily experiences that women begin to understand the articulate female experiences in a new language. Irigaray, like Cixous, delights in the criticisms of the many ambiguities in her thought. For her it indicates her refusal to be pinned down in the male symbol system. However, no matter what the differences are between these three women and others like them, they all offer to women the most fundamental liberation of all – freedom from oppressive thought.

At the same time American feminist consciousness had been growing apace – a feminism greatly influenced by the Civil Rights movement. Its origins have influenced its form. American feminism has always been more pragmatic and action-orientated than the French. British feminism tends to reflect the American approach rather than the French but all forms of feminism – the Anglo-American rights feminism and the various forms of French/continental psychoanalytical feminism – need each other.

The strength of the former lies in its action base, working for change through the laws of the country or Church. The weakness of this feminism is that it can remain at the level of these first forms without a deeper analysis. Hence the charges that women's equality makes little change, if equality is accepted on the male terms inherent within society. The weakness of French/continental feminism is that action appears to be secondary and thought remains where it began at the cerebral stage of thinking. However, the strength of continental thinking lies in its apparently deeper level of gender analysis. Instead of sweeping the issue under the carpet and saying we are all equal or there are few or no differences between the sexes, or that the future will blur the differences, Luce Irigaray's approach challenges all this thinking and claims there are differences between the sexes that do not mean one is better than the other, avoiding any concept of hierarchy between the sexes.

Black women's theory has challenged white feminism for subsuming all women of colour into their analysis of equality and difference. bell hooks and Audrey Lorde, together with other black women writers, have shown ways in which white feminists have presented a common oppression for all women. bell hooks has underlined this problem in her book *Ain't I a Woman*.[23] The importance of the history of black women and their sufferings of racial and sexual violence has led many black women to understand racism rather than sexism as the basic violence. Many talk of the double and triple violence of race, sex and poverty. Furthermore, the feminist model of economic dependency for women often does not apply to them, with the unemployment of so many black men. The women are often the main breadwinners in their societies. The family has a different significance to them.[24] This is why the plurality of post-modern feminism is so crucial in order to avoid the inherited Western tendency to universalize its experience as the way things are.

All forms of post-modern feminism, whether in its French/continental, its American/British and black/coloured forms, now celebrate difference and multiplicity, including different ways of understanding oppression, thus freeing difference from its dualistic either/or understanding to both/and. The temptation of falling back into individualism and even marginalizing men is, however, always present. There is much to be gained by joining these varieties of post-modern feminists in their celebration of multiplicity and difference, for even if 'we cannot be One, we can all be Many. There may yet be a way to achieve unity in diversity'.[25] Like Irigaray we should rejoice in this multiplicity of ambiguities as enrichments and diversity that uncover and heal the many root causes of female and, therefore, societal oppression.

Equality and Difference in Feminist Psychology

In the preceding section, the contribution of the French from a psychoanalytic viewpoint has been touched on. There has also been considerable development in the understanding of how women make decisions and their different ways of understanding reality. Two books in particular are becoming classics in this field, Carol Gilligan's *In A Different Voice* and *Women's Ways of Knowing*, researched and written by four women.[26]

First, Carol Gilligan's classic *In A Different Voice*[27] challenges the sexism implicit in psychological studies of moral development – a sexism that takes male moral development as the norm. Gilligan argues against the notion that women have a less well-developed sense of morality and claims instead women have a different sense of morality from men. She illustrates from her research, based on the moral views of women who were deciding whether or not to have an abortion, that women make decisions not just from abstract principles of right and wrong, irrespective of their personal context, but take into account the context of their relationships as a major part of their decision-making.[28] She later expanded her research to other moral issues.

Gilligan has been accused of essentialism in her work, that is positing an essential, natural difference between women and men. She does, however, stress that she sees these differences not as natural but as a result of the different social factors that influence the lives of women and men. Others have argued in a similar vein over her emphasis that women have an ethic of care. But many women have found echoes of their own experience in her findings on moral decision-making in their own lives and circumstances. Her work is a vital contribution in challenging the universalist claims of traditional male moral philosophy.[29]

Janet L. Surrey echoes this trend of thought in her article 'The Relational Self in Women',[30] where she claims that the differences that emerge in the psychological development of women posit that one cannot speak of equality between the sexes in society because society reserves for women the position of second-class beings, sometimes even non-beings.[31] In a *self/other* understanding of human development, people are transformed and come to a knowledge of themselves through a network of relationships that include differentiation, identification, listening and speaking, rather than through struggles to dominate and fictional categorization. The personal then becomes political in order to effect change.[32]

There is no doubt that the inherited view of rights and its terminology does pose an ethical problem. The enunciation of rights without taking into account the circumstances of the time reduce access to a particular set of rights. Human beings not only have rights but above all they have moral responsibilities to others as well as themselves. Responsibility ethics has a much greater chance of cross-cultural success than a rights ethic, but it must apply to both sexes, to all classes and to all ethnic groups. This form of moral responsibility, at present attributed mainly to women, gives a much deeper understanding of the concept of liberation and equality. It is this more eclectic and complex concept of equality, coupled with an ethic of responsibility for others, that we are searching for. In the process of liberating the individual, it will liberate men and the earth as well as women.

The thought of these writers has been extended further in *Women's Ways of Knowing*, where in broad terms five stages have been identified as women develop in their understanding of reality. The first stage is one of total silence, acceptance of things as they are without question. These are women who have found no voice of their own but only echo the reality they have been taught to live by others. The second stage is termed 'received knowledge', a time when women begin to listen to an inner voice that is, as yet, still too unclear for articulation.

In the third stage, 'subjective knowing', an ability to articulate the inner voice gradually emerges and so begins the long search for personal awareness of who they really are. In the fourth stage, 'procedural knowledge', a shift appears, as articulation and reflection lead to an ability to connect what they have personally learnt from their experiences and how this deviates from their former beliefs of themselves and society. This state tends to be dominated by questioning. The fifth and final stage, known as 'integrating the voices', goes beyond the questioning of reality and moves towards connected ways of knowing, and the birthing of ideas to shape life in a way that reflects their understanding of themselves and reality rather than that imposed by society.

Equality and Difference in Nomadic Philosophy

A further tool in the developing of the equality-difference debate is that of the philosophy of Rosi Braidotti. This she has termed 'nomadic', describing a human being as a 'nomadic subject'.[33] She recognizes a humanity that is always in the 'process of becoming', not necessarily evolving in the physical sense, but in growing beyond the consciousness of the culture of their time into new horizons of change.[34] This is the total opposite of the inherited static perception, termed 'sameness' by Irigaray, of what it is to be a gendered human being. Braidotti refers to this sameness as a 'controlling' and a 'monstrous norm'.[35] Nomadic philosophy, therefore, contextualizes what it is to be human and 'dynamizes' it. This emerging philosophy demands a radically different way of perceiving life. It elevates the importance of the imagination and affective understanding to the same level as the rational, sometimes seeing it as more important than the rational. Furthermore, the basis of a nomadic philosophy is not linear but cyclical and repudiates the dualistic separation of body and soul.

Braidotti, along with many others, believes in the importance of personal experience, which she names as the cartographies or maps of life, which colour our understanding of reality. In this philosophy, women's experience, because it has been repressed, unarticulated and subjugated, is central to the transformation of the world, and imperative for the *metamorphosis* into a more just, fair and equal society. Braidotti names this 'a materialist way of becoming', not in the Marxist sense of material, without the spiritual, rather as a way of explaining that it is through the body that we receive all spiritual experiences. The common term used for this is 'embodiment'. Braidotti calls this a 'process of becoming' underlined by the importance of interpersonal relationships in the growth of self-understanding. This is why it is crucial to shift the understanding of women and hence gender into the social teaching of the Church, where the understanding of gender can evolve in the nomadic cultures of time.

Braidotti in her book *Metamorphoses* agrees with the philosophers of the French school, Gilles Deleuze and Luce Irigaray, that we cannot sweep sexual differences away, as they are at the centre of transformation. Instead, philosophy must now be based on non-hierarchical 'difference',[36] thus developing a new norm for understanding equality away from the old norm of the 'man of reason' as the model for all equality. Women's bodies and experience are both the principle and structure of change and even Irigaray stresses the eventual mutuality of both sexes, once they have begun to rid themselves of the overwhelming male symbolic system in which all have been immersed for generations.

This is why Braidotti believes that the task of metamorphosis of becoming will take so long and has to be strategically planned. For her the days of heroic changes are over, victories will be piecemeal and small but very effective. Successive generations will need to be aware of the task they have inherited and work out for themselves a strategy to educate their times out of inherited prejudices. This passing on of awareness is a sacred task for all educationalists at all levels and in all subjects. Perhaps an awareness and understanding of the importance of philosophy should be reinstated into educational systems. This time, however, it should be a women's critique of the male philosophical dialogue and an education into the new theories of non-hierarchical 'difference' and a nomadic understanding of what it is to be human.

Braidotti's 'feminist philosophical nomadism'[37] therefore

refers to a person who is always in the motion of 'becoming'. A nomadic subject is characterized by mobility, changeability and a transitory nature; 'history is tattooed' on their bodies,[38] not only personally but also corporately. This 'materialist theory of becoming' invalidates disembodied experience as an impossibility in this life: 'embodiment and sexual differences are processes of transformation and this translates into both personal and societal transformation'.[39] Body and nature are slippery terms, since the body itself both physically and psychically is a temporary nomadic subject. Change is written in from birth. It becomes the death knell of sedimented custom and institutionalized addiction and it includes an ethical and ecological dimension to feminism and to change.

All these understandings of women's liberation are found within the women's movements for change irrespective of Church. The diversity of approaches, although often uncomfortable, will lead to a richer understanding of the role and meaning of change, particularly in the Church and the way ministry is understood and practised. Where you stand is what you see. For example, the differing views on priesthood and women's rights over their own bodies cut across the boundaries of all Churches. All traditions, irrespective of their laws, are not written in stone. The concept of a monolithic Church is over.[40]

Historical/Critical Interpretation of Scripture

We owe a great debt to the scripture scholars of the nineteenth and twentieth centuries of both Protestant and Catholic traditions for the growth into the historical/critical method. This method, which is evolving itself, does not do away with the inspiration within the text but it enriches it by not countenancing literal translation but a translation in the context of the historical period of its time, including who wrote the text and why and when. Although Roman Catholicism came to grips with this problem more slowly than some of the Protestant Churches, it is interesting to note that it has now approved historical criticism more officially than almost any other Church.[41] Herein lies a seed for great hope for change.

In the wake of Vatican II this same historical/critical approach was applied and developed by an increasing number of women. Elisabeth Schüssler Fiorenza was the first in the field with her 'hermeneutical approach of suspicion' summed up in her cry, 'Where are the women?' So was born the present-day situation within the Church, where we have those who were reinvigorated by this scholarship and dared to question long-held established systems, and those who wished to retrench back into a perceived safe past. The new scholarship has challenged many former official interpretations. The neat understanding that Christ ordained twelve men to the priesthood and from them the present clerical understanding of priesthood emerged is no longer tenable.[42] Add to this that there were women as well as men at the Last Supper and the whole matter is combustible.[43]

Many terms are used lightly in daily conversation without the full realization of the meaning of the word. The word 'disciple' is probably easily understood in the Christian meaning to be a follower of someone, in this context of Christ. The new word added here is that of a 'discipleship of equals'. Christ may not have used these words but they are implied in his dealings with women. Elisabeth Schüssler Fiorenza's methodology of reading the scriptures is an invaluable source for women who are searching for their real identity in the Christian tradition. Anyone who has attended any of Fiorenza's courses will realize the difference between her approach and other forms of scripture lectures and workshops. She insists on an active participation on the part of all students.

This methodology is explained in her two books, *In Memory of Her*[44] and *Bread Not Stone*.[45] She is not the first to apply a hermeneutic of suspicion to scripture or theology but she is the first to apply this principle in a major way to women's role in the scriptures. Fiorenza calls this method 'a reconstruction of early Christian history in a feminist perspective'.[46] Her suggested methodology is as follows. The first question to ask of any scripture reading is 'Where are the women?', followed by researching the history of the time and the role of women within it. From this vantage point she proceeds to rewrite the text imaginatively from a woman's perspective, including an imaginative reconstruction of women who have been made invisible within the biblical context. The whole process is concluded by some form of liturgical celebration of the subject matter under scrutiny. Fiorenza has been challenged for her methodology but she is convinced of its necessity, as feminism has developed theoretical perspectives and models different from previous interpretations.

It is because the scriptures hold such an eminent place that the rereading of scripture with new eyes is the crucial first step towards any real change. A fundamentalist, literal reading of scripture without reflecting on the historical context with a critical eye, especially a woman's eye, has led to the belief that women have to cover some part of their body in church, often the head, and must keep silent in church. In the RC tradition this is why women cannot officially preach in church. Canon Law still only allows women to give an 'address', but not to preach.[47] The silencing of women has not been very subtle but it has been very effective. But the literal translation of the words of Paul, 'Women obey your husbands',[48] has had the most devastating effects of horrific physical and psychological abuse of women.

Conclusion

This chapter has taken a brief look at where women have come from and at the suggestions of four tools for change – scriptural, theological, philosophical and psychological – that are underpinning women's experience and giving it a reliable theoretical basis. The following chapters continue this theme of the primary importance of the experiences of women. They are stories of women who have been forced to cross boundaries, in their case religious boundaries, not only for their personal survival but also for the sake of the survival of their religious traditions. The final chapter in this book gathers up all these experiences and reflections and imagines what a Church of partnership, a Church of 'discipleship of equals', may look like. It will be a Church very different, and yet the same in essentials, from the present form of high papalism, which is characterized by an over-centralization of authority.

Part Two

Steps Towards Change

4

Bringing Women in From the Cold

Although this book is primarily concerned with women's liberation, the subject and its effects touch men as well as women. Increasingly, men are beginning to realize that a supportive role is not enough – they also have a journey of change to make in accepting that women and men experience socialization differently.

This process can be characterized by three main steps. The first is for men to overcome the tendency to trivialize what they cannot understand or to ridicule what seems different. The second step is for them to understand that simply co-opting women into the present system is not an option. This is a difficult step to take, as co-opting into male structures initially suits both sides, until women realize that there is a glass ceiling to their career development. The third and most difficult step of all is the realization that the need for men to change lies at a much deeper level than can be solved by co-option into the present system. What is demanded is another way of seeing reality and doing things, accompanied by the development of a new, more equitable and just society or Church. This is the stage of deep *metanoia*, of conversion and with it the risk of letting go much that is familiar.

Women's liberation, including women's ordination, goes beyond the social connotations of 'masculine' and 'feminine', as these terms are loaded with historically defined gender expectations. That is why the words 'female' and 'male' are the terminology preferred by many, denoting the biological rather than the more controversial differences mentioned in Chapter 3. There is also much misunderstanding and derision of the words 'patriarchy' and 'feminist'. Both are used as shorthand to denote, in a broad manner, different value and cultural systems. There are wide divergences of opinions about the use of these two words. Many who call themselves feminist do not see it as creating another all-embracing system to which all have to adhere. Feminism is in essence not a system but a way of understanding and critiquing reality and it is a multi-faceted and pluriform critique. What is uniform, however, is that the origins of patriarchy or *kyriarchy*,[1] as many prefer to name the interlocking of all oppressions,[2] deeply affect men as well as women.[3]

Feminism is a fairly modern term to cover a re-envisioned reality where the structures and culture of society and religions are based on the shared reflections of women and men of all races and society. It should be noted that 'feminist' is essentially a white term and that non-white women and men are developing their own terminology out of their own cultures and experiences. Feminism has flowed into an acceptance of pluralism in women's theologies: feminist white theologies, black American womanist theologies, Asian, African and South American theologies. The universal concept of one single theological discourse, a unique way of seeing things and speaking about them, is dying. There is a growing acceptance that the primary methodology for theology is lived experience reflected on and shared.

Patriarchy is clearly visualized in historical artistic images of women, especially in popular art, as handed down in secular and religious history. The pictures of women 'swooning with the vapours' and sitting at the feet of men in order to gain the crumbs falling from their lips have been dominant images until the early years of the twentieth century. A walk through any art gallery is a wholesome reminder of how the Christian message has been seen through male eyes. The famous picture of *The Last Supper* by Leonardo da Vinci is so well known that it has coloured our understanding of the event, instead of just reflecting Leonardo's understanding of that reality influenced by the beliefs of his time, the Renaissance of the fifteenth century. A painting of *The Last Supper*, depicting women as well as men, makes people re-evaluate their understanding.[4] Women artists such as Meinrad Craighead and Judith Chicago have begun the artistic journey out of 'patriarchy', but the artistic revisualization of the Christian message from a feminist or a black perspective is in its earliest stage.

Although some people consider the Church to be beyond redemption, and experience it as a fossilized institution, others are able to detect a movement towards a liberation process within it. The backlash against women's roles and ministries since the 1970s may well foretell the end of the patriarchal concept of Christianity. The corrosive influence of sexism and racism is being stemmed by the global developments in education for women and the communications revolution.

Women throughout history have found some means to cross the restricted boundaries imposed by society and Church. But history also shows that it is well never to underestimate the difficulty and struggle that women have to undergo in order to acquire even a modicum of liberation in the secular sphere, and the ever-present danger of having to reinvent the wheel. To restore women to their true God-given dignity in all religious traditions is proving doubly difficult within the inherited culture and official theology of the RC Church. The Christian challenge is to live with resurrected hope and spiritual freedom to find a path through the chaos of change.

More and more women are overcoming educational boundaries, beautifully played out in a film that has become a classic, *Educating Rita*. There was a woman who wanted 'to grow' – and grow she did into herself and not into a formula of somebody she ought to be. Likewise, a growing number of women want to overcome abusive political and cultural boundaries in all spheres of life.

Political persecution in the twentieth century made it necessary for many women and men of all walks of life to flee war-stricken countries and attempt to settle into more liberal and affluent societies. They were forced to think the new, to travel out and to cross the boundaries – is this the origin of the notion of ongoing revelation? – that is, the truth about God is only brought to life through lived experience. To explore the value system in which one finds oneself means crossing intellectual boundaries as well and deciding what to do there. Women are told from early childhood not to overstep what is right and proper. The behavioural boundaries become bonds that tie girls and women in a way in which they do not tie boys and men. If women overstep the boundaries, they are reprimanded, but if men do so, they are admired for their daring – after all, a man has to do what a man has to do! Although this is a very generalized observation it serves to illustrate the precarious nature of acceptance and non-acceptance of boundaries.

Thus crossing the boundaries is an even more courageous act for women than for men. The stories that follow are present-day examples of the difficulties faced and overcome by women in order to break through the restricted boundaries of their time within the RC Church, boundaries they willingly break, no matter what the cost, in an endeavour that is not just for themselves but for future generations as well.

5

The No Chat Show –
Silencing Women

The history of the public silencing of women, in both secular as well as religious society, has been a phenomenon until comparatively recently. This long and fierce struggle of silencing women, especially in the RC tradition, makes it very hard for women to insert their voices into the 'received' tradition of Church. When they do manage to get their voice heard they are often branded as confrontational and aggressive. This and following chapters break this silence in a public way.

It is well known that public actions of dissent only occur when there is no other way of getting our voices heard. This is the case for women worldwide, from African women who alert the neighbourhood against domestic violence by beating drums outside the offending man's house to Aung San Suu Kyi, who suffered house arrest for at least twelve years in her struggle for the democratic rights of her people, a woman now dubbed 'Burma's Ghandi', who, like him, believed in the 'sacred duty of resistance to injustice'.

Breaking the cultural and psychological silencing of women's speech is in the foreground of this call for justice. It is in the silencing of women that the workings of high papalism stand out. For example, arguments against women's ordination have been scrutinized by scholars and found wanting. Despite the impressive body of research the arguments for women's ordination have not been accepted by those in the Church who have

arrogated authority only to themselves. In the twenty-first
century it is called psychological blocking. Christ, however,
dubbed it 'hardness of heart' and the ultimate sin against the
Holy Spirit.

Despite the long history of being silenced in the Church, there
is clear evidence in the New Testament and the early Church
that women were not excluded from ministry. This was a time
when ministry was charismatic and diverse and women were
able to play significant leadership roles of preaching, proph-
esying and teaching in the early Christian Community. Historically the main blockage to women preaching can be found in the
wrong interpretation of two scripture texts from St Paul and
the historical application of these interpretations out of their
context in later church history. The two texts are 1 Cor. 11:2–16,
concerned with male headship, and 1 Cor. 14:33–35, forbidding
women to speak in church. This culminated in the prohibition
on preaching by the laity by Innocent III at the Fourth Lateran
Council in 1215. History reveals the continuation of this disempowerment in spite of Canons 676 and 677 in the 1983 Code of
Canon Law, whereby permission is given for women to preach in
an oratory or church if necessity requires it. But, as mentioned,
the homily, or sermon, is still reserved to the ordained priest as
it has been since the sixth century.[1]

Because of this enforced prohibition women have found other
ways to use their charismatic gifts of preaching the good news,
particularly in teaching. With the growth of mass education and
mass communication the number finding their voice in both
writing and speaking is increasing fast. At the first international
conference on the ordination of women, hosted by Women's
Ordination Worldwide (WOW) and held in Dublin in 2001, the
Vatican reacted by attempting to silence particular individuals.
Before them many priests had received the same treatment, for
example Tissa Balasuriya OMI, Paul Collins, a former Sacred
Heart priest in Australia, and Matthew Fox, a former Dominican in the USA. It now seems to be the turn of women, especially
women Religious: Yvonne Gebara of the Canonesses of

St Augustine, who was working in South America and challenged aspects of the Church's moral teaching for poor women,
Jeannine Gramick, a former member of the SSND, on the question of ministering in homosexual communities, and Lavinia
Byrne, a former member of the IBVM in Britain, on the question
of women's ordination. It is now openly said by the leadership
in some women's congregations that as women become more
articulate theologically and find public expression for their
views, the church authorities grow more defensive and react by
trying to control these 'loose' women of the Church[2] and bring
them into line with narrow Vatican rules.

A new and growing challenge is opening up for leaders of
women's Religious congregations and their communities when
having to deal with the aftermath of papal prohibitions against
individuals. Ultimately it is a question of where authority lies.
We are fortunate in having guidelines by Vatican II in *Gaudium
et Spes*, no. 16, that of the primacy of conscience.

> In the depths of his (*her*) conscience ... is the most sacred
> core and sanctuary of a man (*and of a woman*) ... There he
> (*she*) is alone with God, whose voice echoes in his (*her*)
> depths. In a wonderful manner conscience reveals that law
> which is fulfilled by love of God and neighbour (Matt. 22:
> 37–40; Gal. 5:14). In fidelity to conscience, Christians are
> joined with the rest of men (*and women*) in search for truth,
> and for the genuine solution to the numerous problems which
> arise in the life of individuals and from social relationships.
> Hence the more a correct conscience holds sway, the more
> the persons or groups turn aside from the blind choice and
> strive to be guided by objective norms of morality.
>
> Conscience frequently errs from invincible ignorance with-
> out losing dignity. The same cannot be said of a man (*woman*)
> who cares but little for truth and goodness, or a conscience
> which by degrees grows practically sightless as a result of
> habitual sin.[3]

The rest of this chapter is a commentary on these words. It opens up a necessary and increasingly urgent discussion on the way forward when people with well-informed consciences find themselves in public conflict with the teaching authority of the RC Church. It becomes a double burden for anyone who works in an official, paid or unpaid, position in the Church and a further burden for Religious, who are under the vows of chastity, poverty and obedience and in consequence place not only themselves but also the Congregation, to which they belong, in a conflictual ecclesiological situation. The answer to this question is fraught with dilemmas for all, but especially for the members of the Congregation to which the so-called 'erring' person belongs. The members literally have to choose between an all-powerful teaching authority or loyalty to their member's conscience.

The Vatican by its very process sets up a situation of divide and rule. Some Religious leave as in the case of Lavinia Byrne and Paul Collins for the sake of their Congregation, having learnt from previous experience the futility of trying to dialogue with an institution that does not use that process. Others transfer to another Congregation, as in the case of Jeanine Gramick, others try to find a way of being true to their conscience and remaining within their congregations. All choices are determined by personal circumstances, but all have one thing in common, the living out of primacy of conscience in a church context. Almost without exception, those Religious or priests who come under close scrutiny by Rome are generally mature people of fifty plus. Their silencing, a form of persecution, seems to come after years of faithful quiet service. They are people suddenly thrust into the public arena by the power of the Spirit for standing up for a need of their time unfulfilled by their Churches. Tissa Balasuriya was seventy-two years of age when the Vatican accused him of 'relativism'[4] and Joan Chittister and Myra Poole were both well over sixty when the Vatican decided to try to silence them publicly.

However, in the case of Aruna Gnanadason, a conflictual

situation arose which was unexpected: the R C Church exerted public power over a non-R C official on the staff of the World Council of Churches, a Council in which it is not even an official member. It is therefore important to publish this action as well as the following stories as they become vehicles for theological reflection on restoring the 'right relationship' between the Church and Religious life and reflections on the serious implications of high papalism for ecumenical relationships.

Reflections on the Dublin Conference[5]

The conference was attended by 370 participants from twenty-six countries. The main speakers were Mairead Corrigan Maguire, Nobel Prize Winner from Belfast, who opened the proceedings, Rose Hudson-Wilkin, Church of England vicar from London, Joan Chittister OSB from the USA and John Wijngaards from London, theologian, author and webmaster of the most comprehensive collection of documents and statements on the ordination of women, the website www.women-priests.org. Through a special fund money was raised for women and some men from Third World countries to attend the conference, as it was paramount to hear representatives from countries around the world. They addressed the conference during the International Panel. At the end of the conference eleven resolutions were passed.[6]

The conference organizers always knew there might be some sabre rattling from the RC church authorities, but in the end they were shocked by the ferocity of the onslaught of which they knew nothing until just before Easter, the middle of April 2001. As the church authorities could not stop the conference from going ahead, they focused their attention on those women over whom they had some form of power: Joan Chittister OSB and Myra Poole SND and one woman over whom they had no overt power, Aruna Gnanadason from the World Council of Churches.

An Ecumenical Dilemma

Aruna Gnanadason is a well-known, highly respected senior officer of the World Council of Churches. She has worked for many years for women's causes in a global perspective and has been highly influential in raising the profile of the severe poverty suffered by women in many parts of the world. Her official title at the World Council of Churches is Co-ordinator of the Women's Programme within Unit III, Justice, Peace and Creation. She is from India, a lay person who has worked in the Church of South India, a married woman with a grown-up family. Aruna is the author and editor of two books,[7] which were the fruit of her work and travels for the World Council of Churches' Decade on Women, 1988–98. Because this was an extremely important initiative, but hardly ever heard of within RC circles, and because of Aruna's credentials as being the key expert in the field of women in ministry, the conference organizers asked her to locate the question of women's ministry in an ecumenical global perspective. She agreed to be a keynote speaker at the conference. She knew that WOW had been founded at the First European Synod of Women in Gmunden, Austria, July 1996, as an ecumenical organization, as its title denotes. It was on this ecumenical basis that Aruna agreed to attend. However, the Vatican thought otherwise as the conference in Dublin focused almost exclusively, but not entirely, on the experience within the RC Church.

At first all seemed to be going according to plan. It was not until just before Easter 2001 that the degree of Vatican intervention became clear. The Church is not an official member of the WCC, but it is a full member of the Faith and Order Committee of the WCC and an equal member of the Joint Working Group on Relations between the WCC and the RC Church. When the matter on Aruna's attendance at the Dublin conference was questioned and pressure put on her, her first concern was not to damage in any way the work of the WCC. Therefore, after much reflection she very regretfully decided she should withdraw. Aruna was deeply saddened by the situation especially as she had already written her paper, entitled 'We Will Pour Our Ointment on the Feet of the Church: the Ecumenical Movement and the Ordination of Women'. The paper, with Aruna's agreement, was published in the conference proceedings.[8]

The organizers of the conference later learnt that official representatives of the Church had even requested that the WCC should demand from the organizers of WOW the return of their generous donation towards the Travel Fund. To the everlasting gratitude of the organizers and participants of WOW, the WCC refused to agree to this latter request.

The conference programme did not suffer as a result of Aruna's withdrawal. Rose Hudson-Wilkin, a Jamaican by birth and presently vicar of two congregations in the East End of London, agreed at the eleventh hour to fill the gap. Her talk gave lucid and humorous insights into the difficulties faced by a black woman in priestly ministry in the Anglican Church in Britain at the opening of the third millennium. She concluded her talk with the powerful poem of Maya Angelou that despite hatefulness, 'Still, I rise'. Rose Hudson-Wilkin urged women to rise above the pain and terror when Churches at present accuse women of breaking up the Churches. 'What women are doing', she said, 'is working to give all Churches a new lease of life.' Her vision was inspirational: 'persevere, persevere; it will come, it will happen'.[9]

'A Priestly People for a Priestless Age'

The second woman to come under the spotlight of Rome was Joan Chittister OSB, a very well-known Benedictine Sister from Erie, Wisconsin, USA, a pioneer of the peace movement and a stalwart of women's rights, especially, but not exclusively in the Church, and the author of many books. Even she, after many years of warnings by the Vatican, was shocked by the viciousness of the attack on her by the Vatican authorities.

The Prioress of her Benedictine community in the USA, Sister Christine Vladimiroff, received a letter from the Congregation for Consecrated Life and Societies of Apostolic Life, CICLSAL, the ultimate official papal Congregation that controls the life of Religious, forbidding Joan to attend and to address the conference. Joan and her Prioress discussed the best way forward. They tried everything in their power to placate Rome. Sister Christine sought the advice of bishops, religious leaders, canonists, other prioresses, and most importantly her own religious community, as well as spending many hours in communal and personal prayer. The Prioress followed this with a visit to the Vatican taking with her an outline of Joan's paper, entitled 'Discipleship for a Priestly People in a Priestless Period'. All was to no avail, further letters arrived until the Prioress was told to put Joan under 'formal obedience', that is to forbid her to attend the conference. This put the Benedictine community in a very difficult situation. For, if the Prioress refused to impose this penalty, the Benedictine community of Erie could be jeopardized and its future, after its service over 150 years as a community in Erie, put into question. The Prioress consulted her community on the issue of the 'formal obedience' required by Rome and to their great credit 127 out of 128 supported the decision that Joan should not bow to the enforced obedience of Rome. The Statement by Sister Christine Vladimiroff read as follows:

> After much deliberation and prayer, I concluded that I would decline the request of the Vatican. It is out of the Benedictine, or monastic tradition of obedience that I formed my decision. There is a fundamental difference in the understanding of obedience in the monastic tradition and that which is being used by the Vatican to exert power and control and prompt a false sense of unity inspired by fear. Benedictine authority and obedience are achieved through dialogue between a community member and her prioress in a spirit of co-responsibility. The role of the prioress in a Benedictine community is to be a guide in the seeking of God. While living

in community, it is the individual member who does the seeking.

She finished by saying:

> My decision should in no way indicate a lack of communion with the Church. I am trying to remain faithful to the role of the 1500-year-old monastic tradition within the larger Church. We trace our tradition to the early Desert Fathers and Mothers of the fourth century who lived on the margin of society in order to be a prayerful and questioning presence to both church and society. Benedictine communities of men and women were never intended to be part of the hierarchical or clerical status of the Church, but to stand apart from this structure and offer a different voice. Only if we do this can we live the gift that we are for the Church. Only in this way can we be faithful to the gift that women have within the Church.[10]

Consequently, Joan went to the conference and was greeted with a standing ovation for her and her community's courage. Her paper did not disappoint the audience. She reignited the courage of all present with her down-to-earth common sense and humour. The following lines with which she opened her address give a flavour of her talk.

> The Trinity called a Divine Summit on holy things and God asked them whether they should have this summit in Jerusalem. Jesus replied with shock horror, 'Are you out of your mind? Ask me about the reception I got there!' Then Jesus in his turn suggested Dublin, to which God replied, 'No, not Dublin, because they don't even yet know I am a "she" there.' Then God said, 'Alright, how about Rome then?' to which the Holy Spirit replied in sheer delight and amazement, 'Rome, oh yeah, Rome, I'd love to go there, I haven't been there for years.'[11]

Then Joan went on to explain with great clarity and seriousness the full meaning of discipleship for the third millennium.

> The problem with Christian discipleship is that instead of simply requiring a kind of academic or ascetic exercise ... [it] requires a kind of living that is sure, eventually, to tumble a person from the banquet tables of prestigious boards and the reviewing stands of presidents, and the processions of ecclesiastical knighthood to the most suspect margins of both church and society. To follow Jesus, in other words, is to follow the one who turns the world upside down, even the religious world. Religious discipleship is a tipsy arrangement at the very least. People with high need of approval, social status and public respectability need not apply ...
>
> If discipleship is what you are here for, be not fooled! The price is a high one and history has recorded it faithfully. Teresa of Avila, John of the Cross and Joan of Arc were persecuted for opposing the hierarchy itself – and then later canonized by them. Discipleship cost Mary Ward her health, her reputation and even a Catholic burial. Discipleship cost Martin Luther King his life. No doubt the nature of discipleship is passion and risk.
>
> Discipleship can only be understood in the living. The Church must not only preach the Gospel but live it. So if a Church preaches equality but does nothing to demonstrate it in its structures and lives an ecclesiology of superiority, it is close to repeating the theological errors that underlay centuries of church sanctioned slavery ... Discipleship is not an intellectual exercise or assent to a body of doctrine. True discipleship is an attitude of mind, a quality of soul, a way of living that is not political ... and may not be officially ecclesiastical but which, in the end, will change a Church that is more ecclesiastical than communal. Real discipleship changes things because it simply cannot ignore things as they are ... Discipleship cuts a reckless path through corporation types like Herod; through institution types like the Pharisees

. . . and through chauvinist types like the apostles who want to send women away. The danger of the present situation is to reduce the Church to the catechism. We must take discipleship seriously or we shall leave the Church of the future with functionaries but not disciples.[12]

The courage of Joan's own life comes out clearly in her writings as well as her talks. Her persecution by the Vatican has been a long journey and continues to this day. Just before the Dublin conference the Vatican, through local church authorities, tried to stop Joan speaking at a religious education conference by refusing to pay for the high school teachers to attend. To the credit of the Leadership Conference of Religious in the USA, they provided the money to pay for the teachers to attend and over 1,500 did so.

Obstructions and silencing continue to this day. The People of God need to be alerted to the machinations of Rome. They do not make good reading to the eternal shame of those who love and wish for a Church of truth and gentleness for all. The culture of addiction to power by those in power and the co-dependency it has bred, discussed in Chapter 2, is nothing short of tragic, as it stops the demise of unhealthy practices and the birth of a healthier Church. The fierceness of opposition, which someone like Joan meets, reflects the anger of those who Christ challenged at his trial in his simple words to Pilate: 'What is truth?'

International Religious Congregations – Strengths and Weaknesses

The situation of Myra Poole highlights a new challenge to large international congregations. A monastic order such as Joan's, where members live together under good leadership, has the opportunity to reach a consensus much more quickly. Large international congregations, on the other hand, find themselves in a new situation without the advantages of the smaller group.

International congregations do sterling work in the poorest parts of the world and have done so for many years. It has not been unusual during the course of their history for members to meet with opposition from the Church. In fact, initially most of their founders suffered opposition when establishing their congregations. The critique in the face of blatant injustice has long been their hallmark when working with the poor, but now there does seem to be a return to the struggles their founders had with the Church and more: their original struggles are reincarnated in an understanding of structural injustice and fuel a growing critique of the present church system. Women and men who have discerned that personal autonomy, arising from an informed conscience, overrules the authority of high papalism.

Myra, a former headteacher and activist in women's concerns, received a letter from her Superior in Rome in May 2001. The Superior had received three letters and to each was added a further signature, till a triumvirate of signatures appeared – Cardinal Archbishop Eduardo Martinez Somalo, Prefect of the Congregation for Consecrated Life and Societies of Apostolic Life (CICLSAL), Revd Jesus Torres, Canon Lawyer, and Archbishop Silvano Nesti, Secretary of CICLSAL. In each of the three letters the pressure was raised until it culminated in the request that Myra, like Joan, be put under 'formal obedience' by the Moderator of her Congregation not to attend the conference and to desist being the WOW co-ordinator. This put all parties in a very difficult situation.

It was at this point that the difficulties appeared and for which the Congregation was not prepared. The situation was complicated by the following factors: the sheer size and spread of her Congregation into all the continents of the world, except Australia; the very group threatening her, CICLSAL, is the same group that accepts or rejects any proposed changes to the Constitutions of the Sisters of Notre Dame, and has the power to take away the hard-won freedoms obtained by the Sisters since Vatican II in the 1960s; it was pointed out that the Sisters of Notre Dame had no houses in Ireland at all and hence no official relationships with the bishops in Ireland. It is noteworthy that Joan Chittister also had the latter point to consider in her deliberations. Finally, there was no process by which the opinion of her whole Congregation could be garnered, or even what their attitude would be to the situation.

Myra's first reaction to the last letter was still to attend the conference and face the consequences. However, she was asked by the authorities in her Congregation to take time with her decision. She asked for advice and was given answers that showed that people were clearly fearful for her at the outcome and cautioned her about the consequences. If she attended the conference, would this in any way jeopardize the constitution of the Congregation and limit the freedoms of the members? In the end, against her better judgement, as she said later on, she decided not to attend the conference. But when it was intimated that she should not even travel to Ireland, she could not agree to this last request. She felt a real responsibility towards the Sisters who were coming from the Third World, and wished to meet and talk with them, for their work in their own countries could also have been endangered.

By the time Myra left for Dublin, she was nearly paralysed by fear, but thankfully also supported by a network of friends. She stayed away from the conference for the first twenty-four hours until the time in the programme earmarked for the International Panel, an address by participants from developing countries. By this time she reasoned that she had to stand by these women who had given up so much to come and speak for the cause. It was at this juncture that Myra went to the conference fearing that her life in her Congregation was over. Joan also felt the same about her situation, neither knew the outcome of their decisions.

The denouement was prosaic in the extreme after the trauma shared by the participants. The heavens did not fall in, as expected. Instead a press release was issued from the Vatican with the following statement from the Pope's press spokesman, Joaquin Navarro-Valls, on 6 July 2001: 'While the Congregation for the Institutes of Consecrated Life had thought the Sisters' participation "inopportune" because of the possibility of outside manipulation, the Congregation never considered taking disciplinary measures.'[13] It is interesting to note that there was no formal communication of this decision to those Superiors who had been advised to put both Sisters under 'formal obedience'. All concerned only heard through a press release!

The question remains: why did they go to all this trouble if it was only 'inopportune'? The letters were full of threats and dire warning, which were not touched on in the press release. The answer lies in the solidarity of women and men in a global context. Through countless messages they showed their outrage at the hierarchical and arrogant stance of Rome, who disavowed free speech in a democratic age. Such was the public outcry when all were informed of the approach and threats by the Vatican that the e-mail messages must have driven home the depth of opposition to the Vatican. All the Benedictine communities in the USA supported Joan and a large majority of the Sisters of Notre Dame, in every continent of the world, when they knew what had happened, came out in support of Myra. Congregations stopped their Chapters to support the Sisters and individuals in quiet places of the world wrote to her to say 'thank you' for standing up for the cause of women.

In spite of all difficulties and previous misunderstandings both congregations proved they had the courage to withstand the dictates of Rome. Both are stronger for it and have set a pattern for similar situations wherever the primacy of an individual's conscience is in danger of being eroded. The Church could be changed overnight for the better, if all Religious, women and men, stood in solidarity and refused to co-operate with the present abuse of power by the Vatican.

In conclusion, one journalist reflected, 'You have started a revolution in the Church.' The failure of the Vatican to silence these women, after repeated threats, denoted a victory of solidarity over Vatican bullying. It was a conference filled with great joy but inevitably marked by the cross. In the words of Soline

Vatinel, of Brothers and Sisters in Christ (BASIC), the ordination group in Ireland, it was a 'time of celebration of women's call to the priesthood'. One Religious Sister, a hospital chaplain who has a vocation to the priesthood, said, 'When I first came on Friday, I was afraid who might see me there. By Sunday I did not care any more, I was no longer afraid.' Another woman said, 'There was a meeting called for all women who have a vocation to the priesthood and who were willing to acknowledge it publicly. The amazing thing was when I got there I found the room was actually too small, so many were there, from so many different countries.' And an Irish grandmother in her late seventies sent a card saying: 'I think every woman left the conference with her head held high.'

Reflections on Authority and Obedience for a New Age

What are the serious theological issues raised by these events? These stories illustrate the particular tension a priest or Religious faces when the primacy of conscience conflicts with the Vatican's understanding of authority and obedience. In the case of Aruna her situation arose from unresolved ecumenical problems of great delicacy and importance. However, this same problem also applies, in a different context, to anyone who works in an official capacity for the Church. In the latter cases it is the threat of loss of job and sometimes means of livelihood. Many who work officially for the Church are frightened to say what they really think, a situation that is very unhealthy for all concerned. The problem of loving what is good in the Church and speaking out about what is hindering the growth of the Spirit is fraught with pitfalls. Those who are and those who have been caught in this dilemma know the anguish of a person or group who decides on loyal dissent for the sake of the ongoing life of the institution. The learning of loyal dissent is hard, but is an essential part of ministry in any Church.

Rosemary Radford Ruether in her article 'Reflections on Joan Chittister's Decision to Speak'[14] elucidates this problem. She speaks of the anguish of Joan Chittister, her Prioress, Christine Vladimiroff, and her Community in coming to their prayerful decision after weeks of discernment. Uppermost in their minds during this painful time was the question of who has the authority in a situation such as this. Ruether believes that in the eyes of Rome this form of prayer and discernment is fruitless. In prophetic voice she says, 'Vatican leaders care not one whit about prayerfulness . . . and in my view the Vatican has no right to agonize us, for one minute.'

The short reflection ends with Ruether arriving at the following conclusions:

1 That the arguments of the Vatican have become so untenable they have to resort to silencing and threats in case the nakedness of their arguments is exposed.

2 If the true sign of Church is the relationship with Christ and each other, Ruether concludes, 'The Vatican discredits its claim to represent Christ when it behaves in a way that suggests it has little understanding of what it means to enter into that relationship.'

3 It is the statement of Prioress Christine Valdimiroff that prepares the ground for a renewed understanding of authority, obedience and the primacy of conscience.

The authors agree with this assessment. Sad to say the Vatican has still not learnt by experience of the futility of this way of acting. The more it responds in this way and the more unreasonable it appears, the greater the resolve of people to attack its stance more strongly. These actions do not lead to silencing anyone, but to further questioning of the morality of the authority that could dare to act in such a way. In every way the Vatican has been the loser, an authority that by its very tactics gave far greater publicity to the conference than it would have had if the Vatican had not attacked it. The ways of the Holy Spirit are truly amazing.

As more and more people find their public voice, and to use

the jargon phrase 'break the silence' on the position of women and all marginalized people in the Church, the velocity of change will rapidly increase. Hildegard of Bingen called the Church to account in her time as did Catherine of Siena. It is now the turn of the People of God, 'to take back the Church after so many failures of leadership by cardinals and bishops'.[15]

The chapters that follow speak with the experience of women and men who are opening up different ways of being present in ministry and being Church in new ways. They find their authority and obedience from within themselves, by the call of the Spirit, and not from any form of external pressure. Some have chosen radical stances in a situation where so many feel marginalized and alienated. The situation is summed up in the words of a five-year-old girl in Pennsylvania when her parents answered her question about women priests saying, 'We don't have girl priests in our church, darling.' The little girl thought for a minute and then responded quite simply but sharply, 'Then why do we go there?'[16]

6

Women's Experiences –
a Source for Change

Preliminary Remarks

Any theoretical investigation into the malfunctioning of systems
needs to be rigorously tested by case studies on the practical
experiences of those working in the systems. This holds true of
the many women – and men – in the RC Church who, while
being faithful to the Gospel message, have become critical of
the way the Church-as-Institution does seem to put sandbags
against the movement of the Spirit. In Part One we set out the
authors' ideas of governance, of what Church should be, a model
for partnership. In this chapter in Part Two we publish the
experiences of eight women and one man, from Canada, Germany, the UK and the USA. They have all been interviewed
and we have corresponded with all of them at length to discuss
the notion of their involvement with church work, their experiences of problems and how problems were dealt with, their
critical stance and desiderata to make the Church listen and act.
The narrative thread of the interviews and correspondence has
been kept as much as possible to present the individual women
and men through their own statements. All quotes are taken
from the interviews and correspondence. At the end of each
presentation the authors have added a short analysis to tie the
experiences into the theoretical framework of the book. This is
therefore not a chapter in which the following nine people just

tell their story, why they work towards church reform and a new understanding of Church-as-People and/or why they want to be priests, but a chapter in which their wishes and their denial by the Church is given space for suggesting ways to think anew about the institution, administration and accountability of the Church. What is Church for?

Some of the interviewees have felt a profound calling for the ministerial priesthood, but because of official denial of their call, became critical and moved into different professional settings. The denial of their call became the very trigger to look at the question 'Who and what is Church?' It was the pathway for thinking about new models of Church, and in many ways for pioneering different ways of interaction, support, partnership and being community. Some have reflected on their relationship with the Church, working in a non-ministerial capacity. What comes through is the tremendously high level of commitment and a reservoir of good will. If all the sheer hard work demonstrated by the nine interviewees, and by many more people around the globe, is not valued and not wanted by the present Church, then it will not only be the poorer for it, but will cease to be the locus of worship, of liberation.

Breaking the Word

Marie Bouclin,[1] from Canada, has reflected on her relationship with the Church over the years, often with sadness and frustration. She has always wanted to 'work in the Church', which made her choose religious life at eighteen. She left her community at twenty-five because she wanted to marry and have a family. To nourish her faith she joined Bible study groups, she became the organist in her parish in order to participate more actively in planning and celebrating liturgies. Only in her fifties did she realize that all along what she really wanted was to be a priest. This realization about her vocation became quite clear after she had been fired from her position as executive assistant to her bishop and secretary general for a diocesan synod.

Refusing to throw the baby (faith) out with the bath water
(the feeling of being rejected 'within' the Church because she
was a woman), she picked up the theological studies she had
abandoned twenty-five years earlier. She loved 'doing theology',
'trying to understand – see – God', and wanted to share her
insights and faith with others, but had no 'ministry'. It was
when she was asked to help women victims of sexual abuse and
exploitation by clergy that she felt a most powerful longing to
bring the healing power of Christ in the form of sacramental
help, especially the Eucharist and Reconciliation, to women who
had been broken by the abuse of power by clergy.

Her role model was Lyn Fisher, an Anglican priest whom she
met at a workshop on spirituality as a source of healing for
women abused by clergy. Lyn is pastor of two small parishes
in Northern Ontario and devotes much of her time to spiritual
direction. When Marie attended Communion and celebrated the
sacrament of Reconciliation with Lyn as part of her own spiritual journey, she wished she could minister to others as Lyn
did. She sometimes recognizes herself as doing priestly work
already. For instance, she gave the homily in her parish, a parish
that closed at the end of June 2002 as no priest was found to
replace the pastor.[2] She also helps prepare children for Confir-
mation. In her base community, she sometimes leads women's
Eucharists, as do at least two other women who also feel called
to the ordained priesthood. She has been called upon as a theology consultant in sexual abuse cases, most recently by General
Counsel to the Ministry of the Attorney General, Dianna Fuller,
of the Superior Court of Ontario.

Marie views her priestly tasks as living as a disciple of Christ,
practising caring, compassion and kindness, first in her own
home and then outside her home, with vulnerable and less fortunate people; making her knowledge of God and her theological
learning available to others as a guest homilist in other churches
or by facilitating workshops on spirituality. She calls this process
'breaking the Word' with the community and applying its message to their daily lives. To her, priesthood is about gathering

the community together around the Word and the Eucharist and celebrating the sacraments, that is using symbols and rituals and leading in prayer to make people aware of God's presence in their lives.

Marie's idea of Church resembles that of many other women: a small compassionate community, a communion of equal disciples who gather together to worship God and then disperse to build a better world. In her understanding, the role of the priestly leadership is to discern, with the community and the help of the Spirit, the gifts of each of its members, to invite them to use them for the greater good of all, to bring into being a network where people support one another.

The old model of Church, something she calls the 'phallocratic pyramid of descending domination', male-centred rather than Christ-centred, with Canon Law taking precedence over Gospel values, she sees as detrimental to true human fulfilment. The old split, between laity and clergy in the personal realm and between body and soul in the theological understanding, is corrosive and cannot possibly contribute to building the kingdom of God. As long as the role of the vast mass of believers, called pejoratively 'laity' as if they were uneducated people, is confined to 'pay, pray, obey', the Church cannot tap into the potential of all its members. In her view, a theology of sacrifice and suffering that condones violence and oppression of the weak and vulnerable is no longer credible. The whole idea of salvation has to be revisited and renewed.

Marie is convinced that a new vision of Church will stress the community life as communion, that is a eucharistic or thanksgiving community. She has no objection to an episcopal model where the community gathers around the bishop, understood as the leader responsible for teaching, governing and sanctifying the People of God. She feels, however, the bishop should come from the people, as should priests, and be answerable to the people.

Collaborative ministry means assigning responsibilities according to the gifts and talents and charisms people have for specific ministries, recognizing the gift of others and working with them. She stresses a much broader understanding of ministry as service, which envelops not just priests or deacons, but is inclusive and open to all, men and women, married or single, each according to their gifts and not their social status. This vision of radical equality and local accountability has grown over the years due to her work with victims of sexual abuse. The Church needs to be local, decision-making needs to be left to the local bishop – not the faraway Vatican Curia – in her/his diocese, or the local priest in her/his parish, with the help of experts from among the community. This also means that priests need to be answerable to their bishops, open to her/his guidance on how 'to keep alive the faith of our fathers-mothers' while at the same time finding contemporary ways of adapting the faith to our own times. However, a priest is also answerable to the community she/he leads – otherwise we are back to the patriarchal model of 'according to Canon Law, I'm the boss in this parish'.

Marie has academic qualifications that would fit her for priestly service. She has a degree in systematic and pastoral theology, but has not been called to pastor to a community although members of her own parish have told her that she would be their choice to replace the pastor who retired. She obviously has no mandate whatsoever from her bishop and her vocation has never officially been validated. But her faith community is a small university parish and a small community of Catholic feminist women who celebrate women's Eucharists together once a month. She has found a place where she can learn and grow with a community that shares her values and passion for a renewed Church.

Marie is one example of a rich talent wasted by the Church. She still offers her services and she is still denied a ministerial priestly role. Her call for collaborative ministry and locally accountable administration is but the logical extension of her personal experiences.

The Imagined *Status Quo*: Reminiscences of King Kanute

'Yes, I would like to be a priest in the sense of being able to exercise a full pastoral ministry in the Church and not being restricted in that because I am a woman. However, I do not want to be a priest in the priesthood as it is currently exercised in the Church.' This sentence is the opening and closing of many a discussion with women who have reflected seriously about their role in the Church. In Anne Martin's case,[3] her conviction grew out of her work as a Religious Sister. Working in education and pastoral settings in Britain and Africa, she would very often have liked to fulfil the pastoral needs of the people she was with, and in particular to give them absolution in the name of the Church. The majority of Catholics in the world cannot go to Mass on a Sunday because there are no priests. 'We are a sacramental Church in essence and to prevent the people from receiving the sacraments because of a church discipline which does not allow married priests or women priests is hardly pastoral and has little to do with Gospel values.'

She is one of many women who have theology degrees and varied pastoral experience, but cannot work, and be paid, in a parish. There are some people, who because they see her as an 'official' member of the Church, engage with her in a directly pastoral capacity, but for the most part her ministry is lived out in her everyday life.

Anne's problem with the system as it is now is not just the way priesthood is viewed; it is how the parish system is maintained. While we should think of Church as 'the People of God', a community, the parish community has atrophied into an administrative unit. Early Christian communities celebrated the gifts of the individual members, valued the individual and focused on the Eucharist in their homes, with the elders taking a role as facilitators. From the time of Constantine Christian communities became increasingly linked with local government. The Church-as-People, celebrating the eucharistic meal in their houses disappeared and the Church-as-Institution took over: the

administrative unit called parish, made up of the households
under the spiritual care of an elder of that community, became
for the convenience of the government the administrative centre
of local governments. This administrative use of the Christian
community organization served the state and the Church well
for many centuries. Today, however, conditions are different.
In the first place: in many countries very few people live and
work in the same place, so the traditional geographically based
parish has little or no relevance in many people's lives. Second,
in the past often the only person who was literate was the priest,
but today many parishioners may be as well or better educated
than the clergy, even in theology. Today a bureaucratic model
of parish is no longer in demand.

A new model of Church needs to embrace all members of the
community. Anne's view of the task of a priest is a person who
facilitates spiritual growth in others. The prevalent role of the
priest, as the person who does everything in the parish and
on whom everything depends and who is not accountable to
anybody, is one that is abusive to both the priest and parishioners. Anne wants a collaborative model of Church, with
mutual learning, giving and receiving. In such a Church, people
would use their talents for the benefit of the community, with
all members being listeners and all having a voice that is heard.
A practical example of this would be to replace, at some times,
the homily by asking members of the congregation to share
thoughts on the readings.

It is important to remember that people in different stages of
life have different stages of faith. Respect needs to be paid both
to the people who have a more traditional style of faith and to
others with a prophetic vision; the Church of the future needs
to allow everyone a place. The Catholic, 'universal' Church has
in the past been all-embracing, accepting throughout its long
history different points of view. The monolithic stance it displays
at the moment needs to be discarded, because such a monolithic
Church only exists in the hierarchical mind, not in history.

Another aspect that needs consideration is whether priesthood should have to be for life. Ideally it should arise out of the community and change as the community changes. The pub church or the house church, meeting in people's front rooms, would emphasize the feeling of belonging far more than being in a building called 'church'.

There is no shortage of vocations today, but there is a shortage of acceptance. The many people with vocations to ministry in the Church, be they married men or married and single women, are simply overlooked, rejected, snubbed, told to go away, to change their denomination, anything as long as they do not bother the bishops further. King Kanute is sitting on the shore, but can he command the waters not to rise and fall? When the needs of the people are not met, and the church authorities behave as if the Church exists for priests instead of the other way round, such a Church is Church no longer. By contrast, we know from history that the Church has existed without priests in times of persecution for many years.

There is a widespread ignorance of scripture and church history. When people are told that Jesus did not institute the priesthood, they are astonished because this is contrary to their understanding of Christian tradition. The only references to priesthood in the New Testament are of Jesus as the High Priest, the priesthood of all believers and the priests of the Jewish temple. Priesthood has its origin in Jesus Christ, but the contemporary role of a priest owes more to Constantine than to Jesus.

Anne, at fifty something, believes that we must work for change and continue to do so, but she is less driven than at times in the past. She feels that events are in progress which of themselves will bring about radical changes in the Church. There simply are not the male celibate vocations in many parts of the Church today which would be needed for a maintenance on the old level.[4] Another factor is that the claims of clerical abuse in the Church and the consequent enormous compensation claims, particularly in North America, are already having an effect on church finances. These two facts will ensure that the current models of priesthood and church administration will buckle and possibly collapse. She does not bemoan these two facts, but calls them 'the moment of the Spirit'. Far from decrying what is happening, we can use crises as levers, as tools for making something new which is life-giving if we have the courage to change.

Whereas in the past religious denominations have been important aspects of personal identity, there is today a much greater sense of ecumenism, and the recognition that there is more that unites than divides us. Many people are in fact attending a church of their choosing because they find a Christian community there that is more in tune with their spiritual needs than their own parish church. There is such a search for the spiritual in life and finding meaning in life, that traditional Catholics are turning to Pentecostalism, house churches, evangelical churches, Buddhism, Quaker meetings, sometimes in conjunction with also going to Mass on Sunday.

The mix-and-match Church is the shape of things to come. If people go back to Gospel values, they will look for a church or Christian community where they live and not be hemmed in by outdated notions of parish boundaries. Particularly in rural areas, with the closure or amalgamation of parishes and the consequent difficulty of getting to Mass on Sundays, it will be unavoidable that people will turn to community or house churches nearer home.

Inevitably the question arises as to the interpretative quality in which the faith is handed on by clerically trained as well as by non-clerical specialists in community or house churches. This is an important question. However, at the moment many of us are asking ourselves, 'Where do we hear the right teaching today?' It is not necessarily through the average homily. The abortion or divorce rates among Catholics are not much different from those of the rest of society, which clearly indicates that certain church teachings are universally disregarded or rejected. People are making their own decisions. Whether in the Church as we know it today or in the future Church, there is a need to educate, to help people have an informed conscience. Anecdotal evidence suggests that this kind of education happens in community groups, the members of which together take their development as Catholic Christians seriously.

Questions about accountability will have to be answered. We might take a look at some religious congregations at the time of the Second Vatican Council in the 1960s. They were highly structured, with a uniformity of life-style and tradition no matter where they were in the world. In the past few decades their uniformity has disappeared and the individual maturity of members has increased with a different dynamic and relationship between members of the community. There has been an increase in discernment and accountability in which each one takes personal and collective responsibility. Whereas beforehand, the direction was from the top down, there is dialogue today, a two-way communication between the individual members and the leadership or Generalate level.

At the moment the church authorities present themselves as a network, like a spider's web, in which the channels of communication are one-way, whereas the future model needs to have channels that are two-way. Because channels today are one-way, those at the bottom of the hierarchy are fearful and those at the top are full of mistrust. With a different dynamic, with those in posts of responsibility being accountable to those who delegate their responsibility, be that at house church or parish level, mistrust can turn into trust.

There is still so much emphasis on Church as a building and a building is rigid. The image of Church as the People of God implies the living dynamic, continually changing and developing and open to the Spirit. Jesus lived and died a Jew. He did not set out to found a new religion; that happened after he had died. Anne is therefore optimistic for the Church. Like King Kanute, the Vatican cannot hold back the sea of change, cannot hold on to the imagined *status quo* as if it could command the seas.

To summarize: the example of house churches, with their individual style and local connection, is attractive to anchor Church far more meaningfully in people's lives in the future.

This is not borne out by a pie-in-the-sky idealism. If one looks at the Free Church or non-conformist house churches, there is plenty of scope for improvement. But the model is workable, a local community, valuing the gifts of each of its members. Anne's suggestions are practical, going further than Marie Bouclin who sees a place for a hierarchical Church also in the future. However, this is not a contradiction, but chimes with Anne's view that people, in their different stages of life, are in different stages of faith, faith practice, needs and need fulfilment.

Community Building in a Priestless Parish

Andrea Johnson,[5] from the USA, served several times as a director of religious education and a secondary level religious education teacher in parishes. She was parish minister in a priestless parish in rural Virginia where she experienced her call to ordination. Having spent many years as catechist, she was hired by an army post chapel to co-ordinate parish ministries for the Catholic congregation. The parish had lost its Catholic chaplain's billet, and depended on contract priests from Washington for the sacraments. The parish was fairly conservative and very Mass-oriented, and was distraught at the loss. Needless to say, they were less than enthralled at Andrea's arrival and the new arrangements. She was the on-site, day-in day-out parish minister. The priest travelled an hour to be with the parish for four hours per week. Andrea started to do the best job of 'co-ordination' that she could.

The process very quickly revealed itself to be a mammoth community building project. A parish council was formed and empowered and people were trained in great numbers for liturgical and education ministries. Adult education and spirituality programmes took off. After six months, the community had bonded. The priests who came on Sundays were happily drawn into the circle. A new way of being a Catholic community came into being. Andrea, the catalyst, felt that she was not in control of all that was happening. She felt stretched doing this work, but was happy to be stretched. She felt part of something very creative. The community's response to her efforts led her to understand her call. It was their interaction with her that called forth the reflection that allowed her to hear the voice of God.

For the moment, she sees her role as working towards the ordination of women through networks promoting this agenda. In her support of women who wish to train for the priesthood, she does priestly work. She has found a community, empowered and empowering, which is engaged in a renewed ministry. This, to her, is the next step, to usher in and promote a new understanding of priesthood, which does not exclude women. Her model of Church has drawn upon the gifts of the members of her community and has fulfilled a number of criteria mentioned by Anne Martin when speaking about house church.

Women's Worship Circle

Judith McKloskey,[6] from the USA, first heard a call to priesthood when at primary school. It did not involve her in pursuing seminary training and the call went into the back of her mind, since the reality was that in the RC Church, women as priests was a forbidden dream. The call, however, never diminished; she joined a religious congregation, but left after two and a half years. Further training, marriage, a family, however, did not obliterate her call. She now understands that this call had never been to sisterhood, but always to priesthood.

Judith had a spiritual director with whom she could talk freely about vocation. She acknowledged it and celebrated her identity as priest after a thorough discussion with him. She discovered a group of women who celebrated the Eucharist on a regular basis. It was called the Women's Worship Circle, which at that point in her life became an important place for her. 'Whatever the glitches or foibles or disparate visions, that group, which no longer meets, manifested God to me ... What did matter was that here was a group of women who stopped waiting for permission that wasn't forthcoming – women who took our

authority as baptized Christians into our own hands and worshipped our God in a multitude of creative ways.' She prepared
and led services, valuing most the authenticity of the group.
Members cherished their experiences of God, while Judith
appreciates the creativity that was released in this circle.

In Judith's story, the value of small groups becomes clear, as
she took the experience of that group into the larger community
in which she serves today. Today, she lives out her priestly
identity as fully as possible. In her parish she has been commissioned as a lay preacher, one of a group who preach at
Sunday Eucharists presided at by priests. She presides at week-
day communion services when the priest is away. She listens
and responds when women come and ask her to 'hear my
confession'. Frequently, she encourages others to respond fully
to their baptismal calls. She takes the many little steps necessary to bring priestly presence in people's lives – echoing Mary
Hunt's 'Priests, Priests Everywhere and not a Single One
Ordained'.[7]

Judith's work brackets both tendencies, the one formulated
by Marie Bouclin and Andrea Johnson, to work within the given
structures, as well as the other, formulated by Anne Martin, to
set up your own structure. The range of priestly activities exercised within the institutional set-up gives her space to function
as priest as fully as possible. She is happy to have found this
space and will, no doubt, expand it in due time. For others this
is not enough, either in scope or in recognition. For her it works
for the moment and might well be the middle way that will be
chosen by many women to follow, not only in pursuit of priestly
ministry, but also in their understanding of church organization
and to this end she is applying her gifts.

It is Essential to Remove Prejudice

What is the changing perception of women in the Church today?
Having been brought up a Catholic, Mary Ann Rossi,[8] from the
USA, found that because her husband was not a Catholic, she

was not allowed to be married on the altar of an R C Church. The parish priest Monsignor William Botticelli, in Torrington, Connecticut, in 1954, maintained that he could merely bless the marriage with a fifteen-minute ceremony. To her it felt like the exclusion her parents suffered when her elder sister who was born dead was prohibited from being buried in a church cemetery because she was not baptized. The baby was buried in an unmarked grave, not in consecrated ground.

Mary Ann and her husband decided to join the Episcopalian Church and brought up their four children in that Church. When her daughter married a Catholic in 1982, they were still not allowed to receive communion at her daughter's bridal Mass.

In 1976 the Episcopalian Synod in the USA voted to ordain women priests. But the bishop of Mary Ann's diocese of Green Bay had a meeting after this vote and announced to the congregation in the church that although the vote was taken, there would never be a woman priest in his diocese. He was crying when he announced this. At that point something clicked in Mary Ann. She suddenly realized that she could not set foot in that church again, which she did not do until twenty years later, for the funeral service of her daughter.

The short biographical sketch is important as it provides the key to understanding Mary Ann's next steps. She wondered where were the women in the church leadership, finding it difficult to believe that women had been excluded from the beginning of Christianity. She then turned to church history to discover what was the perception of women in the early Church. She immersed herself in research and found evidence that women have always been 'there', speaking out, ministering to the needs of the people and fulfilling the role of a caring and a loving Church in society. She therefore took the questions 'Why is the Church silent about these women?' and 'Why have they been silenced?' as her research topic. She studied archival sources which made it plain that from the Council of Trullo in 692 onwards there has been an imposition of silence on women in the Christian Church. Although this Council is not seen as an

ecumenical Council, decisions taken there were incorporated
into the body of orthodox Canon Law.[9]

At best women were ranked among the simple-minded, who
needed protection from corrupt and wicked men or vagrant
monks, while at worst they were seen to constitute an equally
dangerous tendency towards un-Christian behaviour in society.
These polar opposites meant that women were perceived as a
source of both innocence and corruption. The fear of female
potential triggered the determination to keep women under control. Both aspects are typical of medieval societies, but their
influence can still be felt today, in the current gag order of
the Vatican to prevent discussion of women's ordination to the
priesthood,[10] still in line with canons first formulated at the
Council of Trullo in 692. These were then included in the Nomo-
canon, the most important medieval compilation of civil and
ecclesiastical law, which remained influential to the fourteenth
century. It was a Canon Law instrument that prescribed and
legalized a cultural construct, the 'defect' of women's behaviour,
within Church and society. The echoes of this legislation are
heard today in all church documents on women. Mary Ann
agrees with Judith Herrin, that 'This Council in Trullo marks
the source of a long process of excluding women from active
participation in the liturgy.'[11]

In her studies Mary Ann came across Giorgio Otranto's
research in the Vatican library,[12] notably his findings about grave
inscriptions naming women priests in the early Church. She
translated Otranto's articles from Italian into English and published them and thereby brought to public attention his evidence
that women were indeed ordained in the early Church, em-
barking on lecture tours to spread the good news. She found it
inexplicable that this testimony had not been acknowledged
before. The traditional perception of women has blinded people
to documentation, such as that about Leta, specifically called
'priest' of the town of Tropea in Catania, Southern Italy. Her
husband is referred to as 'maritus' while she is referred to as
'presbytera'. Otranto's contention is that if the husband had

been the priest of Tropea, he would not refer to himself as 'maritus'. Leta must be a priest in her own right, 'presbytera' meaning a woman who has been ordained into the holy orders as leader of the community and has assumed the duty of preaching, residing and teaching, the three duties that define the role of those admitted to the sacrament of priesthood.

Mary Ann began to realize that historiographers of the Church have been blinded to such testimony as Leta's by their preconception that women could not have been ordained. In their view the title 'Leta Presbytera' must be construed to signify 'Leta, the wife of the priest'. But Atto of Vercelli, a noted scholar of the Church in the eighth century, makes clear that 'presbytera' signified both 'priest' and 'wife of a priest'. Of the two meanings, Atto says he prefers the first. Yet of the many ecclesiastical lexica, only the *Glossarium* of Du Cange[13] includes the definition of 'presbytera' preferred by Atto of Vercelli.[14] Such devices for narrowing down or outright erasing of women's presence have been detrimental to all women.

Mary Ann continued to find sources that would irrefutably demonstrate that women exercised priestly ministry. But the question arises as to how this leadership role would be exercised today. If women were ordained, the Church would need to transform its perception of women as subservient and subordinate. Since women comprise the majority of church membership today, they must no longer agree with the two assumptions, that of the exclusively male leadership in the Church and that women are second class. By virtue of the sacrament of baptism, women are eligible to be ordained.

The ordination of women in many Churches of the Anglican Communion has changed the perception of women. Mary Ann finds a sense of justice, of rightness, seeing women officiating as priests. Of course, she is fully aware of the fact that there is still discrimination against women priests in those Christian Churches that ordain women, when women are put into posts that male applicants do not want. The main task therefore is to remove from the consciousness of all women the deleterious and persistent self-hatred that is imposed by the received teachings and the customs and the law of the Christian Churches. Every breakthrough of awareness, such as the knowledge that women have always performed priestly ministry, have always contributed to the community, have always suffered with the community and achieved things for the individuals and the community, will open the door to women's realization that they are fully human and fully qualified for ministry. For far too long have they been convinced of their inferiority by the woman-hating convictions of the Church Fathers, ingrained in the doctrines, mandates, and canons of church law.[15]

Women can only achieve this goal by constantly chipping away the artificial limitations put upon them. In 1993, a group of women founded Catholic Women's Ordination, CWO, in London. The group has met monthly at the Piazza of Westminster Cathedral, with a display of banners with slogans such as 'Hope for Women Priests' and a prayer vigil. Mary Ann, whenever in England, has joined these vigils and has noticed that passers-by, often women, pour vitriolic scorn on those gathered for prayer, and shout: 'Why are you always here?' and 'You won't go away, you are destroying the Church!'[16] Mary Ann takes this as an important example, showing the full acceptance by some believers about women's subservient place. More important, it shows the knee-jerk obedience to the law of silence imposed on everyone by *Ad Tuendam Fidem*. Seeing a small group of women and men praying for women's ordination exasperates such people.

The acceptance of women's ordination in the Church is a necessary step, similar to gaining the vote, to provide role models for women in parishes worldwide, thus for the first time developing the full inclusion of women in all aspects of church life. One way to achieve progress might be through the house church movement, with small groups concelebrating and sharing their lives. It is essential for the Church to do what it can do best: remove prejudice. Once the future Church has accepted this role, the path for true inclusion and growth is open. Seminary education will become a thing of the past; the present catholic culture limits both human and the consequent spiritual maturing. Living by example, maturing together, might be the way to achieve a renewed Church.

For Mary Ann, going to the sources, studying church history, became the method with which to find answers and a prophetic insight into what is needed today. Her life is embedded in the gifts offered by a sacramental Church. For her the community aspect of Church is important, be it in a traditional parish set-up or a more prophetic house church context. An enormous task of education needs to be started, that of re-educating women of their own worth and men of the intrinsic worth of women, on all levels of Church and society. The goal, to remove prejudice, is the echo of the goal of Suffragettes campaigning for women's suffrage. Sexual discrimination in state and society is banned, it has to go also in the Church. She has investigated the faulty view of 'tradition' with its ban on women priests and has come up with a much older tradition with its priestly profession for women. She works as scholar and campaigner to chip away presumptions and prepare the way for a partnership of women and men in Church.

Why We Must be Heard

Whenever Sue Williamson[17] thinks about Church and her own place in it, she confesses to being torn by conflicting feelings. Ideally, if the Church were relatively democratic with structures for true dialogue to take place, then it might be possible to stand back from the brink on which she now finds herself. As the Vatican is gradually reversing the reforms of the Second Vatican Council, she feels the crisis in the Church is becoming more and more acute. For Sue, being committed means being active and radical and critiquing institutions of state and Church, as her grandparents and parents did. Members of Sue's family had been actively involved in setting up the Trade Union movement and the Labour Party.

In her youth Sue believed she had a call to priesthood, but when she discussed it with a Redemptorist priest, he replied uncaringly, 'We cannot have bunnies on the altar!' The misogyny and fear of women's bodies in that statement only had its full impact on her years later. She has met many committed believers, in Secular Institutes, in Religious Orders, especially members of the Grail and the Sisters of the Sacred Heart Congregation as well as radical Jesuits. In her student days, she organized liturgies that she called 'unofficial', but which nevertheless ensured that she and those celebrating with her participated fully.

In her professional life as a teacher she has met many women who would have been splendid priests and bishops, but would dispute that they had such a vocation. They could not or would not follow such a calling and Sue felt angry on their behalf. Through taking additional courses in theology, pastoral studies and Biblical studies she hoped to be able to work as a prison chaplain. Chaplaincy posts only seemed to be open to those who were recognizably religious, that is nuns or priests, so Sue became a special education teacher in schools and colleges, eventually qualifying to help those with dyslexia. Latterly she became head of Basic Skills in a high security prison in London.

The Iona Community has played a very significant and special part in Sue's life. This ecumenical community, which has its spiritual power base on the island of Iona off the west coast of Scotland, where St Columba founded an abbey and community, is deeply committed to justice and peace, as well as being totally egalitarian. Celtic spirituality also influences its prayer life. The experience of being with the Iona Community made Sue realize that what really mattered was Christianity, not denomination. This gave her the strength to continue working with a deeper vision of what Christianity might be. In this process there was also a feeling of being alienated as a single woman, not fitting into the categories of wife, mother or nun.

When the Synod of the Church of England voted to admit women to the priesthood with a two-thirds majority in 1992,

Sue felt an extraordinary sensation: all the pent-up anger and frustration of years came flooding back and yet she did not know anyone else felt like her. Having been a member of two radical women's organizations, St Joan's Alliance, founded in 1912 to campaign for the ordination of women, and the Catholic Women's Network, set up in 1984, she was invited to the inaugural meeting of what was to become the British organization for the ordination of women in the Church, Catholic Women's Ordination, CWO. There were many present at the first AGM in 1994, who, over the years, slowly dropped away, but Sue felt she had to stay and fight for women's ordination if she were to remain a Catholic. She met with some people who were seasoned campaigners on other issues, and those who had not yet taken that route. Together, however, all realized that making the issue visible was essential. So began the various actions taken by the group, such as monthly vigils on the Piazza of Westminster Cathedral in central London and a prayerful presence at the Chrism Mass in Holy Week in front of several cathedrals in Britain. Sue became a networker in Catholic Women's Ordination and a member of the National Co-ordinating Group.

The Augustinian understanding of the Eucharist, where the priest elevates the host saying 'The Body of Christ' and the congregation respond 'I am', is essential to Sue's vision of Church and the priesthood within it. In her view, any true priest would facilitate the transformation of the community into the Body of Christ. This was the vision of the early Church, the discipleship of equals, where leaders emerged from their communities, and women as well as men were 'presbyters' and 'deacons', as Mary Ann Rossi demonstrated.

In recent times, the model of the base communities in South America and Paolo Freire's three-step model of discernment[18] have provided workable ways to enable others to express themselves liturgically and to facilitate networking and political awareness from the grassroots. The concepts of hearing the voice of the people, of being inclusive and participatory, need to become the concepts of a renewed Church. So much has been

said about the option for the poor, the priority for a prophetic
Church, for justice and peace. For too long a distorted theology
has diminished the actual representation of the divine in the life
of people – a thought more fully expressed in an article by
Matthew Fox: 'Somehow we have to start putting these concepts
into action, to embody them worldwide, as the agenda for our
twenty-first century.'[19]

Sue's political credo is the motor for her understanding of
Church. The Augustinian understanding of the Eucharist presents a practice that is much more important, because inclusive,
for her. She desires a prophetic Church, which is far less involved
with hammering out rules and regulations and much more concerned with the basic needs of people.

The Story of a Purple Stole

The theologian and Religious Sister Ruth Schäfer,[20] Medical
Missionary of Mary, SCMM, demonstrated her support of
women's ordination by wearing a purple stole during the ordination ceremony of male ordinands in the diocese of Essen, Germany, on 29 May 1998. The colour purple as the liturgical
colour of mourning and the stole as the priestly symbol have
first been worn by women in the UK and then adopted by
women in many countries as symbolic expression of mourning
for women's lost gifts in all Churches.[21] The RC Bishop of
Essen, Hubert Luthe, decided to act quickly and ordered Sister
Ruth to a meeting with him. The press statement made clear
that since Sister Ruth had not been prepared to change her views
on ordination, he thought it better to save her further pain by
not renewing her contract with the diocese to train pastoral
assistants.

In spite of this edict Ruth was asked to deliver the homily on
the World Day for Vocations in 2000. It is published here
as an example of the problems faced when tensions remain
unresolved.

Dear Sisters and Brothers,

Instead of preaching on the biblical text on vocation itself, I would like to tell you of my own experience with vocation today. Maybe you know some of it from your own life? I hope that my thoughts might be such that you understand what determines my own conviction.

Many years ago I thought that vocation was something for somebody else. Vocation was something for experts in piety, notably priests. I had not thought that it was something that would involve me. After all, I have not always been a Religious Sister. Nobody in my group of friends had ever spoken seriously of having had a vocation. Friends wanted to train for a profession, not for a vocation.

And then, relatively young, I joined a community, which meant that I changed sides. Now everybody thought of me that I must have had a vocation – maybe a vocation which still needed to be tested, but nevertheless a vocation. Talk of it was quite clear: if a woman joins a religious order, the process of discernment for one's vocation was thought to be one of the most important facts. Personnel for just such developments are made available. It was then that I learned to pay attention to being in tune with feelings and to take decisions consciously according to these feelings and before God.

In a certain sense everybody was happy. I was happy with my vocation to the religious life, my impression that this way of life before God was fitting for me. My society gave me permission to take the vows of the community. And the Church seemed to be happy to have a young Religious Sister once again.

Then I read theology at university and recognized another facet of my vocation. I have found that I could imagine a life as priest. I had the training to test my vocation and I did so according to the same standards as before, with the result that, against all expectations, my own impression hardened to a subjective certainty. I felt called to be a Religious Sister and also a priest. After all, why should there be different decisions for me from my fellow students, simply because I was a woman? I decided to talk about this aspect of my vocation in public. The scandal for the diocese was huge, I was told, but what have I done which was so bad? Many communities and parishes suffer from the fact that they no longer have priests and I could contribute to alleviate the situation.

Today, I stand much more critically in front of you after having taken my decision. I have learnt that talk about having a vocation is relatively arbitrary. It is permitted to some and not to others. What does it mean, 'I have a vocation?' I do not 'have' a vocation, rather, the vocation has chosen me. It led me to a decision that I had never thought I would have to take.

Having made the decision I stand much more convinced – and if you want, much more believing – in front of you. I have become totally convinced that it makes a difference how we look at life. What helps me is the trust that God knows me, that he points me to a good way through life. If I experience myself as having been put by God into a certain situation, then I will work differently and will develop great inner strength.

Really, we may trust Christ, when he said, 'I am the good Shepherd, I know my flock.' Who should know us better than he? Let us try to go our way with him, or first of all to find our way with him. Then the second part of the Bible quote will become reality, 'I am the good Shepherd, I know my flock and my flock knows me.' Amen.[22]

This homily encompasses Ruth's understanding of Church. Renewal does not depend on big words and unwieldy plans, it happens all around us, unseen at first. As a woman from Germany she experiences a rich Church, a well-oiled bureaucracy paying its priests high salaries. There are committees for everything, in short the institution is a complicated machinery. It is involved with itself, struggling to follow directions or find directions. What is missing is credibility. Often the well-funded exterior covers up a spiritual void.

The Church is sated. Ruth, however, is hungry for simplicity. 'At bottom, our faith is simple.' People who search for and find God are simple; they are not naïve. They do not need to hide behind complicated phrases. It is the gift of simplicity that stands against the lust for careers, the intrigues and fights for power in the Church. This gift opens the heart for the poor. It goes without saying that structural change for the sake of justice, and in particular for the case of gender justice, is dear to her heart. And yet she feels that the power to usher in such change, and with it the renunciation of power by men, springs from the simplicity of one's personal relationship to God. The hunger of people cries out for those who have spiritual experience, who try to live their faith and not just talk about it. Therefore, in Ruth's eyes, the future of the Church depends on the 'increase of simplicity'. It is nearly always enough to do that which one realizes as right in the eyes of God. It is not necessary to do more, neither for the new beginnings, which have to happen again and again in one's personal life, nor for the reforms in our Church.

Ruth, while working within the Church, is a visionary, a prophet, a campaigner. The call for 'simplicity' in the Church and faith life resonates with so many calls by many groups actively engaged in working towards better solutions for a greater mass of people. Whether they are environmentalists who are serious about the grave dangers posed by misunderstood 'development', whether they are campaigners for the rights and dignity of big numbers of people who suffer discrimination, the call for 'simplicity' is the call for structural change, in society as well as in the Church.

Ministries in Prisons – Prophets not Priesthood

This last section is giving space to a husband and wife team. It is therefore somewhat longer than the previous analyses, because it highlights the work-in-partnership. Petronella Phillips-Devaney[23] is a member of the RC chaplaincy team at Pentonville Prison in London, where she and her husband Barry share a music ministry, providing the musical accompaniment and leading the choir of prisoners who sing at Mass each Sunday. HMP Pentonville is a Category B prison, which houses around 1,000 male inmates; some are there for a short time on remand, awaiting trial, others are serving long sentences for serious and sometimes violent crimes. Petronella and Barry work with the prisoners each Saturday and Sunday, and as a long-time teacher of meditation, Petronella has introduced her prisoner choir members to this form of prayer. It is a service of commitment, which Petronella loves and which, she says, has deeply enriched her life. What does a woman with Petronella's background and talents and faith have to say on the question of making faith life meaningful, creating community for those who are forced to live with each against their will?

To begin with, working with prisoners is not like working with people in an ordinary parish, free to come and go as they please. Her husband claims he can no longer imagine a Sunday service where the congregation is not body-searched – all the inmates are body-searched before coming into the chapel. The prisoners cannot choose which Mass they attend – there is only the one Mass on Sunday morning – nor can they just pop into church for a quick prayer during the week. Above all, there is no parish priest in the normal sense. Each week a different priest is saying Mass, and there is no priest with responsibility to the prisoners. This role falls to the married deacon who is the senior member of the RC chaplaincy team. The priests who say Mass come and go each Sunday, some reappear but there is little sense of continuity.

Petronella has become convinced that the structure of priestly ministry needs to be reviewed and reformed, and with it, liturgy and worship. In any case, the current lack of vocations in terms of male celibates will instigate change in spite of the present resistance from the topmost echelons of the hierarchy. Like many Catholics who love the Mass but also long for the opportunity to explore other forms of liturgy, where everyone has a chance to contribute and share, Petronella feels that the way forward is, at least in part, a matter of smaller groups meeting regularly and creating liturgies that reflect their own situations and understanding of God. Priestly ministry, she thinks, is important, but she sees no reason at all why it should be confined to male celibates. At Pentonville, the senior Catholic chaplain is a married deacon, and the Anglican chaplain is a married man also. The fact that they have normal family lives makes it possible for them to relate to those they serve in a way that they would not be able to otherwise. Often priests seem to have an idealized and unrealistic idea of married life and parenthood, one that ordinary people find it hard to relate to and even harder to live up to.

One of the longest serving Catholic chaplains at Pentonville is a woman, a Religious, and she is often asked for advice by the prisoners when they need to talk and confide their hopes and anxieties. Petronella has found that many prisoners, carrying their burdens of guilt and shame and worry, long to make their confession and to receive absolution. But they need to do this with someone they know, who they have a rapport with: they are after all incarcerated and marginalized and it is not easy for them to open up. The Catholic chaplains hear what amount to deep acts of confession day after day, but because they are not ordained priests they cannot absolve, and the confession is not sacramentally graced.

The 'Shadow' Side of the Church

In examining the possibilities for new approaches to liturgy within the normal context of church worship, Petronella feels that an obstacle arises due to what Jung called the 'shadow', and which can be described as the dark, hidden side of an individual or an organization. If you want to know your shadow, you have to explore all those things that cause feelings of shame, disgust, disappointment. In therapy you have to start dealing with these very powerful elements, and then, along with an awareness of the formerly repressed contents of the shadow, the creative side emerges and, most of all, the creative female qualities. Normally, women do not allow the whole range of female traits to emerge, only a small, narrowed-down way of being a woman. Women have tended to portray the effeminate as opposed to the female, to act out caricatures of true womanliness, and as such they have suffered a sense of powerlessness and low self-esteem. The Church has, consciously or unconsciously, pandered to false images of femaleness, perhaps because the Church itself does not admit its shadow – it does not like to admit that there is a dark side. But in the search for God you have to go into the dark. Jung used the word 'shadow' for darkness, the unknown, and meant the same thing.

One example of the dark side, of what is hidden, is the recent plethora of accusations of paedophilia against priests, particularly in America, but elsewhere, too. What does it say to us if hundreds of priests stand accused of sexually molesting children, of sexual misconduct with adults, men and women? How do the paedophilia cases that have come to light strike the ordinary Christian? Petronella made a connection: it struck her that the priests are inculturated into a system that encourages them to see themselves as fathers, as father figures. And if they are the fathers, the laity must be the children. 'My child', a priest might gently address a lay person, without in the least meaning or causing offence. But it makes for an odd, unequal relationship. Only in the last generation has it commonly become accepted to call the priest 'Father'. But there are negative patriarchal overtones when using such a title, which in its real context is earned by a sexual act, something a Catholic priest is vowed not to engage in.

We have, according to Petronella, reached a stage where it is very difficult to examine the dark side the Church carries. It is quite painful and repellent for people to see the institution that embodies the Gospel values enmeshed in such evil acts as paedophilia or adult rape, and even worse to know that these crimes have been deliberately concealed by the Church's bishops. In prison, those committed for such crimes have to be segregated for their own safety. Prisoners are generally tolerant of others; but the ones in segregation are considered untouchables. When things emerge from the shadow, they usually provoke an ugly and violent reaction. In an analysis or therapy situation it can even end the analysis. But it can be a good as well as a hard moment. 'In the Church, when things emerge from the shadow, from the hidden part, when weakness and wrongdoing are exposed, it can unleash all hell,' Petronella says. The Church does not allow that this shadow side, what is suppressed and what is dark, is talked about – this stands as a gigantic obstacle in the way of growth and change. Petronella has in herself recognized growing pains and the wish for change, and she is aware that, in one's desire to continue to belong, one has to be immensely careful that one is not sucked into a mentality that resists growth.

The New Spiritual Home

Two years ago, Petronella experienced a long and difficult period of depression. She suffered a sense of spiritual emptiness, and in particular a disenchantment with the Church. After what seemed like a long time, she went to France and found herself in Lisieux, where she experienced a spiritual renewal. It was not about going back, but about knowing that she was all right. And on her return to London, quite out of the blue, she and her husband Barry were invited to take up the music ministry in Pentonville, which she now calls her 'chosen parish'.

She no longer sees Church as a hierarchy of orders, in fact she has many concerns about the question of women's ordination. 'What sort of priests would women be?' Women would not fit in to the present model of priesthood. She has thought a great deal about vocation and ministry, and asks why someone today would want a role that sets them apart from everybody else in the Church, that confers a different status. Shouldn't we all be priests to one another? Baptism already initiates us into a royal priesthood. In seriously considering the ordination of women, we should also be exploring new ways of being a priest.

For Petronella, the Church of the gospels, even with its problems, is still a treasure and her own spiritual way. She says there is an aspect of the Catholic Church that is 'incredibly healthy', encompassing in Jungian terms the positive archetypal imagery of the Saviour, the Divine Child, the Great Mother, the Loving Father, representing energies that have always existed. She calls the Church a living entity, grounded in profound ritual, the health and healing that comes from its empowering symbolism. On the other hand, there is the danger of what is repressed. On the whole she finds that Catholic spirituality has a greater extent of healthy symbolism than shadow images, but from the outside, the shadow is what is more easily perceived.

The Question of Ordination

Ordination becomes an issue for anybody who is on her/his spiritual journey; not just ordination to the priesthood, but the whole question of calling; what am I called to be? Is one person's calling higher because they are sacramentally ordained? Can we not be priests without being ordained? What are the possible alternatives? Petronella detects clues in liturgies that are joyful, energizing and inspiring. She is no longer keen to be a passive person in a liturgy, an observer, somebody who has things done to her, nor is she keen on being the person who makes everybody else passive.

What then would be a workable model of Church for Petronella? Maybe there is not *one* model; for the moment she is happy to work with small groups, where everyone is involved, without any one of them being superior. She quotes Jung, who said there is only one point to therapy, and that is not to fix problems, it is to create the possibility of the analysis and having a direct experience of the divine. Without this direct experience a person is spiritually empty, people spend their whole lives yearning, but nothing will completely fill or fulfil them. They will sublimate their need for God in material things, pleasure seeking or excitement seeking. The prisoners in the choir at Pentonville are serving time for a variety of crimes, all of them anathema to the ordinary law-abiding citizens who make up the average parish. Nevertheless, Petronella has experienced more love and acceptance, courtesy and kindness in the prison choir than anywhere else. Serving, she has discovered, is not a matter of 'doing good', or even just of giving of oneself and one's abilities, but of being open to receive from people who you might think of as having nothing to give. 'Those Jesus called the "little ones" also happen to have the biggest hearts. They are generous and unhampered by the things that concern ordinary people. If we all in the Church *really* focused our attention, as Christ directed us to, on the poor, the sick, the homeless, those in prison, on our neighbours in need, we would all be transformed and so would the Church. And the world would be a better place.'

If people want to follow a spiritual path, the Church must encourage people to seek God themselves. The Church has always worked to instruct the child, but not the adult, in fact the opposite: it infantilizes the adult. And male spirituality does not necessarily fit female spirituality. A lot of the imagery and language of the Church is alien to women. There have been many women mystics who managed to break through, but this kind of breakthrough depends not only on spiritual progress but also on how far a woman has gone on her journey as a *woman*. This is why some women cannot bear the idea of women priests. When a woman is not comfortable with her own femaleness, her negative sense of self as a woman is projected on to other women, and it is then natural that men come to represent the positive, that which is good and desirable.

An Ekklesia *of Prophets*

When, Petronella maintains, we deal with Church on a tribal level all prejudice under the sun comes out. More than women priests, we need women prophets, we need prophets today, women and men who are inspired, who are clear in their own connection with God and themselves and who can talk about God, who can speak prophetically.

How do you 'prophesy'? Prophesy means telling the truth about God from your own experience. Petronella has belonged to a meditation group in which each member has the opportunity to prepare and lead the meditation. Part of the growing comes from everybody having to go away and think about the reading, the meditation, the prayer and the music. It is a way to becoming centred. In following such a practice you come to feel the Spirit guiding you. This is what everybody needs more than anything else. Nowadays Petronella feels less worried about what has to be done, how to organize, how to plan the meditation session, about whether somebody might say something stupid and make the group uncomfortable, or any of the other things that could go wrong. Experience has shown her that she can have faith and trust in the process when God is held at its centre. 'Let go and let God' is a slogan she likes very much. And in fact, she feels the same way about the Church. It is the Spirit who will bring about change, and everything else is arrogance.

Nevertheless it is sad that for so many the experience of Church is of it being boring and fossilized. Stereotyped people do not get the opportunity to express their own spirituality. Mass often seems to be the only service on offer, a Mass that appears to centre on the celebrating priest rather than on God and on the individual and collective experience of the entire congregation.

In a very important insight Petronella likens the small worshipping groups to an A A (Alcoholics Anonymous) meeting. Members often start by knowing that something needs to change in their life, and that they are looking for something they cannot create by themselves. They acknowledge their need for something greater, and through the love and support of the group they are able to begin the voyage of discovery, to understand the need for humility, which is not easy to connect with at a Mass where the majority of people are unknown to each other. A huge group, any huge group – and the Church *is* huge – cannot please everybody. The nascent Church began with a political injunction, 'Go and baptize'. We have to move forward with and from this command if we are to be honest in looking at renewal. When Christianity started it was tribal, it lived in a context that is gone; today the Church has to function in a context that is global and individual.

Petronella says that a part of her is still fascinated by the grandeur and history of the Catholic Church and its ceremonies and with her own history within it. She admits that she gets a lump in her throat if she tries to image 'letting go' to the point of being outside all that. But there comes a time when letting go is a vital step in spiritual development, one that includes asking not only what is priesthood, what is ministry, what is the model of Church, but what does it mean to be a Catholic? In what way does being a Catholic help an individual to become a more complete human being? To grow and develop you have to learn to cope with change. In terms of practice, this can definitely be better facilitated in a small group in which you feel held safely. The church group should function like a container, holding but not restraining the energy.

At present, the Church is not always a safe container. Sometimes it is more like a straitjacket. We are, all of us, Church. And we can change it. Movements start with a few like-minded people who care enough; if what they do and experience is authentic, the movement will thrive. It will attract others and it will have universality/catholicity because it does not exclude anyone. Petronella is convinced that the way forward with small groups as the locus for individual growth will evolve and will release creativity. 'We need to have faith, we need to support each other in living the values that make us Christians and Catholics. Theology and doctrine will go, disappear, become esoteric. People will study them like they study the classics. We need to let go of a lot of the baggage in order to get a new understanding.'

Barry Phillips-Devaney's Music Ministry for Prisoners

Barry, Petronella's husband, is a gifted guitarist who has long been involved with music for liturgy and who currently assists with his wife at the weekly Mass in Pentonville Prison. Every Saturday and Sunday finds this husband and wife team among the prisoners, first in leading a choir practice on Saturday morning and then leading the music at the Sunday Eucharist. The dedication of this married couple is evident and shows in their outreach work, as the prisoners relate well to them and are impressed by the way a man and woman can work together as real partners.

The question of equality is a difficult one to answer in a prison situation, because the prisoners have clearly lost their outer freedom, if not their inner freedom. Barry talks of how much he feels is given back to him by the prisoners every weekend. It is opening up a new understanding of ministry for him. From his experience he particularly feels there is a growing need for more varied forms of ministry and a good beginning was made with the introduction of permanent deacons to the role of prison chaplain, a role he would like to see open to women as a matter of course.

In talking to Barry the word 'humanity' was mentioned more than once. As Barry himself has step-sons, some of the prisoners are delighted to find someone in a similar situation to themselves, who is either remarried or married to someone whose first marriage or partnership broke down – in other words whose life is reassuringly messy. Although there always have to be the necessary boundaries between the prisoners and himself, Barry feels that many of them can relate to the situation of his own personal life, and an obviously happy married life is proving a great witness to the prisoners. Petronella and Barry are not deliberately developing a new concept of partnership, but by their very presence they provide an example of what partnership can be. Because they feel they work better together than alone, the concept of partnership becomes credible.

During the interviews the question of the role of prisoners and preaching came up and Barry explored the benefits and possibilities of prisoners sometimes sharing in homilies with priests to help them articulate their experiences to other prisoners. Obviously these shared homilies would have to be tightly focused and well prepared beforehand. If the men were occasionally, under controlled conditions, allowed to express their faith in a public setting, it would then become possible for them to experience something positive themselves: being of value to others. Thus, a very public affirmation within the framework of the Sunday liturgy would help them and assist their faith through these times.

When asked what kind of future he sees for the Church, Barry's answer came through very clearly – one of inclusivity for all those who felt or in fact were marginalized by their prison sentences, sexual orientation or refugee status. He worries about prisoners when they leave prison and go back to their parishes. Most do not seem to find a worshipping community where they feel they belong. This is why Barry and Petronella are now developing a music and prayer group that would welcome prisoners after their release. A further growing concern Barry has is the number of men who are reoffending and return to prison, often because life is too hard for them or they are too unused to life outside.

When he entered the prison for the first time and the prison gates closed behind him, Barry began to realize that passing through those gates a person really did enter a 'different world', not the kind of a 'different world' advertised over the doors of the luxury store Harrods in London, but a world where former codes and mores do not apply. Barry's call to prison ministry came through another's call and, although initially reluctant, it proved to be a turning point in his life. He found people who really came to pray, and not out of duty or because they wanted to get their children into Catholic schools. They came because they had an understanding of their great need of God. When all self-esteem had been stripped away they felt they were still completely loved by their maker. One regret Barry has is that 'micro' and/or hidden ministries such as Petronella's and his are not recognized publicly by a special ceremony of commissioning or financial recompense. Money is not their top priority but perhaps the Church needs to reassess its financial priorities and dignify this and other ministries in a public way, for the sake of the ministers, for those they serve, and not least for the Church itself.

Petronella and Barry serve in an exceptional place. Their priestly work is much appreciated by everybody they reach. They have made things happen, they have enriched many people's lives by their presence and witness. They, like so many people, stress the importance of small groups, where individuals feel comfortable and secure. Their vision stresses the prophetic side of Church, the need for presence beyond rules and regulations.

Summary

These nine stories present a microcosm of views held both privately and publicly by many people. They exemplify the intensity of those who have chosen to live on the margins. The focused way of living, according to their understanding of the gospels, means that these people are 'seed crystals' of the present for the sake of the future. Some have been led to a more radical stance than others. The case stories illustrate the rainbow colours of this transitional age. All experiences narrated are the fruit of their particular circumstances and cultures reflected in the work of Braidotti, which she names as 'embodied experiences'. Stories such as these expand our own consciousness from a monolithic concept and perception of Church to a diversified and contextualized understanding of following the gospels. Just as in the world in general, a momentous shift is happening also in the Church 'and because of the web of all life, progress in one field accelerates progress in all fields'.[24]

'Breaking the word' is important for Marie, accountability for Anne, renewal for Ruth, the Church as container, holding, not restraining one's energy for Petronella, Christianity and not narrow denominationalism for Sue – to name just a few points raised in the case stories demonstrates that the overall aim is making our concerns visible, making our agenda seen and heard. From Barry's practice of micro ministry to the many calls for small worshipping groups, stress is on the prophetic insights and gifts.

The three following chapters continue this discussion by highlighting more public forms of living prophetic and priestly lives.

Ludmila Javorova's Call to Priesthood –

'Welcoming, Listening, Forgiving, Encouraging, Leading People to God'[1]

The American Medical Mission Sister Miriam Therese Winter visited Ludmila Javorova in the 1990s, when the story of an ordained woman priest in the underground Church in Czechoslovakia was splashed over the title pages of newspapers from Europe to America. The fruit of her many discussions was the book *Out of the Depths* in which Winter gave Ludmila space to tell her life story. Winter's book is not so much a book about Ludmila, as the provision of an opportunity to put into writing what Ludmila was not allowed to do in those long years of communist rule in her home country.

A hallmark of any underground Church, and indeed any underground movement in general, is the mutual trust between members, with no paper trail. This lack of documentation, in particular, proved to be a problem once the country found a way out of communism in the six-week long 'Velvet Revolution' in November and December 1989, a revolution that was a testimony to the political maturity of the citizens who did not engage in a bloodbath to overthrow a hated government. The lack of documentation about decisions, training methods, the names of ordinands, the names of ordained priests, bishops, flow of directives, etc., have made it nearly impossible to counter innuendoes of incompetence, of arbitrary resolutions, and of heresy once the Church was about to emerge from the underground. The fact that an underground Church operated against the state with its spy and security set-up and against those priests appointed by the regime, meant that its moves had to remain opaque, to say the least. When dozens of priests were ordained and worked clandestinely, bringing the sacraments to the people, their situation was difficult enough. But when the political situation had changed and the Vatican demanded to be shown records of the studies of these priests, expressing itself dissatisfied with the lack of records and/or the quality of the priests and ordering them to undergo another round of training and ordinations, it must have seemed like a slap in the face for these men and women. It reminds one of the fate of the Falasha communities in the Highlands of Ethiopia who followed Judaism long before Christianity was introduced into Ethiopia and continued to the late twentieth century. They faced such extreme difficulties in the political situation in the 1970s and 1980s that they were airlifted to Israel. Here they faced the stark reality of having to undergo lessons in Judaism and initiation into the faith – the very reason they had been 'rescued' from their ancestral lands.

The Context of the Underground Church of Czechoslovakia

Ludmila Javorova was born in 1932, in Brno, the capital of Moravia, in the Czech Republic. When the Communist government took over in 1948, Pope Pius XII replied in 1949 with the proclamation that Roman Catholics who supported communism would be excommunicated. This was the cue for the government to embark on a series of measures to destabilize church institutions, seminaries and theological faculties, and to put in diocesan administrators to control the Church from within. Religious orders were disbanded, church property was seized and Catholic pupils were not allowed to pursue higher schooling.

Ludmila had to start work at fifteen years of age; she wanted to enter a religious order, but this was no longer possible; she then wanted to train for nursing, but ended up in a clerical job in a carpet factory. She was one of ten siblings, born into a very pious family, where family values were coterminous with traditional RC values.

A friend of her father, Felix Maria Davidek, was ordained priest in 1945 and subsequently studied medicine and gained his medical degree in 1948. He had a plan of setting up a Catholic university to counteract the repressive measures of the state system of education. He established a philosophy faculty under the name 'Catholic Atheneum Chrlice', a part of Brno where he gathered a group of young men and women around him who wanted to study. Davidek, working as priest and physician as well as organizer and lecturer, a charismatic man, was well-known to Ludmila from his near-daily visits to her father. His activities came to the attention of the authorities and he decided to cross the border to Austria. However, he was apprehended and accused of training students to turn against the state and imprisoned as an enemy of the people's democracy for fourteen years from 1950.

In prison, Davidek had organized a clandestine system of classes with lectures being given during outdoor exercise periods and repeated by one prisoner to the next. He celebrated the Eucharist using raisins dunked in water for wine and bread, while also assisting fellow inmates as physician. He ministered to women prisoners on the other side of an enclosure wall by shouting the words of absolution across to them, for they had no access to any sacraments. Ludmila summarized his realization about the asymmetry in the sacramental life of Catholics: 'That men had access to the spiritual support of a sacramental life, while women in prison were denied this simply because of their gender, seemed to him unjust and contrary to the ways of the Spirit. If only the women had priests among them, like the men had, the harsh conditions of their present life would be easier to bear.'[2]

The Establishment of the Underground Church
Platform 'Koinotes'

Upon his release in 1964, Davidek returned to his friends eager to continue where he left off all those years ago. He made contact with the Javorova family and asked Ludmila to help him find men who wanted to become priests but could not do so because they did not want to submit themselves to study in communist-run seminaries. Ludmila and her family knew a number of such men and from that moment her co-operation with Davidek began. For the first time in her life she realized there was a possibility for her to develop spiritually. Hours of conversations and lectures to a small group of people who were introduced to Davidek by Ludmila followed. He worked with whoever was available, judging people by their attitude, not their credentials.

He knew that he was watched from the day of his release onwards. Part of his training of priests involved knowing how to avoid drawing attention to oneself, how to detect and evade surveillance. He impressed on everybody never to take notes or disclose information to third parties. He fitted the members of his classes to function in a hostile environment. Together with another priest, Stanislav Kratky, he worked out an ordination course and began secretly to prepare the members for ordination and priesthood. In his courses he stressed creativity, the ability to discern new ways of operating in a given situation. It was important to him not to leave things to spontaneity only, but to direct his students in their learning process. He understood leadership as an act of guiding and teamwork rather than manipulation of power or the exercise of control.

Ludmila became responsible for the organizational aspects of running seminars, lectures late into the night, surreptitiously moving from one private residence to another. Issues of security were paramount. The programme, called 'Koinotes', a Greek word meaning community, was not a narrow ordination course and from the very beginning it was not just for men. Davidek envisaged a community of believers which he called the local church, who would find a way of living their values and who would be ministered by priests of compassion. Ludmila started with home visits and hospital visiting: 'I would ask those who were bedridden to offer their illness for the Church, because the Church really needed it at that time.'[3] Davidek found a job in a children's hospital disinfecting bedding, which gave him an excellent start in getting in touch with caring professionals. After three years he had prepared a number of men for ordination and was looking for bishops who would ordain them. However, Czech bishops refused to ordain the candidates he had prepared.

Some Czech priests, on the other hand, had contacts with East German priests and in particular with the Bishop of Görlitz, Gerhard Schaffran, who agreed to ordain the men. Travel restrictions meant that it was very difficult to cross borders, even borders of 'friendly' communist countries. To obtain travel documents was difficult, but after a number of attempts was possible. What was much more difficult was to send documents to Bishop Schaffran describing the ordinands, the courses they had completed, etc. A system was devised which had a venerable pedigree: the indenture. A legal document used in the Middle Ages, cut into two halves with zigzag lines that fitted into each other, to prove ownership of property, was the model: a picture would be torn apart and the bishop would be sent one half and the ordinand was given the other half to present to the bishop on arrival in East Germany. The candidate would arrive in the evening, and be ordained deacon and then ordained priest the following day. No documents were kept as they would only endanger the new priest and the ordaining bishop.[4]

This was a workable arrangement, albeit a clumsy one. It was clear that 'Koinotes' needed its own bishop who would ordain its ordinands. In 1967 Felix Maria Davidek was consecrated bishop by Jan Blaha, a member of 'Koinotes' who had himself been consecrated bishop by the Bishop of Augsburg, Josef Stimp-fle. Ludmila understood that approval for the consecration of Blaha and Davidek came directly from Pope Paul VI.[5]

Davidek was now able to ordain the men he had trained, of

whom there were twenty-one in 1968. Some of them had been waiting many years to receive the sacrament. The new priests established small clandestine communities in the areas where they lived. They would come together for prayer, worship, teaching, catechism and pastoral work. 'Koinotes' expanded into an ever-widening circle of small communities, the existence of which remained well hidden. 'Koinotes', in the eyes of its priests and bishop, was the local Church, the sacramental presence in the world, a Church with a non-territorial status. Bishop Eugen Kocis from the Greek Catholic Church ordained six married men within 'Koinotes' with bi-ritual faculties, which meant they could celebrate the Eucharist in either the Greek or Latin rite. The long-established Greek Catholic Church had been forced to join the Greek Orthodox Church in 1950, with the result that those who did not comply went underground and joined 'Koinotes'. The first of the married priests was Ludmila's brother Josef and in 1978 Davidek ordained Ludmila's father, Frantisek Javora.

The Council of the People of God and the Issue of Women's Ordination

In 1969, Davidek appointed Ludmila his vicar general, his administrative right hand. From his prison days Davidek knew that women under harsh prison regimes had no access to the sacraments. Ludmila when visiting prisoners and ex-prisoners felt their deprivation as though it was her own. In September 1970 Davidek called a 'Council of the People of God', to take place in December 1970 to discuss what was appropriate practice for a particular place at a particular time. One of the issues was the ministry of women. One day before the Council meeting, however, pressure was put on her to cancel the whole meeting – not all sixty men and women would be able to attend and not all of them supported the agenda any longer. The Council did start, with notable absences, but many participants complained about the issue of women's ordination. It was felt that such a major break with traditional practice should not be undertaken. There was precious little time and it was spent on talking about the agenda rather than making decisions. When it came to voting on the issue of women's ordination the Council was split in half.

The Council broke up with one side accusing the other of heresy. The pressure of time meant that the question of women's ordination remained unresolved. Two developments followed. On 28 December 1970 Davidek asked Ludmila whether she wanted to receive the sacrament of ordination and, late at night, witnessed by Davidek's brother Leo, Ludmila was ordained and celebrated her first Mass. Davidek promised her to inform the Pope. The other development was that a new group emerged, which while using the old name 'Koinotes' was against the ordination of women, not knowing that Ludmila had been secretly ordained.

Ludmila was not allowed to tell even her parents that she was ordained a priest. She celebrated Mass on her own and secretly concelebrated at the liturgies of the rump 'Koinotes'. 'On the day of ordination one does not become a priest; one accepts one's ministry.'[6] She lived her priesthood through everything she did throughout the day. One year after Ludmila's ordination, Davidek ordained three other women, but they left the priesthood after a time. Lack of support and acceptance as well as an absence of pastoral opportunities contributed to their decision: 'It was hard enough to be called to the priesthood in a secret Church, but to be a secret within the secret, as the women priests were forced to be, was a very large burden to bear.'[7] In 1976 Pope Paul VI sent Monsignor John Bukovsky to meet Davidek. He brought greetings from the Pope, they discussed women's ordination; soon afterwards Davidek was informed that he should stop consecrating bishops and ordaining priests.

Davidek wanted to travel to Rome himself and inform the Pope of having ordained women, but circumstances would not permit it. Ludmila was not comfortable with this situation and decided to take action herself. She wrote a letter to Pope John Paul II, took it in person to Cardinal Frantisek Tomasek in Prague and asked him to deliver it into the hands of the Pope.[8] Tomasek promised to do so, but added 'It is invalid', referring to women's ordination. It was then that Ludmila told him that she had been ordained. Despite his promise to call her upon his return from Rome, he never did so.

Her situation was not resolved as Bishop Davidek died in August 1988 and one year later, after the overthrow of communism, the network 'Koinotes', established by Davidek, had no need to function any longer. The priests who had been working secretly for many years came into the open and expected to be accepted unconditionally. That did not happen. The clergy who had collaborated with the regime, called '*Pacem in Terris*' clergy or less favourably 'Pax Terriers', continued their active service, whereas the clergy who had chosen to work in the underground, precisely because the Vatican prohibited co-operation with communists, were investigated and official recognition of their priesthood was withheld. Their status remains unresolved.

A Question of Trust

In 1990 Ludmila received approval from the bishop's office to work as catechist and to teach religion. It was only in 1995, when pressed by Austrian journalists, that she admitted openly that she had been ordained a priest. In 1996 she was formally forbidden from exercising her priesthood, which the Vatican considered invalid. Her comment was 'While I do not have a public ministry, it doesn't mean I am losing my priesthood.'[9]

Ludmila's story is intertwined with the vision and work of Felix Maria Davidek. The political situation, forcing a rethink on what it meant to be Church, eventually brought about a new understanding that this new Church needed women priests. Problems remained, however, about the application of such an understanding.

Evaluating the situation after the event, it is very difficult to

comprehend the dangers posed by the society in which 'Koinotes' operated. The achievement of 'Koinotes' in producing
priests in a priestless society is in line with many an underground
movement, from the Catholic priests in sixteenth and seventeenth-century England to Anglican priests in the twentieth century in China and the ordination of the first Anglican woman
priest, Miss Li Tim Oi. In 1944 she crossed enemy lines to meet
the bishop in Macao and was ordained a priest by him. The
sad thing is that her licence was withdrawn at the Lambeth
Conference of 1948 – opposition was so vehement that Bishop
Hall and Rev Li submitted to the pressures exerted on them.
Out of loyalty to Bishop Hall, Li Tim Oi did not exercise her
priestly ministry, although she did not resign her orders. In 1971
her status as priest was restored by the Anglican Consultative
Council.[10]

The parallelism of both stories is impressive. In times of utter
hopelessness, hope flourishes, not in the old bed of 'tradition',
but in the new bed of exigencies. Both Ludmila and Li Tim Oi
were loyal members of their Churches. Both had visionary
friends or superiors, who recognized that the women wanted to
become priests because the political situation demanded it from
those who were serious with providing a sacramental presence
in society. After having played their part, in a new situation,
the women were told that it was a mistake, that they were the
reason for 'schism' or 'heresy' and that they should forget ever
having been ordained.[11]

Micro Ministry

The 'Koinotes' model of Church was in fact a 'micro model';
the place of work, the place of one's family, the circle of one's
friends, were all to be enriched by a priestly presence. In Winter's
book, Ludmila explains her role as one of finding her congregation herself. Her role was to alleviate the pain of the sick, the
solitude of the prisoner, the humdrum everyday life of a family
and its ups and downs, raising children, coming to terms with

jobs or lack of jobs, financial bottlenecks, in short, the whole experience of the 'everyday'. Her ministry was a ministry of presence, where she would find those in need. It was not a question of a local group adopting her as its leader and priest or making her accountable to the group.

Could such an experience point to a new model of Church, requiring a different kind of commitment, of living in the community, being undetected, being witness, being prophet, creating centres where thoughts can be nourished, hurts be healed and decisions mature? Such a role is lonely and needs support on a level not yet explored institutionally. While in many countries there is no need for an underground Church, it can be argued that in others there is every need for a personalized micro ministry, which touches people on a far deeper level than mere Sunday worship or coming into contact with 'Church' when services for 'hatching', 'matching' and 'dispatching' are called for: baptism, marriage and funeral. Micro ministry might be understood as presence, to assist in particular life stages.

The model of the micro ministry is one that will appeal to many because of its grassroots aspect. However, it requires a radical rethink about the training of community leaders, whether they are called priests or not. Teaching on a one-to-one basis inevitably reaches fewer people, though its quality will inevitably be significantly better. A new balance needs to be struck between what and who is available and what and how skills are going to be used. The old understanding of sacramental priesthood with its training in philosophy and theology will have to accommodate more people-oriented practices such as psychology, counselling and advocacy and more specific skills such as being with people, listening to and assisting them in a practical way. Questions arise as to how such training can be given. Such questions arose over the years in 'Koinotes', although the group understood itself as following orthodox R C tenets albeit with unorthodox methods. The existence of smaller groups of committed believers will blur the line between consumers and providers of sacraments. The needs of the day, in a particular locality, with a particular group of people, will vary and will most certainly not meet the requirements of a centralized structure used to issue rules. The world is full of tensions between 'how we should' and 'why we can't' and any new development will run up against counter-arguments.

In the last analysis, the question of new and workable models of Church will not so much hinge on the question of accessibility or the opportunity for local activists to minister to their community, but more on the question of which argument carries the group, which interpretation is credible and which way forward has the greatest support.

As has been demonstrated by this Czech example, something was built up, requiring enormous personal cost and devotion, time and energy. In time, one item, the ordination of women, proved to be the watershed, the point of no return for half the group. There will always be such points and it will depend on the trust within the group as to how the group will solve the problem. Often it is a clash between the charismatic innovators and the ordinary supporters. Ludmila kept her vow of secrecy until she was exposed by a newspaper. Whether it was opportune to do so or not is not the question. Ludmila's role grew in an organic way and when she was asked whether she wanted to be ordained, the time was ripe for her to agree. She was not so much the firebrand innovator, but an example of a woman who was a priest long before she was ordained. Her ministry did not change after or with her ordination. Her very presence made things happen on a micro level.

8

Christine Mayr-Lumetzberger and the Ordinations on the Danube

This chapter profiles Christine Mayr-Lumetzberger through her life story and her own writing[1] in the first section and through an eyewitness account of the ordination to the priesthood on 29 June 2002 in the second section. At the time of writing, Christine has been officially excommunicated by her Church. This event, a media sensation when it broke, did not change Christine in any way. She was prepared for it and accepted that her work would lead her into confrontation with the powers that be. Not that she sought confrontation; she persevered with her life's vision and was prepared to take the consequences. She lives her life as priest as she did before she was excommunicated.

Commitment in the Church

'Everything I need to know about life, I learned from Noah's Ark. Maxim *One*: Don't miss the boat.' This – and the following remaining nine maxims – were sent to us by Christine by way of explaining her persistence with her vocation. Her imagery of a boat was to become prophetic. The maxims from Noah's Ark mirror the fighter Christine is and her strong sense of urgency, not wanting to miss the boat of opportunities for women.

Her sense of urgency is heightened by her sense of service. She was born in 1956 into a Roman Catholic family in Linz,

Upper Austria, and grew up deeply imbued with a sense of belonging. The altar server in the family, her grandfather, was a formative influence on her, telling her about the 'holy things', the sacred vessels. Christine attended a school run by the Holy Cross Sisters and had her fair share of indifference to religious education and quarrels with nuns. After her A-levels she trained as a nursery teacher, but very soon, in 1976, she entered the monastery of the Benedictines of the Immaculate Heart of Mary in Steinerkirchen, Upper Austria. She felt that her life in the monastery would inexorably lead to priesthood, as many of her co-Religionists worked as pastoral workers in practical parish work. The community was founded in 1949 by Norbert Schachinger OSB, with the express intention of training Religious Sisters for pastoral ministry. In Christine's understanding, a training for parish work would inexorably lead to priestly ministry. After her novitiate she wanted to study theology but was not sent to university, instead she went to a teacher training institute to train as a teacher of religion. During the last years of her studies she was also teaching religious education in a special needs school run by the RC Church. The training was good, but it was not enough for Christine. Doubts arose, conflicts with superiors followed. Christine decided to leave the monastery after five years, a step she did not take lightly. She felt she had failed to find what she really wanted while at the same time had been given a spiritual treasure that even today she credits to her formative years in the order; 'In my inner self I have remained a Benedictine.'[2]

On leaving the monastery in 1982 she met Michael, who had four children from his previous marriage. Christine and Michael married and Christine immediately ran into difficulties when applying for posts in RC schools. It took her years to overcome being isolated and marginalized. She was unemployed and vacancies in the church educational systems were closed to her. In 1988 she started to work, on a voluntary basis, as hospital visitor. Here she found herself accepted and did work that suited her. It was during this time that her inner longing matured: that of becoming a priest and of ministering to a community. In the 1990s she gained more qualifications, chiefly in working with the severely handicapped. In 1996 she started a part-time degree course in theology at the Religionspädagogische Akademie in Linz, besides having a full-time teaching commitment.

Apart from hospital visiting, where she became accepted as 'priest', Christine was increasingly asked to perform priestly roles such as blessing and preaching at gatherings, in pubs, at outings, etc., and was accepted much more easily by those present than would have been an officially ordained priest. Over the years she met many priests who had relinquished their priesthood in order to get married. Christine found it increasingly sad that they had given away something that was out of reach for her.

Maxim *Two*: 'Remember that we are all in the same boat', so obvious to Christine, was not obvious to those who had left. Christine experienced that on the one hand she was accepted as pastor, while on the other she saw men withdrawing from their pastoral roles simply because the Church could not accept their gifts as married men. Not being in church employment, Christine realized that she enjoyed a freedom that these men did not have. It dawned on her that the message is important, not the system, and that being a member of a community, a group, the biblical 'two or three gathered', meant that the group itself was gifted, empowered to nourish their spirituality themselves and to celebrate the Eucharist and to give thanks. Christine met women in church employment who openly confessed that they put their hopes in women like her, who needed not to fear losing their livelihoods if they did what Christ charged them to do – celebrate his memory.

As developments for a more modern Church started to unfold in Austria when the We Are Church movement was started in 1995, Christine was voted on to the board of its Upper Austrian section as deputy chairwoman. One of the five demands[3] of We Are Church was a rethink on priestly ministry, as a ministry of inclusivity, a ministry shared by women and men. In 1999,

Christine mooted the idea of an ordination course for women, a course organized and taught by women, to bring their gifts and experiences to the community.

Maxim *Three*: 'Plan ahead. It wasn't raining when Noah built the Ark.' Christine and the women around her have waited patiently while the men in positions of responsibility have told them again and again that the time is not ripe, that they have to be patient; many women have grown old and have nearly lost hope in the process. After long years of thinking, praying, fasting and discerning, they came to the realization that Rome will not act. And so the women started an ordination course for women covering topics they considered would be important and necessary to cope with life in the third millennium: conflict resolution, psychology, teamwork, mediation, ecumenical respect, in short accompanying people on their way through life in all the situations life throws at them.[4] The programme is arranged in such a way that women who already have a degree in theology are trained in the practical aspects of priesthood; if necessary, experts are invited to teach specific topics.

Fifteen women from Germany and Austria signed up for a three-year course, an integrated learning experience of weekend contact classes of ten units – weekend seminars, with one spiritual text, group work in theory and practice, personal reflection and liturgies as well as reading, essay writing, course work and pastoral work in between, under the supervision of a spiritual director.

The process of 'each one teach one' has many examples in the Bible and in church history: women in other Christian denominations had to convince their church leaders of their call for justice and their own vocations. By setting up the ordination course for women, Christine has given the demand for priestly ministry names and faces. She has come out and gone public, because not doing so is no longer an option for her and her group – 'We are on our way . . .'

Three years later, eight women finished the course and after a process of discernment and months of discussion and rigorous interviews, decided to go ahead with ordination.[5] They knew that the system had not changed, they knew they wanted to have the visibility of being ordained priests, not a clandestine priesthood. They knew that the present situation in the R C Church would not allow their local bishops to ordain them. Given all these constrictions, the question arose what model of Church Christine envisaged that would accept her gifts.

The Ecclesiology of Small Communities

Maxim *Four*: 'Stay fit' and Maxim *Five*: 'Don't listen to critics' prove practical no-nonsense pieces of advice. Maxim *Six*: 'Build your future on high ground' and Maxim *Seven*: 'For safety's sake, travel in pairs' encapsulate important lessons – create your support group, do not do things on your own, as you can be picked off far too easily, but invest time for solid preparation. Maxim *Eight*: 'Speed is not always an advantage' – the snails were on board with the cheetahs! – points to an organic process of maturing, examining, deciding – effectively the three-pronged method of reflection/action/reflection.

Christine's thoughts and actions have been shaped in a way pointing to a model of Church somewhere between the patriarchal model of Church-as-Institution and a radical model of life beyond an institutional Church. In a Church that values relationships, it will be immaterial whether the members of the group that celebrates in memory of Christ will be led by a woman or man. What is important is that the members are seeking God and want to proclaim the message of 'love your neighbour'. There seems to be a need for a loose organization or affiliation of groups. Thus, for Christine bishops, female and male, will have a role as overseers of the groups. Such people would be radical justice-seekers and not create injustice by promulgating laws that create exclusive privileges for some.

She advocates a college of Elders with responsibility for the worldwide Church, not as a unified model, but one that takes in local needs and practices. She is adamant that this college should not exercise power as it is exercised at the moment by the Holy See in Rome. The whole question of church capital, financial assets and church finances needs to be opened up to public scrutiny as the financial situation of large groups in society needs to become far more transparent. The leadership question on the local level should embrace a shared priesthood, a priesthood of the community, inclusive on all levels.

There are and always will be conflictual views on how things should be organized and run. What in Christine's view is therefore required are mechanisms of settling disputes peacefully, conflict resolution by experienced people, accountable to both sides, involvement of the community and the group, rather than the process of no-discussion, threats and even excommunication that are the models at this moment in time. Leaders are invested with authority because of their personal competence and gifts. Women and men with a calling for leadership will then emerge from the communities and be trained by and for them, while living their lives in their families, with their partners and children, or celibate, if they so wish. Remember Maxim *Nine*: 'The Ark was built by amateurs; the Titanic by professionals' – we all need the space to start building, to start growing.

Christine discerns 'priestly people', women and men, in every community. Many are trained theologically, but this should not be a pre-condition to leadership posts. Most of them have a calling to priestly leadership, have a job, have a family or live a lifestyle in tune with their own wishes. They take turns in presiding at liturgies, know the people in their groups and accompany each other on their way through life. Christine wants to be with people, to celebrate the sacraments with them.

Ordination will have little influence on her pastoral work as she will continue with her professional and voluntary tasks: she will counsel people, accompany groups, teach children, visit the sick and the dying, celebrate the sacraments, accepts invitations to preside at Eucharists, preach, continue to give advice. She will help people who are trying to find their way to God. She is a priestly presence among her friends, among them a group of sportsmen and women as well as women's groups. It is heartening for Christine when parish priests ring her up and declare their solidarity with her. She regularly writes in the Catholic papers and is available for radio and TV work. She says of herself that she is not a theoretician and cheerfully acknowledges her lack of a theoretical approach in her thinking despite her years of studies. She recognizes herself rather as the one who applies the theories, who is the doer, translating new thoughts into practice.

Why Now?

Christine stresses that Christians everywhere console each other with the thought that we are 'at the end of a pontificate', meaning, that for some time to come, nothing will change. A millennium has just finished which has not excelled in showing justice to women. Over the last two millennia women have served their Church and have accepted – in the majority of cases – that it was God's will to do so in a secondary role. Be that as it may, many women do not want to do so any longer. They want to expand, not to sever their service in the Church. Many women, it is true, have disengaged from Church, have lost their interest in a Church that, using the phrase 'God's will', discriminates against women and negates the idea that they can possibly have received a vocation. Men in priestly ministries have received this vocation, the joy and pain of having been called to serve God. Christine asks, 'Have the men forgotten this joy and pain?' And do they really think only men can receive this joy and pain? A vocation that forms one's life in such deep ways must not be negated, explained away or pushed aside, as to do so would be a sin against the Holy Spirit, the Holy Ruach. The passage in Acts comes to mind, where Gamaliel, a 'teacher of the law', cautions the Pharisees, 'If what they have planned and done is of human origin, it will disappear, but if it comes from God, you cannot possibly defeat them. You could find yourselves fighting against God' (Acts 5:38 ff.).

Over the last few decades women have searched for ways in which they can express God's will – not the narrow will of the Church – in their lives. These thoughts have nothing to do with wanting to split the Church or wanting to destroy the Church, but rather wanting to build up the Church, from its innermost kernel and from the grass roots, to rejuvenate it, to plant justice so that it can grow and overcome misuse and injustice. After the end of the second millennium of the Christian era it is high time, the right moment, the *kairos*, not to be silent any longer.

An 'Unreasonable' Demand?

Christine does not want to break with the system; she is clearly in the camp of reformers, who, weighing up the value of tradition, want to gift their understanding of what is necessary in order to change the model of Church as it is now, to nudge the present model into a more inclusive one. She therefore has to answer questions, frequently posed by journalists, whether what she wants is an unreasonable demand. Her reply is that to demand of more than half of all church members that they, the women, are forbidden to aspire to the ordained priesthood is certainly unreasonable. Frequently the question is also posed whether it would be more appropriate for her to work for the abolition of priesthood rather than demanding the ordained priesthood for women. She reasons, however, that there is no need to do away with a good institution. Priests have a place in the community, they invite people to participate in the Eucharist and in giving thanks, in strengthening individuals in their hours of need through dispensing the sacraments. Nevertheless, for her, with women in priestly ministry, there is no doubt that the office of priesthood will change.

Inevitably, she was asked, before the ordinations in 2002 and before the excommunications in 2003 of all those ordained, how they have avoided excommunication. Her reply was by her baptism she became a member of a community of Christians and the sacrament of baptism is an indelible sign that cannot be taken away. The Cardinal of Austria, Christoph Schönborn, advised her to leave the RC Church and become a Lutheran. Christine found his suggestion an offence to fellow Christian Lutherans, and regards it as sinful to invite anybody to commit apostasy and leave the RC Church. The problem would not be solved if she became a Lutheran, as the injustice in her own Church cannot be swept under the carpet of another Church. Before her excommunication she was asked if she fears punitive measures being taken against her. She replies that there are not enough priests, and people want pastoral care, so who should punish her? She works in her pastoral role, in groups, with the sick and the dying and at her place of work, where she is valued and understood. The threat of excommunication did not worry her and the implementation of the threat has not changed her conviction either.

When Christine started her course, there were two more centres in Austria, in Innsbruck and Vienna, where women fol- lowed a similar ordination course. The two courses have not continued and the women have therefore not had to decide whether or not to go ahead with ordination. The organization We Are Church has distanced itself from the group run by Christine and did not support its decision to go ahead with the ordinations. Christine was also a member of the steering committee of Women's Ordination Worldwide, WOW, and here again, not all the members of the steering committee were behind the decision the members of Christine's group had taken. The stumbling block was the question whether an RC bishop would be the ordaining bishop. However, Christine did find full support in some countries, once the decision to go ahead with the ordination became known. The Canadian group Catholic Network For Women's Equality, CNWE, stands for many in its comprehensive and detailed response:

The crux of the issue is best expressed by Hubert Feichtlbauer of We Are Church Austria (document 5). He says they do not support the ordination because 'no actions should be taken which do not correspond with valid church law'. He later adds: 'But with all the understanding for such women, who through the attitude of top church officials find their vocations not taken seriously, and they are discriminated against and marginalized, the committee of the Platform doubts that a change in church rules can be achieved by the actions such as those now being planned.'

Two points: First, we are already technically not 'corresponding with valid church law' by the very fact that we are discussing the issue of women's ordination (you will recall that *Ordinatio Sacerdotalis* (1994) said that 'this matter pertains to the Church's divine constitution and . . . this judgment is to be definitively held by all the Church's faithful'). Secondly: if we do not take these vocations seriously, if we marginalize the women who go forward and seek ordination from a dissident or retired bishop or a bishop from the Old Catholic Church (whose episcopal ordination can be proven to be in line with 'apostolic succession'), sadly, we are no better than the hierarchs in Rome.

Christine and the group of women seeking ordination have undergone serious theological training and scrutiny. According to document 4, 'They would remain Roman Catholic and would celebrate the sacraments with those who would request them to do for them.' Elsewhere there is some indication that they would follow the model of the Worker Priests in France, in other words, priestly vocations which are centered on bringing the Gospel of Christ, from within the Catholic tradition, to those with whom these priests live and work. Their concern for communion and unity within the Church is not about power and governance (i.e. 'running' a parish, etc.) but about witnessing and discipleship. This, in my view, is what Joan Chittister meant by a renewed priesthood. The most recent news out of Europe and Ireland is that the dissenting voices of Roman Catholic bishops are finally beginning to be heard. But *at the moment*, women who want to live out their call to priestly ministry have *no option* other than seeking ordination from a dissenting bishop, probably in secret, or from a bishop of another rite. We believe this is a prophetic gesture on their part: they are following an inner imperative from the Spirit rather than conforming to human canonical regulations. On a historical note, it would seem that it was only when Episcopalian women (in the US) sought ordination from older, retired bishops that things began to move in that Church. What about the women who were ordained in secret behind the Iron Curtain? It meant the survival of the Church in many instances. We must do what we have to do and DO IT NOW. For if not now, when?????

The American voice is advocating 'working from inside the Church'. There are no women 'inside' the hierarchical structure of the Church, there are only hundreds of thousands of women on the outside supporting this patriarchal and androcentric *structure* which is more concerned with maintaining an untenable posture of power and infallibility than with proclaiming a liberating Gospel. That is the hard reality we need to remember. Women's energies are being co-opted so we will preserve 'canonical validity' at all cost, at the expense of true communion among ourselves as People of God and followers of Christ.

To conclude, the National Working Group of CNWE expresses its wholehearted support for the women moving forward for ordination.[6]

The press got wind of it and had a field day – the women were quarrelling among themselves! Myra Poole stepped into the debate by saying: it is the Church that is forcing women into this action, of going ahead with the ordinations despite the express prohibition by the Holy See. 'Women have been driven to do things like this because of the Church's attitude to their role within the Church.'[7]

While the e-mails were going to and fro around the globe, a report on a vote in the European Parliament made headlines. The motion, written by Maria Izquierdo Rojo from Spain, condemned the 'administrations of religious organizations and the leaders of extremist political movements who promote racial discrimination, xenophobia, fanaticism and the exclusion of women from leading positions in the political and religious hierarchy'. The report was adopted by 242 to 240 votes on 11 March 2002.[8]

A German solicitor has started a court case against the German state on the grounds that the laws regulating church life in Germany stipulate an income for bishops by the state. This means that being a bishop is akin to a civil service post. By not employing women as priests and bishops, because of church law, they break state law, therefore the laws on equality have been broken. The court cases will be heard by the European Court of Law.[9]

The final Maxim *Ten* from Noah's Ark: 'No matter the storm, when you are with God, there's always a rainbow waiting', puts it all into perspective. Fuelled by one's vision, there will be movement, movement of argument and eventually change in the situation. Christine and the other women are passionate about their vision and believe that eventually more and more people will become sympathetic to their action. Whether the new priests will be able to share their gifts in larger groups and be accepted by the wider Church is not an issue for the moment. Their step was historic as it was done in public, after the necessary training and supported by RC bishops.

Illegal but Valid

The ordination of seven women to the priesthood in the RC Church on 29 June 2002, on board the MS 'Passau' on the Danube in Germany and Austria

Preamble

For forty years, since the beginning of the Second Vatican Council (1962–65), women have used theological arguments to refute the reasons for exclusion from ordained priestly ministry. In the post-conciliar period numerous scholarly and popular articles, books and publications in favour of the ordination of women have been published worldwide with a view to presenting the case. The leadership of the R C Church, the Congregation for the Doctrine of the Faith as well as the Pope, has so far ignored these writings, even when they were produced by the papal Biblical Commission, to wit the report of the Biblical Commission of 1976. Through repeated declarations like *Inter Insigniores*, 1976, *Ordinatio Sacerdotalis*, 1994 and *Responsum ad Dubium*, 1995, the leadership has instead confirmed the exclusion of women from priestly ministry.[10]

The Facts

Experience has shown that no amount of discussion has so far convinced the hierarchy that women no longer regard themselves as unable to image Christ in the priesthood. Christine and the women of the training course have therefore chosen the path that is technically called '*ordinatio contra legem*', against the law (CIC: Canon 1024).[11] As the official R C position is clearly stated in Canon Law they had no other option but to opt for a step that is contrary to Canon Law, Canon 1024, which stipulates that 'Only a baptized man can validly receive sacred ordination.' For these women and many others, who were not a part of these ordinations, this canon or paragraph contravenes the basic human right of equality between the sexes and is therefore no longer acceptable in the secular sphere and even less so in the canonical sphere, as it ignores the status of women as baptized and confirmed members of the Church.

The group decided to contravene Canon Law. The members have been engaged in pastoral work, teaching, nursing and counselling. Years of patient training, research and collaborative ministry have not shifted the Vatican 'no' regarding the ordination of women. On the contrary, injunctions, prohibitions and threats of excommunication have been bandied about. Fortunately – depending on one's point of view – even some theological experts and the famous women and men in the street have found these explanations wanting. Members of the group have for many years felt themselves called to the ministerial priesthood. Some of them are elderly, who only want to live their call before they die.

They all found themselves in a situation of grave conflict of conscience. On the one hand was their strong call from God, and on the other church officials who refused to recognize the call of the Spirit within them. The women always realized their ordination would be viewed as 'illegal' in the eyes of the official Church, but they understood their action as prophetic protest against the official Church, in line with a number of thinkers, saints and founders of religious orders, who have sensed that the official Church was lagging behind developments in the secular sphere. In consequence, the group completed its training and started a six-month process of discernment: each member of the group had a soul friend, a pastor, accompanying her in her training. They were theologians who were not involved as the women were with the ordination agenda, but provided valuable reflection and analysis.

In January and February 2002 it became clear that a number of them, but not all, wanted to go forward with the ordination to the diaconate and the priesthood. Some women were interested in the diaconate for the time being, while others wanted to wait altogether to put themselves forward for ordination with the next batch of female ordinands.

Those who after a period of discernment were clear in their mind that they wanted to go ahead with ordination to the diaconate and the priesthood wanted to follow the rite of ordination as prescribed by Canon Law. This meant they needed one or more bishops who would ordain women and not just men, as Canon Law prescribes. Christine, who had initiated the whole process, started to look for bishops who would ordain the women rather than ask the communities they were serving to do so. If the women had followed the latter path the stress would have been on the notion of apostolic succession lying within the apostolic community that they were serving. Such a step was too radical for some of the women and, most important, was not in tune at all with Canon Law. What the group wanted most of all was to follow the official line as much as possible.

The question of who was to ordain these women was a very delicate one and led to much misunderstanding as the women wished to shield the bishops from adverse publicity. The group decided not to publish their names, as a number of them requested their names remain secret. Such a scenario was neither satisfactory nor actually helpful to the group.

The Problems

To prepare for such a step, never before done in public by a group of candidates from three different countries, is rather like climbing a mountain, without maps, paths or compass, and possibly missing the right way. Nevertheless, the members of the group celebrated their ordination to the diaconate on 24 March, Palm Sunday, presided over by Bishop 'Augustin Miller', a pseudonym, for his identity cannot be revealed.[12]

The second celebrant was Monsignor Dr Romulo Braschi, an Argentinian, a Marianist priest for forty years, who had courageously taken on the military dictatorships in South America in the 1960s and 1970s when standing up for workers' rights. In 1974 he was imprisoned for one year in Argentina and, on his release, told to stop working as a priest with left-wing organizations. The hierarchy was obviously supportive of the military junta, so Braschi did not return to his pastoral ministry but joined a charismatic Church in Argentina called the 'Catholic Charismatic Church of Christ the King'. He was eventually consecrated bishop by the former RC Bishop Roberto Garrido Padin in October 1998 and by RC Bishop Geronimo José Podesta in January 1999. Romulo is a charismatic, a faith healer, a married man who has ordained men and women in the past few years. Rumours in the press that he extorted money were found to be utterly baseless; he has no criminal record and the accusers lost their court case.

Therefore in the eyes of the women who wanted to be ordained, Bishops Romulo and 'Augustin' were in full possession of the 'apostolic succession', the term used to denote the laying on of hands from apostolic times onwards to the present. The apostolic succession of bishops, that is the uninterrupted chain of one bishop ordaining priests who in turn would become bishops and ordain priests, had been broken several times in the course of 2,000 years of Christian history. However, as a symbol it is a potent marker that connects Christians across centuries and millennia and continents to apostolic times. Today, the episcopal succession is generally felt to be less important as a criterion for authenticity, since everybody who is baptized stands in the apostolic succession. But the symbolic concept of succession was sufficiently important for the candidates to look for a bishop or bishops with full apostolic succession. Equally important for the ordination of the candidates was the call from their communities.

The group met with 'Augustin' and Romulo several times and together they worked out the programme for the ordinations, the texts to be used, the music and rubrics. On 9 May 2002 Romulo ordained a former Benedictine monk, Ferdinand Regelsberger, as bishop, the rationale being that if anything happened and neither 'Augustin' nor Romulo could attend the ordination of the women, Ferdinand would be able to act in accordance with Canon Law.

In the meantime, preparations for the ordination began. To be absolutely certain of an undisturbed event, the organizers hit on a wonderful idea: to charter a large river cruiser on the River Danube. Thus access could be rigorously controlled and those intent on disruption excluded from the start. A river boat was to leave Passau in Germany, travel downriver into Austria to Neuhaus/Untermühl and return to Passau.

The Ordinations

'Today the boat is our church' – these were the first words of the opening address on board the motor ship 'Passau' on 29 June 2002. It was a very shrewd move. By celebrating the ordination on board ship, the boundaries of dioceses were blurred, but it also gave rise to a number of unanswerable questions: will the boat gather momentum and speed or will it land on the rocks? Will it start something new or will it be a one-off event?

The press was after news, the more sensationalist the better. Journalists kept ringing Christine in Austria and another candidate, Gisela Forster, in Germany continually from 6 am at intervals of a few minutes for weeks on end. Some opponents to the whole event had rung every convention venue in Upper Austria to find out whether there was a block booking for 29 June 2002. The date was known, the venue not. Eventually, the boat company confirmed a block booking, but stood by the contract with the women, even after threats had been made that it would be financially ruined if it went ahead with the booking.

In May 2002, Christine was asked to participate in a television discussion with Cardinal Archbishop of Vienna, Dr Christoph Schönborn. However, he declined to participate, but stated to journalists that he would advise her to become a Protestant if she wanted to become a priest. She called this statement totally out of tune with the spirit of ecumenism and a total misjudgement of the situation – the issue of women priests in the R C Church would not go away, even if the Cardinal wanted her to do so.

Two weeks before the ordination, two Canon Lawyers among the group sent a 'Statement regarding the Ordination of Women in Austria' to the press, again setting out the injustice done to women and the reasons for taking matters into their own hands:

All Catholic women who feel themselves called to the priesthood, now find themselves in great distress due to the current legal status of women in the Church, which Pope John Paul II has exacerbated even more with several decrees ... Because of their vow of obedience to the Pope, all Roman Catholic bishops are obliged to reject the ordination of women. They all accept this obligation without exception. This is the reason why women's numerous attempts in the past to find Roman Catholic bishops as celebrants for an ordination of women *contra legem* have all failed so far. It is therefore certainly understandable that the group of women prepared for ordination has accepted an offer from validly consecrated bishops willing to ordain women, even if this includes or could include bishops that are technically no longer members of the legal institution of the R C Church. The women called to priesthood find themselves faced with a choice of either accepting an ordination that is sacramentally valid, but jurisdictionally controversial, or else continuing to accept exclusion from the office of priesthood for an unforeseeable period of time.[13]

One week before the ordinations, when all the women had more than enough to do with getting chasubles made, hand printing their silk stoles, issuing invitations, organizing the music, the programme booklets, etc., the Bishop of Linz, Maximilian Aichern, Christine's local bishop, issued a pastoral letter to be read out at the Sunday Masses threatening that anybody taking part in the ordinations would be excommunicated. On 27 June 2002 the same bishop wrote a letter to Christine threatening interdict according to CIC 1378 para. 2 no. 1 and excommunication according to CIC 1378 para. 3, as ordinations were only legal for male ordinands.

Some 250 people stepped on board the 'Passau' early in the morning of 29 June 2002, the feast day of the Apostles Peter and Paul, a traditional day for ordinations, although this year some dioceses could not celebrate a single ordination because of the dire lack of male candidates. Outside, the green banks of the River Danube flew past, the waves and currents made for rapid progress; the Danube is a fast-flowing river, a truly European waterway, breaking through gorges and accelerating over rapids, forging its very own course. The ceremony followed the RC rite, but Braschi in a short address stressed that he could not ordain with RC authority. Thus the sacrament conferred was technically illegal, as conferred without authority and counter to the 'man only' rule, but valid, because the orders were conferred by a man who has apostolic succession through the Bishops Padin and Podesta, thus keeping to the letter of Canon Law.

There were seven candidates, Iris Müller, Ida Raming, Pia Brunner and Gisela Forster from Germany, Christine Mayr-Lumetzberger and Sr Adelinde Roitinger from Austria and Angeline White from the USA.[14] Adelinde was told that by being ordained she would excommunicate herself, the so-called *eo ipso* rule. She had been a member of her order, the Halleiner Schulschwestern, for forty-eight years. None of the soul friends, who had worked with the women, were on board, nor any priest or bishop from the dioceses from which the women came. However, a woman priest from the Old Catholic Church in Austria and a woman minister from the Lutheran Church in Germany attended. And what of Bishop 'Augustin'?

The boat cast off late, since the train lines to Passau were interrupted by building work, and the participants had to wait for the arrival of a shuttle bus. When the last passengers had arrived and 'Augustin' was not among them, consternation on the faces of the organizers became visible, likewise raised eyebrows on the faces of a number of passengers; there were no explanations and no phone calls as to why 'Augustin' was not on board. It was then clear that Romulo would be the ordaining bishop, something which a number of passengers clearly found inadequate. He was not helped by the fact that ceremonies were conducted in German, but he spoke only Spanish; this meant that everything had to be translated, not always theologically correctly or even acceptably.

A number of participants, co-travellers on this epic voyage, would have liked a different bishop to officiate. A Peruvian music group played, shipped in by Braschi at the last minute as a blackmail tactic: 'Either you accept them or I do not ordain you!' This was twenty-four hours before an event of mould-breaking significance in which symbolism was of great importance. On the day before the ordinations he changed texts and music so that the published booklet could not be used. The group was caught up in an impossible dilemma: either accept Braschi's demand and be ordained or send everybody off the boat and call off the ordinations. The trust that was built up over the months between Braschi and the group had disappeared, aggravated by the non-appearance of the other bishop. But the group decided to go ahead, even though some now had grave reservations.

Five days later Christine received an e-mail from Bishop 'Augustin'. He had, prior to the ordinations, spent a few days in a monastery with priest friends. On the day of the ordinations he planned to leave early, to take a train to rendez-vous with all the passengers at the appointed place. However, in his e-mail he reported that his clerical friends had locked him into his room to stop him attending the ordinations. He had no phone and no way of communicating with the organizers. True, he could sue his 'friends' for involuntary incarceration, but it is unlikely that he will ever do so. The women respected his privacy and did not wish to risk a court case.

A small number of participants, for various reasons, decided to cancel the trip at the eleventh hour. Some because they did not want to be associated with an event, which in their view, gave undue weight to the fact that the presiding bishop acted without authority from Rome. To them, the 'illegal' facet of the ordinations was more important than its 'valid' facet. On board the boat two views prevailed. One stressed very strongly that the message of the R C Church was bigger than Roman Catholic interpretations embedded in Canon Law. The other more dominant view was that the women's actions were prophetic, breaking with male imposed rules and regulations, a call of the Spirit to be a beacon for all.

The ordination service, with the promises of the candidates, litany of saints, laying on of hands, prayer of ordination, investiture with stole and chasuble, anointing of hands and presentation of chalice and paten, re-enacted the age-old ritual of conferring the sacrament of orders. Outside there was the landscape with its green pastures and colourful meadows of wild flowers, its dark forests and small villages on the river bank, and inside the ceremony connecting the people to all those who have ministered to Christians throughout the centuries – it all flowed together and created an atmosphere of calm. When the candidates lay prostrate in front of the bishops, when they were standing and felt the hands of many on their heads and when they received their chalices, some had tears in their eyes. For too many long years they had waited for this moment – an end and a beginning. They have chosen a very hard and stony way. They need every bit of support, however far or near, whatever one's attitude to the ordaining Bishops Braschi and Regelsberger. The women decided on an ordination *'contra legem'*, because they want the Church to acknowledge the spiritual vocations of women for priestly ministry. These women have had many critics for deciding to act *contra legem*, but the real criticism should be directed to the present R C Church that refuses even to discuss the situation within the Church, let alone ordain women. Therefore it was not surprising that some women felt called to act. Their frustration and sense of injustice had become uncontainable, when people clearly need new forms of priestly ministry.

The Vision

For the seven women everything and nothing has changed. In their eyes everything – because they believe they have achieved something that no women for many centuries has achieved, public ordination to the priestly ministry in the R C Church. On the other hand nothing – because they have lived their priestly ministry for many years, being pastors to their families, friends, different groups and the people at their places of work. The accusation that 'all they wanted was being ordained' is unfounded. They sought the visibility of ordained ministry so that their groups who authorized them to seek ordination could receive the sacraments.

The ordinations were not ego-trips, as some press have written of them, only to add hastily, 'The time is not ripe, these women should have waited, been patient and obedient.' However, the seven women and many more around the world have waited patiently and experienced that when it came to women's ordination, the time was never 'ripe' in the eyes of the law-givers. For them the *mañana* attitude and mentality has no value, when they experience Catholics deprived of sacraments because there are no pastors. Not that the women want to be accepted simply because male candidates do not come forward. The women want to be accepted now, because above all they were helped to discern their call from God and willingly followed a three-year training programme, often at great cost in time and money to themselves. It is noteworthy that the median age of the seven candidates was fifty-nine and all had lived lives dedicated to the well-being of the Church.

These women are viewed by some as a blessing to the Church, by others as an obstacle. Whatever a person's view, the fact remains that they have challenged the present concept of Church and opened the possibility of a new perspective on ministry. Although they were not unreservedly happy with the choice of bishop, what, in the prevailing climate, was the option? They are heartened in their decision by the very fact that many women have applied for the next ordination course. This most important work will be complemented by the priestly tasks they are engaged in already: pastoral care of individuals and groups, particularly women who have distanced themselves from the Church, and ministry to those people who request the sacraments whenever a need arises.

With women in priestly ministry a different dynamic flows into serving their community. They understand themselves as R C priests, commissioned by their communities, obedient to the ordaining bishop. They understand their ordinations as a small but immensely important step towards living out the Gospel message of equality in Christ. It is not a step to complement the male hierarchy, not even to become 'hierarchical' themselves, but rather a demand for equality. They do not want to create structures of exclusion in parallel to the male structures. They will develop the scope and task of being pastors and will celebrate the sacraments if and when asked to do so. Theirs is a *vocatio interna*, an internal call or conviction that compelled them to go down this road.

Afterthought

On 10 July 2002 Cardinal Joseph Ratzinger issued a statement, *Monitum*, in which he called the ordination of women a 'simulated act'; the sacrament has therefore been conferred illegally. The ordinations broke Canon Law, the bishop who ordained the women belonged to a 'schismatic' community, and the event damaged the right promotion of women who have their 'own specific place in the Church and in the society'. These are the reasons why he threatened the seven women priests with excommunication if they did not recant their ordinations by 22 July 2002 and ask for forgiveness and show contrition.[15] Gisela Forster and Christine Mayr-Lumetzberger called a press conference in Munich on 22 July 2002 and refuted every allegation in the Statement from the Vatican. A letter with the decree of excommunication, dated 2 August, was sent from the Apostolic Nunciature to the seven ordained women. The women had two weeks to register their objection against the excommunication, which they did, without any reply by 2 September 2002. On 27 January 2003 the threat was implemented; the seven priests were excommunicated by Rome.

9

Public Action

This chapter is about making the vision of equality visible. The first case study deals with the public action of one woman, followed by examples of the growth of group action around the world. Many people talk privately about the problems within the present cultural forms of Christianity, and may even welcome the idea of priesthood for women, but at the same time they often find it hard to accept that some women and men feel called to bring the matter to public notice in ways that some would call extreme. Also, many Christians are not happy with the word 'protest', possibly because protest can have violent connotations. But the reclaiming of non-violent Christian protest in the cause of justice for all has a long history in the development of women's consciousness.[1] This form of protest is often referred to as going from 'notional to real assent'; a person, or more frequently a group, realize that all other ways of bringing a certain injustice to the notice of relevant authorities has failed, and silent stoical suffering is for them no longer a viable option.

Action is a last resort and the ultimate call for change, giving voice to resistance against an injustice that cannot remain hidden. It comes at the end of a long process of developing personal and group consciousness, which becomes so strong that it inevitably bursts out into the public arena in its cry for change. As it is played out in the public forum, people's attitudes are challenged and the demarcation lines between responses become clearer. It inevitably leads to misunderstandings on many sides, including those nearest to them. The following case stories of both personal and group involvement serve to illustrate the consequences faced by those called to this the most challenging Christian calling.

Janice Sèvre-Duszynska's challenge

Janice's[2] actions for women's ordination are a culmination of her many years of experience as a seasoned campaigner. Janice learnt much of her art of successful campaigning from the School of the Americas. In 1990 Roy Bourgeois, a Maryknoll Missioner, founded an organization called WATCH in Fort Benning in Georgia devoted to close the School of the Americas, which is operated by the US Army and supported by tax payers' money. So far the School has trained 60,000 Latin American soldiers in civilian-targeted warfare against the poor of that continent. The soldiers have been responsible for the death and suffering of thousands of innocent victims throughout Latin America. WATCH, like so many movements, began with a hunger strike.[3] Twelve years later, Janice used the same tactics during Holy Week 2002 to draw attention to women's ordination. Over many years, women have participated in campaigns, notably in Great Britain, when women successfully campaigned outside the US army base at Greenham Common to achieve the removal of weapons of mass destruction.

Janice's move into public action for women's ordination reflects for our time the difficulty women face in getting their voices heard to speed up the process of change. In many ways this struggle relives, in another context, those of the early Suffragette movement when women's determination to get the vote led them to face arrest. Janice is from a Polish-American Roman Catholic family whose daily lives revolved around the extended family, the neighbourhood and the parish. From her earliest years in Milwaukee, Wisconsin, she remembers her aunt and uncle helping to run a parish. Her formative years were no different from those of most young Catholic girls of her time:

a Catholic education, daily Mass and all the usual activities of initiation into this tradition. However, early on Janice reflected on a girl's role in her church. Why did girls always do the ordinary jobs but were never allowed on the altar? However, she did not pursue this question until later in life. She married and had two sons and trained as a teacher of English. At the same time she found she had a talent for writing poetry and plays, an aspect of her life that has become more and more important as she has matured. Her greatest grief was the loss of her son Brian at the age of eighteen years in a car accident. The effects of this accident were catastrophic in her life, and her marriage ended in an acrimonious divorce. But the final effect on Janice of her son's death was her determination to live life to the full. 'Death', she says, 'strips away the denials we live with.'[4] Janice committed herself to her teaching and the study of early Christian history and theology. In the course of her studies she became more and more aware of the egalitarian nature of Jesus' relationships with women and the swift erosion of these relationships as the male-dominated Church became a historical reality.

As the papal announcements on women's ordination became more and more hostile in the 1990s, Janice, like so many other women in different parts of the world, began to meet with others at women's ordination conferences and discuss the question of their very limited role in the Church and the pseudo-theological basis for this. The discussion groups developed and the need for prayerful and liturgical expression grew. Janice took part in small group Eucharists, but still felt something was missing. She decided on her first public witnessing on the occasion of the ordination of a male candidate on 17 January 1998, presided over by Bishop Kendrick Williams in Lexington Cathedral, Kentucky, Janice's home cathedral and a place where she had worshipped for several years. Out of courtesy she wrote to the male candidate for ordination to inform him of her personal call to priesthood, and the strong compulsion she felt to give public witness to her calling. Janice dressed in what has now become her trademark – a long white priestly alb with a red cincture around her waist. In later demonstrations she was to add a purple stole; purple being the colour of both mourning for women's lost gifts and simultaneously celebrating their priestly call.

On this occasion as Janice prostrated herself in front of the altar, the bishop said to her, 'I understand your difficulty and that you are called.' He later denied saying this, changing the words to 'you *think* you are called'. But he asked her to return to her seat, calling her actions disruptive. Before acquiescing to the bishop's request, Janice wanted to make sure the reason for her action was clear: 'I am here', she said, 'to represent all women, past and present.' But her anger was aroused by the presumptions implied in the word *disruptive*, as her action had been the result of considerable prayer and reflection. Although the courage demanded from Janice in this form of public witnessing had increased her self-respect, her action was received with the inevitable criticism that always follows anyone who crosses the boundary between private and public witness for justice. Such misunderstandings nearly always include adverse comments from those who support the cause but are not convinced of the wisdom of the action.

Janice was not deterred by this opposition. In June 2000, she participated in a street demonstration at the US Bishops' Conference in Milwaukee. She gained entry to the meeting room of the Conference, following observers into the room. When the roving microphone passed close to her, she quickly took it and began reading out her justice statement, entitled 'Become Easter Morning Men'. The assembled gathering was stunned by her intervention. It took a few moments before the bishops realized the full impact of her intervention and the microphone was immediately switched off. Janice then sat down on the floor in protest at being silenced. When the bishops broke for lunch Janice remained on the floor and prayed about her action. After ninety minutes police ordered her to leave the building.

Janice's Action at the Bishops' Synod, Rome, September 2001

The International Movement We Are Church (IMWAC) was planning to hold its second 'Synod of the People of God', a 'Shadow Synod' in Rome, at the time of the Bishops' Synod in autumn 2001.[5] Janice joined them to make the cause of women's ordination visible during the Synod. The best way forward seemed to be a large banner display of the BASIC poster featuring a woman priest holding the host and chalice during the Eucharistic Mass and the words 'ORDAIN WOMEN PRIESTS' in Italian, Latin, Polish, German, English, Spanish and French. The banner was displayed as near the Vatican as possible with the approval of the city authorities. The events of 11 September 2001 did cause doubts on whether the proposed scheme should go through. In the end it was decided to carry on, 'hopeful that the presence of women priests on the altar, our perceptions and stories, would be seen as a sign for justice to free people from violence throughout our world'.[6]

Press releases were sent out to the media of the world on the feast day of St Thérèse of Lisieux, 1 October, patron saint of women's ordination. Janice and a friend flew to Rome and saw the banner go up for the first time 100 metres from the Vatican's Sistine Chapel. After attending the 'Shadow Synod', women's ordination supporters processed from Piazza Cavour to Via Porcari wearing purple stoles; Janice wore her priestly garments, the same alb and cincture she had worn when she first asked for ordination nearly four years previously. Janice and Soline Vatinel, spokesperson for the 'Shadow Synod' and member of BASIC in Ireland, led the procession, holding placards proclaiming the same slogan 'Ordain Women Priests' in five languages. All in the procession wore the purple stoles that have become the symbol of the call for women's ordination. At one point they were confronted by police and asked for legal documentation to process in the streets. This was duly handed to the police from whom they parted on good terms.

It was a historic moment as this was the first time such a banner had ever been displayed in Rome. Janice said to the assembled press: 'We would like this banner to encourage the Pope, the bishops and the Curia to re-examine their attitude and position on this issue. We also hope it will generate a positive grass roots response from the community to welcome women's vocations.' Soline Vatinel summed it up in the following way: 'It is all about opening hearts and minds to what the Spirit is doing in our Church today. The banner is literally one of the signs of the times. We are hopeful that prayer and fruitful dialogue on this issue is possible.'[7]

Action in the USA in 2001-2002

Janice continued her witness at the US Bishops' Conference in Washington in November 2001. Helped and supported by friends, as she has been all the time, her action was preceded by four mailings to three hundred bishops. In these mailings the bishops were urged to embark on a course of justice for women and every bishop was sent a purple stole and asked to wear it and to speak out on women's ordination at the next Bishop's Conference.

She and her friends went to the Cathedral of the Immaculate Conception and Janice read out parts of her justice statement 'Become Easter Morning Men'. Wearing her alb and cincture as she walked straight down the aisle and right up to the sanctuary where the bishops were sitting, she stopped at the communion rail, genuflected, turned round and walked to her pew. The all-male cathedral procession and the gathered assembly began to sing Psalm 72:1-2, 7-8 with the words 'Justice shall flourish in our time'. Janice waited until the singing was over and then in one almighty voice of anger, which reverberated round the cathedral, cried out, 'How dare you speak about justice when you refuse to ordain women called by God to ordination!' The bishops were alarmed and the police arrived instantly. Her arms were held to her side and she was marched out of the cathedral. As she was walking out Janice turned round, looked the bishops straight in the face and with deep conviction said, 'How can you call yourselves bishops? Get rid of your fears. Ordain women. *Become Easter Morning Men*.'[8]

Meanwhile outside the basilica a priest told the police to remove her from the property. Janice replied, 'This is my property. My mother and father worked for it . . . My aunts and uncles, my grandparents and the immigrants I came from.' The police moved her gently and asked the priest whether they should arrest Janice. The priest answered, 'No, unless she tries to re-enter the church.' Janice felt her actions had been sufficient to raise the profile of the cause and decided against arrest.

Janice offers a challenge, to women and to men and especially to the hierarchies. She is clear that in the third millennium, women, especially in the economically comfortable West, are called to stand up for their beliefs to further the will of God. With this in mind she continually invents new ways of raising consciousness. On 2 February 2002 in Atlanta, Georgia, Janice was arrested on criminal charges, when she entered the cathedral to pray at an ordination ceremony, accompanied by two friends. On entering they were informed that ordinations were by invitation only. Janice responded that ordinations were open to everyone and Christ welcomes everyone to his table. They were threatened with arrest and men came forward as if to push them to the door. Janice immediately sat on the floor and said, 'I guess you will just have to arrest me.' Her two friends stood either side of her. By the time the Gospel was read, Janice was handcuffed and arrested by a young police woman. When in the back seat of the car, the police officer removed the handcuffs, as they hurt. She then thanked Janice for all she was doing for women, even though she was not a Roman Catholic. Six hours later after payment of a bond of $500, Janice was released from prison.

The good news is that a judge in Atlanta has dismissed the civil suit filed against her by the Archdiocese of Atlanta that tried to bar her from its churches. During Holy Week in March

2002, she called on others in the USA to join her in the fast and vigil that she planned from noon on Palm Sunday to noon on Holy Saturday. During this time Janice spent some time each day in front of the tabernacle in Lexington Cathedral, Kentucky, as well as fasting from solid food during this time. The locked tabernacle represented for her all who had been abused or excluded, including those who had been locked out of priesthood.

Janice has crossed boundaries. She is the first woman who has been handcuffed and served with criminal trespass for the cause of women's ordination. Will the next thing be a prison sentence for women's ordination? This is a situation that would cause the greatest embarrassment to the authorities, as no one has ever been jailed for a cause such as this and the last thing the R C Church would want is modern-day martyrs and heroines. Her call to priesthood, for herself and for women in general, informs her action. To many she is an inspiration of courage, to others an uncomfortable fanatic. What is clear is that she puts her reputation on the line for something she believes in passionately. What sort of Church will ordain her is not her ultimate concern. To her, the eradication of the ban on women priests is the goal and once reached, the women's presence at the altar will change the Church.

Women's Alliance for Theology, Ethics and Ritual: WATER

The form of protest of Mary Hunt[9] and Diann Neu[10] who founded WATER, the Women's Alliance for Theology, Ethics and Ritual, in Silver Spring, Maryland, in 1983 has taken a very different form from that of Janice, although they themselves have also been deeply involved with the women's ordination movement in the USA almost from its foundation in 1976, and are no strangers to multiple forms of direct action. They, however, decided to focus their energies in founding a special centre, WATER, for, as they say, 'they were all dressed up for ministry in the Catholic Church but had no place to go'. What is remarkable about WATER is that their collaboration is based on a deep and tested friendship and is a living example of the understanding of women's friendship, which Mary theologically illustrates in her book *Fierce Tenderness: A Feminist Theology of Friendship*, 1991. It is a theological reflection on the difference between the male concept of friendship handed down through the Christian tradition in the writings of the early Fathers of the Church as well as the treatise on 'Friendship' by Aelred of Rievaulx, a thirteenth-century monk.[11]

The topic of the book, female friendship, investigates the differences between the inherited traditional view of friendship and the long-neglected genealogy of female friendship. Mary critiques the Aristotelian concept that only a few friends are needed with her strong conviction that women need many friends, not few, in order to survive, a thought incidentally mentioned frequently in black women's theology.[12] Mary defines women's friendship as 'justice seeking friends in unlikely coalitions'.[13] Thus female friendship has the potential to reverse some of the values of male friendship by its numerous networks and the way women stand in solidarity with each other for justice, refusing to be divided, even when there is an inevitable variation of views. Women's friendships are then understood as friendships for justice equivalent in the present day to the networks of women working for change in all areas of women's lives.

Mary and Diann's friendship grew not only out of mutual respect for each other and shared interests, but also out of their shared experiences. It was this friendship, like many other women's friendship in history, which has been the driving force in their work together. WATER is now a famous feminist educational centre with a wide network of justice-seeking people. It began in response to the need for theological, ethical and liturgical development for and by women and some men. This organization allows them to work locally, nationally and internationally.

The two women work as a team, fulfilling different roles in WATER. Mary is the resident theologian, as her books, articles and frequent lectures testify. She is a well-known speaker, especially in the USA, articulating new thoughts on the Christian tradition. Mary frequently says that one day the institution will follow the Holy Spirit.[14] She reflects on women's sense of 'practical wisdom', or 'worldly ways', of their sense of being with people and celebrating with them so that one day bishops will have no choice but to appoint highly qualified, highly motivated and very competent women – Mary's definition of a priest.[15] Years ago, no one would have called these women priests, but today women bear witness to their vocation by their work as chaplains. They exercise ministerial, but not priestly roles in the traditional sense. They provide pastoral care, spirituality and theology, but they are still unacceptable as priests to the church authorities. While ordination might be the way for some women, others do not find the concept of ordination into a faulty system attractive. Mary and Diann decided to stop 'knocking on the church's door and begging admittance. We began simply *to be Church*.'[16]

Mary and Diann both have a rich experience of finding new ways for expressing sacraments and solidarity and have been involved for many years with the ecumenical movement known as Women-Church that does not exclude men who understand the need for equality and sharing of gifts. Understood as the gathering of people who seek to engage in sacrament and solidarity, linked with other groups around the world and over time, it is the locus where justice can be voiced, can grow and can issue into action. Elisabeth Schüssler Fiorenza's phrase of 'a discipleship of equals' imagines a Church organized according to egalitarian principles. Its aims are participatory and democratic, involving members to the full extent of their potential in decision-making and action. Further, the Church needs to be both local and global. The local expression is the primary experience for most people, but an important component of 'being Church' is living in connection with other people in other parts of the world, who share the same commitment to sacrament and solidarity. They believe that without such a global connection local groups can become isolated, and similarly without a local expression, universal notions of 'Church' can become useless abstractions. Their experience has taught them that a growing number of people not only need parish worship but also small groups, because it is in these small, often experimental, spaces that people are affirmed and spiritual growth in individuals and groups takes place.

WATER as a feminist educational centre, with a network of justice-seeking people, allows Diann, the resident liturgist, to work liturgically locally, nationally and internationally. Her work with Mary includes programmes and projects, publications and workshops, counselling and liturgical planning, which enable people to be part of an inclusive Church and society. Both work together on tough ethical issues that the institutional Church refuses to discuss – reproductive choice, lesbian and gay rights, women's ordination, married priests, divorce and remarriage and same-sex unions. Mary and Diann have become community builders and guides for many kinds of marginalized people.

As a feminist liturgist, Diann has been celebrating the Eucharist for a number of years and now understands her calling to be one of creating liturgies and workshops for communities and justice groups worldwide. She also co-ordinates a women's liturgy group through WATER and participates in Sisters Against Sexism (SAS), a local Women-Church group that has been meeting and celebrating liturgy in the Washington DC area since 1979. Her liturgies are published in *WATERwheel*, WATER's quarterly publication, and in liturgy books such as *Women-Church Source Book*, *Women and the Gospel Traditions* and *Together At Freedom's Table*, published by WATERworks Press.[17] Diann's special joy is in creating and celebrating life–cycles liturgies, such as baptism, first menses ceremonies, weddings and holy unions, house blessings, cronings – celebrating one's old age – and memorial services. Her prayers and liturgies are published in many languages around the world and she is currently preparing an anthology of liturgies she has created over the past eighteen years.

Diann also ministers as a spiritual director and psychotherapist who comforts and heals. Her particular ministry is with those who are hurt and have been marginalized by the Church and are looking for other ways of being Church and ministering to others. She also counsels those alienated from institutional religion: lesbians and gays, divorced and remarried, women who have had abortions and those who have been abused. Her power comes from her understanding of Baptism. She feels passionately that by Baptism we are called to be healers of one another. Both women work tirelessly for systemic change and their energies are focused on helping Women-Church base communities develop participatory, egalitarian models of shared leadership and partnership in ministry. For Diann this involves encouraging and teaching women to develop the liturgies their lives need, and to lead and develop an understanding of Eucharistic worship. Diann also co-ordinates a coalition of thirty-one Catholic women's groups, and is active with peace and justice groups worldwide. WATER has a special link with South America and is gradually expanding to wherever people feel a vacuum in the Church as it is now experienced. Although they are themselves Roman Catholic their organization crosses all denominational boundaries.

Their fruitful and many-faceted ministry of over twenty years in WATER and the desires of its founders are best summed up in the following prayer written by Diann, for all women who are ministering in any way as priests around the world:

Let us bless those among us who are in healing ministry: those who work in hospitals and hospice, those who are in mental health, providers, spiritual directors, ecologists and gardeners.

ALL: Blessings on you.

Let us bless those among us who are in political and activist ministry: grass-roots organizers, lobbyists, housing advocates, those who hold political office, marchers and protesters, those who vote.

ALL: Blessings on you.

Let us bless those amongst us who are in educational ministry: teachers, parents, mentors, writers, theologians.

ALL: Blessings on you.

Let us bless those amongst us who are in ministry through the arts: dancers, performers, authors, visual artists, musicians.

ALL: Blessings on you.

Let us bless those who are in liturgical ministry: liturgy planners, preachers, prayers, Eucharistic celebrants.

ALL: Blessings on you.

Let us bless those amongst us who are in family ministry: those who work with children, with elderly; those who care for pets.

ALL: Blessings on you.

Let us bless those amongst us who are in leadership ministry: community leaders, fundraisers, pastors and associate pastors, elected officers, team leaders in sports.

ALL: Blessings on you!

Let us bless those amongst us who are in the ministry of

creating a discipleship of equals: women, married priests, lesbian and gay people called to ordination.

ALL: Blessings on you!

Let us bless the unnamed, unacknowledged, yet no less important among us.

ALL: Blessings on you![18]

Group Actions

Important as are the various individual initiatives written about above, they are all supported and have grown out of the knowledge of worldwide dissent in Churches on the question of women's role. The struggle has been and still is long and hard but the persistence of group action has become the backbone for raising consciousness in all continents of the world. The consistency and the similarities of these actions are striking.

In the latter part of the twentieth century, women theologians in various parts of the world, especially in the USA, began to expose the weaknesses in the inherited approach to doing theology. Experience as a source for theology, although not unknown in other times, did not dominate the theological thought until after the 1960s. Liberation theology from South America dared to question Western theology and its limited basis for theologizing. But even the best of liberation theologians were still European trained and failed to do any sexism analysis until conscientized by women theologians from their own countries and elsewhere.

Feminist and coloured women's theology has always resulted from reflection on personal and group experiences. This is why women are developing other ways of doing theology that are not just based on the present university methodology. Theology, too, has begun to expand beyond the limited academic boundaries of the past and is being returned to the experience of God in people's own lives. People generally, but especially women, are beginning to trust their own experiences more than official edicts, as their level of education in all fields and forms of knowledge has dramatically increased over the last two to three generations. The growing development of accepting multi-cultural sources from which to theologize – poetry, prose, music, including Negro spirituals and the slave narratives of former and present times – without neglecting the scriptures, is gradually enlarging the horizon of our understanding of the greatness and infinity of God. Above all, all good contemporary theology is based on the experience of those who suffer most from the present dominant economic and cultural reality – the poor of whom the greatest number are women, summed up in the words of Elisabeth Schüssler Fiorenza, 'Until all women are free, no woman is free.'[19]

Fiorenza's biblical scholarship and interpretation of scripture was the cutting edge of the understanding that change was a requirement for the life of the Church. To look for women in the scriptures, the suppressed or nameless women, became for many the key to critiquing the 'received' tradition. As this scriptural and theological process became more sophisticated and informed, so also the various responses of women and men towards the Christian tradition took on different forms. The long painful journey and transition out of patriarchal Christianity had begun.

The theological and scriptural critique, known as deconstruction and reconstruction, has always gone hand in hand with both public and private actions for justice. Various reform groups grew and began to organize and co-ordinate their efforts. Theology arises from personal experiences, from learning from others and crossing boundaries and at the same time its authenticity is judged by its source, the people's life experiences of God in the cultures and times in which they live. Groups that gather to discern what is the place of Church in their lives are springing up everywhere. And in countries where no groups have started up, individuals join groups in other countries and in this way

strong inter-national and intercontinental network and communication groups are growing. The presence of so many
women from different continents at the WOW Conference in
Dublin reflected this development.

At the beginning of the third millennium, these groups can
be found in large numbers in the USA, Europe and Australia.
Groups that began with a catalogue of desiderata have specialized
on joint issues and now often place women's concerns at the top of
their agenda, along with the question of homophobia. Although
women's groups have become a particular feature of our times,
there are a growing number also of mixed groups dealing with
women's concerns.

All groups are born out of a particular need and when all of
their needs are met will cease to exist. For example, men who
left the priesthood to marry bonded in groups to promote the
idea of a married priesthood. In a similar way as women began
to listen to their call to priesthood and that of others, similar
groups developed making women's ordination their key issue.[20]
In 1995 Austria led the way with the initiative of a referendum,
known as We Are Church[21] and issued a five-point charter for
change in the Church in which the women's question was given
the highest priority. What all these groups have in common is
a desire to work, as far as possible, for change within the
Church. The proliferation of groups in the RC Church – and
using the internet as an indicator there are now hundreds of
them – denotes the present state of unease in the RC Church
and the desire of the people for radical reform within that
tradition, based on the experience of all.

By the end of the twentieth century, a group action on the
question of women's ordination began to emerge from these
groups for women's ordination under the umbrella of Women's
Ordination Worldwide, WOW.[22] This ecumenical network is
open to include any Christian denomination that does not as
yet ordain women to the orders of deacon, priest and bishop.
The stringent silencing on the ordination debate by the Church
fuelled a desire to speak and act publicly against the injustice.

Just as the Suffragettes chose the colours green and mauve as their campaign colours, so do women's ordination groups. Purple has become the colour for mourning women's lost gifts in all Churches. Purple stoles, scarves or ribbons are worn not only by Roman Catholics but increasingly by other denominations in sympathy with the cause.[23] Purple has become a hallmark of supporters at Mass or at prayer vigils for women's ordination. The latter has become part of the regular form of witness outside the main cathedrals of the world for certain events, such as male ordinations, in the case of Janice Sèvre-Duszynska, and the monthly vigils of prayer, in the case of many ordination groups. Yearly prayer vigils are held during Holy Week, especially at the Chrism Mass when the priests recommit themselves to their calling. Catholic Women's Ordination (CWO) in Great Britain has held from its inception in 1993 monthly prayer vigils on the Piazza of Westminster Cathedral in London every first Wednesday of the month. During Holy Week, CWO has a presence outside a growing number of cathedrals in Britain. On the continent of Europe there is the Purple Stole Movement, engaging in public witness. The communication between these groups has been greatly helped by modern technology and by the interest of the media of the world. The binding characteristic of these groups is the passion they share for a truer understanding of the real Christian message.

We Are Church, which began in Austria, has developed like WOW into the International Movement We Are Church (IMWAC). It has already held two 'Shadow Synods' in Rome, when the bishops of the world were meeting, the last in September 2001. IMWAC's aims are laid out clearly in its Manifesto.[24]

Conclusion

For those people who are now seasoned campaigners the very process of public witness has become an important stage in their own understanding of Christianity. As essential as public witness becomes at a certain stage of consciousness raising, these forms of action have to be continually informed by personal and communal prayer as well as theological reflection. People begin to want to know why a tradition has developed in a certain way and how it can be put right without throwing the 'baby out with the bath water'.

All movements for change show that they follow a similar pattern in certain stages of development to get their voices heard. The human spirit as part of the divine Spirit can never be quelled forever. Truth in the end always prevails, no matter how long it takes. Many do not understand the need to expose in public the weaknesses of a tradition they love, as the many jibes and comments received by those who do witness attest. But the history of peoples shows that public witness is an essential element in any process for major change. The resistance of those who will lose power from the change proposed is always strong. It is never stronger than within Churches that have built a system of power to obstruct these changes and who have such an emotional hold over the minds and hearts of those whom they treat as subjects and not as partners. In this context an interesting parallel exists in secular society: many people have lost their trust in the political system in this early part of the third millennium and have taken to public protest for many issues. The latter is always a sign that a system is no longer tenable and a shift is required. The length of time in which change will occur depends on the rootedness of the system. Those institutions that find themselves unable to change become the 'museum pieces' in Alvin Toffler's understanding, places people like to visit out of curiosity but not inhabit.

Part Three

A Vision for the Future

Making All Things New

The authors have introduced the reader to underlying problems within the Church tradition as the twenty-first century opens. Of particular concern was the recent historical development of centralization, high papalism, which is currently weakening the power of the local church. The stories told bear witness to this inherited imbalance within the understanding of who is Church. As the nature of the Church is not only institutional, but prophetic and mystical, the authors' preferred model of Church is the more fluid concept of the mystical body of Christ. This model has the potential to incorporate the two primary models from Vatican II, that of the *People of God* and the *Church as a Servant*, dynamized by the scriptural vision of Church.

The historical discourse on equality and difference has a direct bearing on the understanding of inclusivity and of the attempt to shift the theology concerning women from systematic theology to that related to the evolving social teaching of the Church. The inherited Western philosophical tradition of equality on male terms is being critiqued from a feminist theoretical, theological, psychological and scriptural viewpoint. And the reflection on experience and theory has given rise to the development of 'Women Church' as a movement for change in reshaping the understanding of sacraments, liturgy, theology and spirituality from women's own experience.[1]

The Church needs women to bring their experiences to new forms of leadership and ministry. There is no point in the ordination of women as priests unless this is accompanied by a significant shift in language and liturgical expression, accompanied by a wider debate on moral issues from the experiences of the marginalized. Christianity calls every generation not to replicate every jot and tittle of the past, but to preach anew in every age the following words of Christ, 'to preach the good news to the poor . . . to set at liberty the oppressed' (Luke 4:18–19).

Language and Church Buildings

Although there has been considerable discussion and writing[2] on language change there has been and still are great obstacles in using new language and metaphors for God. If people really believe that God is male, to the extent that they cannot pray to a Mother God, a Sister or Friend God, or change he for she in psalms and other biblical texts, then for them the male really is God, and the tradition has been severely distorted in their minds. Yet most Christians also believe in an all-powerful, loving, compassionate God with qualities society has traditionally attributed to the female. God is not the Father Christmas of this world, dealing out 'goodies', as some images might imply. To be able to pray and understand God in both genders and beyond gender is crucial in changing false consciousness. Using Luce Irigaray's term, it is moving back to the awareness of the *semiotic* before the all-pervasive intrusion of the male symbol system in which all generations have been immersed. It is interesting that most of the great mystics, male and female, use gender-free language for God, referring to the 'goodness', 'the compassion of God' as well as 'the Motherhood of God'. The term 'Mother Jesus' occurs frequently in the writings of Bernard of Clairvaux as does the term of 'Motherhood of God' in Julian of Norwich. This leads not only to changing and understanding words and phrases but to the writing of different forms of liturgical material, hymns and prayers, as all ages have done before us, from Thomas Aquinas, Charles Wesley and Father Faber to Janet Morley, James Cotter, Carolyn McDade, June Boyce

Tillmann and Janet Wootton. The three last-named are fast becoming well-known women feminist hymn writers of this century.

Therefore, following the French writer Luce Irigaray, the most adequate strategy consists in '*working through* the stock of accumulated images, concepts and representation of women, of female identity, such as they have been codified by the culture we are in'.[3] This strategy is coupled with the process of revisiting language, and its multi-faceted complexities, to regain lost images of God until the concepts of God become as pluriform as the multi-cultural society we all live in.

In like manner a new interpretation of reality will reform the place and structure of church buildings.[4] The original layout of a meeting hall has been transformed to mirror the division in church society, the high table and the low rows. The challenge for present and future feminist architects, male and female, is to build churches more suitable for forms of worship in order to facilitate new spiritual practices. The space given over to altars of devotion in the past is now being reclaimed in some churches for discussion groups, prayer groups and play areas for children. Multi-purpose buildings may well replace churches built only for Sunday worship. Too many church buildings lie empty most of the week and their maintenance costs can often no longer be met. A reorganization of church buildings, places and different forms of ministry requires risks but above all imagination, trust and hope.

Ecumenical Dimensions for Change – the Sheffield Report

The Sheffield Report of the World Council of Churches, *The Community of Women and Men in the Church*,[5] marks an historic moment in time. This is a pioneering report, based on wide consultation. The chapter written by Elisabeth Moltmann-Wendel and Jürgen Moltmann, entitled 'Becoming Human in New Community',[6] does not blame Christianity for introducing patriarchy but for its lack of ability to overcome it. This is a document produced by women and men in mutuality of thought and action, not making women the scapegoats of the evils in society. For example on marriage and the break up of family life the report welcomes women's entrance into public life and work, not as 'freedom *from* the family' but as 'freedom *in* and *for* the family':[7] family is seen as the new community of mutuality and sharing of roles rather than conforming to designated cultural roles. It is interesting to note that this inclusion was in response to African women who sensed the danger of undue Western influence in downgrading family involvement.

Member churches of the World Council of Churches as well as Roman Catholics and conservative evangelicals, neither of whom are members of the WCC, shaped the report, which was not so much a 'theology of the laity' (a term that would presuppose the existence of a 'theology of the clergy') as a 'theology of the Church',[8] based on a process that did not tell people what to think but invited all to do their own theological work.

The word 'community' is highlighted as the key to opening up the 'women's side': 'to talk about "women" and "men" is to position the issue on two parallel tracks, rather than to see that the problems of women have to do with the problems of men'.[9] The following are listed as steps towards a new community:

1 Women with women, having the opportunity to reflect, develop and affirm their own gifts, talents and priorities.
2 Women with men, finding their way to be partners where the women's side of the partnership can make a difference in the justice and quality of relationship.
3 Men with men, discovering in this new dialogue with women the personal resources for their own self-critical reflection and renewal.
4 Women and men together becoming more human in community.[10]

This report is not to be taken as a naïve listing of idealist desiderata. It states the problems and the difficulties that have to be surmounted by direct consultation and action. For example, women's views on the effect of a male hierarchy on their lives should be sought by intensive study and reinterpretation of both theology and scriptures from the perspective of women. The report strongly advocates language scrutiny coupled with images of inclusivity for God and symbolism more in line with scriptural images. How difficult it has proved to implement a change in God imagery from the dead metaphors of our time is illustrated from the furore that first greeted the publication of the Church of Scotland report, *Motherhood of God*,[11] and the non-inclusive language and symbolism in the present R C Catechism.[12]

Towards a Partnership of Equals in the R C Church

A people without vision is a people with no future. The following are suggestions for discussion and pointers to gaining a renewed vision of Church.

Listening to the past

- Recognize the omission of women from biblical texts.
- Recognize the texts in which women's lack of authority is constructed from a faulty understanding of physiology.
- Explore the importance of women's role in the post-resurrection embryonic Church.
- Listen to the experience of women throughout history.

Listening to the present

- Listen to women's experiences from all nations, creeds and colours.

Preparing for the future

- Combined action by women and men on all the above.
- Worldwide prayers towards repentance and change.
- Services of reconciliation for sexism.
- A new catechism published this time including the thought of women.
- A concerted effort into the re-education of all members of parishes and dioceses.
- Setting up new structures for the Church with equal representation of women and men on all official bodies of the Church.
- All offices in the Church open to women.
- Preferential option for women in all positions in the Church.
- Meticulous monitoring of all positions in the Church so that fairness is achieved.
- Built-in assessment of performance by all church officials.
- A listening, reformed papacy that acts from a concept of collegiality.
- Rethinking of parish structures and the present role of the priest.
- Adoption of the correct title of 'Presbyter' or 'Elder' to signify that a mature adult leads the group.

Final Reflection

How much change is appropriate, how fast it should be and in which major areas, will differ from person to person and the pace will reflect the need of the time and the community concerned. There is clearly no easy way to becoming a Church of inclusivity, only persistence in the truth and a growing linking of gender-aware and ecological understandings of Christianity. Change is embedded in the notion of the *mystical body of the Church*.

The ability to 'hang in there' has a high risk factor, but we have to make the leap of faith. Braidotti uses the concept of 'bungee jumping' or 'the art of hanging in there',[13] to impress upon all the need for courage. The whole risk is summed up in the following words:

> We have to cut across sedimentary memory by undoing the structures of domination by careful, patient revisitations, readjustments and micro-changes ... we have to be willing to undergo a long apprenticeship to minute transformations, endless repetitions. This will replace the royal road of revolution of one single point of resistance and insert instead the constant flows of metamorphoses ... activating it by deprogramming it out of the dominant mode. Becomings are a creative work in process.[14]

The emergence of communities of learning, of sharing tasks and gathering of contributions produces new levels of interaction which can break down barriers and draw on resources of good will, time and talents. What is needed is a space of love, not fear, that releases new energy levels to grow in passion and commitment for a renewed and just world for all. It is not a question of being 'accepted' by somebody else, we need to accept each other as we are, 'warts and all', irrespective of colour, sex or creed.

The examples in the preceding chapters of women training and being ordained, of women preaching and running priestless parishes, of musicians appointed as music ministers, have led to a much wider interpretation of ministry. Women pursue their own leadership through writing, running Christian groups, engaging in high visibility public witness and action, advocacy, teaching and campaigning; all these examples show a huge level of commitment and vision. None of them provides a single blueprint for the universal Church. All of the women concerned have an inner calling for serving God internationally as well as locally. Their work is about 'Making All Things New'. The welcome they get is the encouraging sign that beyond Church-as-Institution the Church-as-People of God is living and breathing.

Afterword
Autonomy versus Authority?

JOHN WIJNGAARDS[1]

The members of the Catholic Church have changed. In this Afterword I will reflect on that indisputable fact. We are claiming a degree of Christian sovereign dignity that the faithful of past centuries could only vaguely have dreamt of. We are rediscovering autonomy as a lost property, part of our Christian heritage that has somehow been overlooked. Authority structures will need to be changed.

I will blend observation of fact, social study and theological reflection.

Test Case One: Should Women be Ordained?

In 1976 the Congregation for the Doctrine of Faith set out its reasons for opposing the ordination of women.[2] As opposition intensified among theologians, Rome heightened the stakes. In 1994 Pope John Paul II declared 'that the Church has no authority whatsoever to confer priestly ordination on women and that this judgement is to be definitively held by all the Church's faithful'.[3] One year later the Congregation for the Doctrine of Faith stated: 'This teaching requires definitive assent, since, founded on the written Word of God, and from the beginning constantly preserved and applied in the Tradition of the Church, it has been set forth infallibly by the ordinary and universal Magisterium.'[4] This means that, according to the Congregation, the teaching has been infallibly decided by the collective body of bishops worldwide. It was the highest and strongest endorsement it could give to the ban on women priests.

However, the reception by Catholics in the developed world has been overwhelmingly negative. Surveys in the USA show that 63% of Catholics would want celibate women to be ordained priests, 54% married women; 63% also state that the laity should have a say in deciding the question whether women should be ordained or not. Among Catholic college students in Australia, 62% believe priestly ordination should be open to women. By the most recent statistics, Catholics in other Western countries also favour women priests: Spain 71%, Ireland 67%, Italy 58%.

It should be noted that most Catholics who support the ordination of women do so because they feel strongly that openness of women to Holy Orders is implied in our faith priorities. They sense unresolved contradictions: 'I hate the double standards the Catholic Church produces. Our school is an all-girl school and we are encouraged to be strong women of our time. But the views of the Pope and the Church just hold women back. Will the Pope ever understand the injustice that women have suffered? When will the law on women in the priesthood be changed? The Church will never have my full support until women receive the equality they deserve.'[5] Or: 'I have sometimes wondered whether this is not a logical deduction: the premise that it is impossible for women to be ordained implies ultimately that women cannot receive *salvation*. If Christ had to be incarnated as a *man*, if he can only be represented by *men*, he saved only *men*. I think it would be possible to prove the connection – thus giving the lie to the premise as there have been many women saints.'[6]

People Speak Up

Vox pop, 'the people's voice', the opinion of ordinary folk interviewed on the street, can be lively, funny, dramatic, precisely
because people often reply with astonishing wit and honesty.
The same is true of people who respond to a website that I
manage. The site promotes the ordination of women in the
Catholic Church. It is called www.womenpriests.org, and is the
largest website of its kind on the internet, with academic as well
as pastoral dimensions. At the time of writing, the site attracts
more than 100,000 visitors a year, from all over the world.
Most of them read a selection of our documents – over a million
during the past twelve months – and thousands send in their
questions and observations. Our *vox pop* will be drawn from
those. They will only be representative voices, chosen somewhat
at random just to give an idea of how variously people react.

As could be expected, considering the nature of our website,
many visitors reflect on the *arguments* the Roman authorities
give for their ban on women priests. Quite a few visitors to
womenpriests.org enter into the debate by offering their own
insights. It is impossible to summarize their numerous suggestions, questions, remarks and doubts. Consider some typical
reflections, both for and against, on Rome's contention that it
was Jesus himself who excluded women from the priestly ministry. Notice how the conviction that even ordinary people should
think for themselves underlies the discussion.

- 'How can you say that Jesus didn't exclude women? He
  only chose twelve men to be apostles. They were the only
  ones present at the Last Supper. Women are mentioned as
  being present at other times in the Gospel. I don't think
  that the writers of the Gospels had an agenda to exclude
  women.'
- 'A significant point against the ordination of women as
  priests is the event of the Last Supper. No one was present
  at this except the apostles. Part of this meal was

instructional. "Do this in memory of me." Note that there were no women involved. This fact would lend weight to the case why women cannot preside at the Eucharist.'

- 'Regarding Rome's argument that Christ did not include women among the twelve and thereby set a norm which the Church has no power to change; the Gospels tell us that Christ did include at least one married man among the twelve and even made him their leader. The Roman Church apparently had no difficulty in changing that norm! They can't have it both ways. As someone who, regretfully, was forced to choose between the practice of my ministerial priesthood and marriage (I have never regretted choosing marriage, but bitterly regret the inflexibility that forced me to choose) I think Rome's arguments, to put it somewhat less than academically, stink!'

Similar discussions take place on such issues as the ordination of women deacons in the early Church, the ancient prejudices surrounding menstruation, the claim that women cannot represent Christ, or Paul prohibiting women from teaching. People want to know the *reasons* for church decisions, and if these reasons do not measure up to expectation, they are dissatisfied. In a way people assess their leaders' sense of judgement, and it is here that the social shift manifests itself. As well they know!

- 'Congratulations on your attempt at accuracy and fairness. I myself have mixed feelings about women's ordination – but the real issues are how one envisions the Church, the ministry of service in teaching, the effective and obediential response to tentative teachings (or even so-called definitive/ non-infallible declarations).'
- 'The Church is organized and presided over autocratically by an ageing and numerically diminishing clergy ... All organizations are in constant need of reform but reform becomes more difficult when it has to be carried on against

those who have imposed themselves historically as sacred rulers.'

A Question of Authority?

I am always careful to present the case for the ordination of women respectfully, as loyal dissent within the Catholic Church, as a loyal member's duty to protest. This is, however, not how some visitors perceive it. A common objection voiced by conservatives rests on the claim that the Pope and the congregation for the doctrine of the faith cannot be wrong. They are guided by God. And even though the teaching authority may make mistakes, it should be obeyed. The argument is thus moved to the more central issue of authority. Is it significant that this objection is usually voiced by men?

- 'The Pope has declared this a forbidden issue. The argument is stale, and has been proven wrong. The Catholic Church doesn't have the power to ordain women. It cannot change the sacraments established by Christ. You should put your efforts into increasing vocations to the priesthood, not being in serious contradiction (and heresy) with your Church. The issue is closed, Peter has spoken infallibly . . . [*sic!*] Women cannot be ordained.' (a man commenting)
- 'Remember, the Church is not a democracy. The Church is directed by God, and no amount of pushing can change basic doctrine that God has set forth. Remember that the Bible is not the work of any saint but the work of God. Therefore, if St Paul wrote he rejected woman priests, God rejected women priests. Also remember the infallibility of the Pope. Don't be a cafeteria Catholic. If you don't like what the Church says, then leave it.' (a man commenting)
- 'Do you believe that Pope John Paul II is *the Vicar of Christ*? If you don't, then I see why you are pursuing the issue of woman priests. If you do, then why not be humble

and listen to him concerning this issue? Remember, the first
sin of man was *disobedience*.' (a man commenting)

- 'As faithful Roman Catholics we should bow to what our
  Holy Father teaches, even though sometimes it contradicts
  our own understanding. The teaching authority of the
  Catholic Church was instituted by Jesus Himself, so that we
  should allow our erroneous conscience to be corrected.
  Who is the author of Catholic doctrine? Theologians?
  Philosophers? Councils? or JESUS HIMSELF? ... Any
  conscience or understanding that contradicts the teaching of
  the Church is always an erroneous conscience ... Don't
  indulge in liberal thinking, because liberal thinking will
  bring you to heresy. Just become a good Catholic. The
  Pope is the successor of Peter and the Vicar of Christ, so
  what makes you think that you are more Catholic than the
  Pope himself?' (a priest commenting)

A number of correspondents state explicitly that they would
change their position if Rome were to turn round. Basically,
Rome's rejection of women priests is their only problem. In a
way they renounce their own right and duty to think as responsible members of the Church.

- 'As much as I respect your very scholarly and sensible
  approach to this matter, I respect the guidance of the Holy
  Spirit through the Magisterium and the Holy Father as the
  Vicar of Christ more. I believe you when you say you are a
  very committed Catholic but so am I. I am a Vatican II
  Catholic in every sense of the word and Vatican II itself
  says nothing about possible ordination of women.
  Assuming that women's ordination were possible, and Pope
  John Paul II along with his predecessors have made their
  approval abundantly clear, then I would agree with you. I
  know you feel your arguments for female priests are
  stronger than Rome's but I don't see it. If it were possible
  that one of Peter's future successors were to infallibly allow

women to be ordained then I would graciously accept it.' (a
man commenting)

- 'How can you prove beyond reasonable doubt that the
  Church should ordain women? Such a momentous break
  with tradition would require the Church to be absolutely
  certain that this was God's will. When the Church began to
  admit Gentiles, Peter had the vision described in Acts 2 and
  the baptism of Cornelius and his family followed soon
  after. If God gave to the Pope some special vision or
  inspiration that women priests was His plan for the Church
  and an Ecumenical Council on both Catholic and Orthodox
  Churches concurred, then I would have no problem at all
  with women priests. I would be a bit surprised granted but
  if it was definitely God's will no problem. But you just
  can't have that degree of certainty. Do you believe that God
  does guide the Church through the Pope and Bishops in
  Council or don't you? If you do then you have to accept
  what the Spirit seems to be saying to them and all the talk
  about Roman repression is, forgive me saying it, mere
  paranoia. God bless.' (a priest commenting)

The notion of *paranoia* is extremely interesting in this context.
For 'paranoia', which has come to mean psychotic delusions,
refers to some force being active outside the rational mind. And
this is precisely what is at stake. We are witnessing a shift from
a previous, authoritarian mindset to a more autonomous acceptance of responsibility for our beliefs. It is not the arguments,
but the mindsets underlying them that count. Could this psychological assessment be near to the truth?

- 'If you listen to the language of church documents that
  prohibit women's ordination you hear in their rhetoric a
  panic that shows they know they are wrong. For instance
  by saying that the Church has no authority NOT to ordain
  them. When the Church argues that women cannot *image*
  Christ on the altar, the notion of in whose *image* all of us

have been taught we are made reverberates under the surface. It is as though they are so frantic in their opposition, they actually provide the counter-argument in defence of women's ordination in their very proclamation. This is what we might see as linguistic Freudian slips that echo just beneath everything officially said on the issue. I find this subversive use of language interesting at the least, hysterical at best.' (a woman commenting)

• 'The primal flow in the present Catholic Church is the ancient sin of the arrogant lust for power legitimized by illusions. Ultimately, the institution bases its authority on power rather than service, on demands for unquestioning obedience rather than love.' (a woman commenting)

But if people challenge authority, what is happening?

Social Change Towards Greater Autonomy

The present crisis in the RC Church is due to a multiplicity of factors. One is a mismatch between the existing institutional practice and a new sense of self-worth among Catholics, especially in the developed world. People are better off. They are healthier and more educated. They have a greater control over their own lives. They participate in media discussion and political decision-making. All this has given them a new sense of personal autonomy, an autonomy that clashes with the antiquated authoritarian structures of the Church.

The change is documented in Gallup research known as 'The European Values Systems' study. It examined 210,280 Europeans from Great Britain, Ireland, France, Belgium, West Germany, the Netherlands, Spain, Denmark and Italy who expressed their opinions in interviews covering 480 questions each. It is the most extensive survey of this nature ever done and covers the whole of life: relationships, leisure, work, politics, religion, the meaning of life, family and ethics.[7] The European Values Studies of 1981 and 1990 have documented a steady shift in people's basic motivations. From having been *security seekers*, people are gradually becoming *fulfilment seekers*.

The terms 'security seekers' and 'fulfilment seekers' are my own.[8] They need to be carefully explained. The older generations in Europe are security seekers. Having experienced the uncertainties surrounding the Second World War, they are chiefly motivated by the need for economic and physical security. They cling to traditional certainties in the family, at work, in ethics and religious practice.

The younger generations become progressively more fulfilment seekers in the sense of being motivated more strongly by the needs of self-realization, belonging and quality of life. One consequence is a growing resistance to religious creeds and to organizations that impose restrictions on one's views or personal behaviour.

There are marked differences in attitudes. Within a family context, security seekers stress marriage stability and the traditional role of women: fulfilment seekers stress a woman's right to work even if she is a mother, and prefer divorce to an unhappy relationship. In their job, security seekers give priority to hard work, good manners and obedience; fulfilment seekers want interesting jobs. They rate imagination, creativity, independence and tolerance.

Security seekers tend to be traditional in their religious convictions. They believe in a personal God, adhere to orthodox doctrine regarding heaven, hell, sin and the devil, and are committed to traditional moral standards. Fulfilment seekers on the other hand are more likely to see God as a Life Force, to have doubts on orthodox doctrines, to be more permissive in morality and to be more critical of the Church.[9]

Comparative studies through the years document a steady shift towards the values of freedom and autonomy. In 1981, 33% of Europeans were outright security seekers, 14% outright fulfilment seekers, and 53% mixed. In 1990, the outright security seekers were down to 21%. Outright fulfilment seekers were up to 21%, mixed fulfilment seekers to 58%. That makes the total of fulfilment seekers 79% of society.

These social changes have also affected the Christian Churches even though the Churches proved, to some extent, havens of traditionalism. A significant proportion of the Churches' core members (weekly church attendance) are security seekers. The unchurched are predominantly fulfilment seekers. The intermediate group of marginal Christians (the 41% who occasionally attend a service) are also mainly fulfilment seekers. Indications are that people in this middle group are aware of their religious needs, but feel out of tune with institutional Christianity.

A number of follow-up studies in Australia and the USA demonstrated similar trends in other parts of the Western world. Of particular interest to us is an analysis of the Catholic Church in the USA which describes a parallel shift among Catholics from 'security seeking' to 'fulfilment seeking'. The author, Eugene Kennedy, speaks of two cultures which I will characterize as *external-authority culture* and *internal-authority culture*.[10]

According to Kennedy, external-authority Catholics emphasize the stability of the institutional Church. They are concerned about the credibility of the Church and its persistence as a social institution. These Catholics are rooted in the traditional, hierarchical exercise of authority. They stress the importance of private confession, where priests, representing the external authority of the institutional Church, give counsel and absolve sins. Kennedy argues that this cultural orientation is found most often in Catholics who were raised in the pre-Vatican II years of the 1920–40s.

Internal-authority Catholics conceive of religious authority as internal, flowing from the exercise of one's conscience. They believe the locus of authority is within the believer – that God speaks through the experiences and reflections of individual Christians. From this perspective, Catholics are to take personal responsibility for their faith, which is intimately related to daily experience in the world. According to Kennedy, this cultural orientation is most common among Catholics raised in the post-Vatican II years of the 1970–90s.

It is obvious that we are speaking here of two poles, rather than two clear-cut divisions.[11] For our purpose it is enough to observe that a major social change has taken place and that it has also made Catholics different. Many of us have, to a varying extent, become fulfilment seekers and internal-authority believers.

Numerous other studies confirm these findings. They show the far-reaching psychological and cultural changes that have changed the Catholic community in the decades following Vatican II. The Pro Mundi Vita study *The Roman Catholic Church and Europe* (1976) is informative for our purpose.[12] Research was done on the Catholic Church in England by Spencer (1975), by Pro Mundi Vita (1978) and especially by Hornsby-Smith (1979), whose book was at the time hailed as 'the best study of Roman Catholics in England and Wales to date'.[13] An extensive research was conducted in the Netherlands known as *Opnieuw: God in Nederland* (1970, 1979). Also worthy of mention in this context are the study of Dutch Catholicism by the American sociologist Coleman (1978), and a number of excellent reports by the Dutch research centre Kaski.[14] Information on Catholics in Australia is available through the National Catholic Life Survey (Mason 1997, 1998)[15] and through research on Catholic students preparing to be teachers (McLaughlin 1999).[16] Data about Catholics in the USA can be found in three successive Gallup Surveys (1987, 1993, 1999).[17]

Test Case Two: The Use of Contraceptives for Birth Control

Ever since Pope Paul VI published *Humanae Vitae* in 1968, the official position of the Church has been that artificial birth control goes against the natural law and is intrinsically evil. In 1987 John Paul II reiterated that 'this teaching of the Church has been written by the creative hand of God in the nature of the human person'. Disputing the doctrine, he said, is 'equal to refusing to God himself the obedience of our intelligence'.[18] This assessment is rejected by the vast majority of Catholics in the Western world.

In the USA, 73% of Catholics maintain one can be a good Catholic while using contraceptives, 61% believe the Church should not interfere in this: it should be left to one's own conscience. Even among weekly Mass-goers, only 21% say this is a matter for church leaders to determine, nearly half (45%) consider it a matter for one's own conscience. In Australia only 2% of students accept the Church's teaching on artificial contraception; 89% indicate it is a personal issue for the couple involved.

The Church's teaching on birth control is almost universally ignored by Catholics in developed countries.[19] The important question is: why? Has Rome's stand been rejected by a lack of self-discipline, by a surrender to convenience, by moral degeneracy?

Though such factors may always play a part, the decisive element is the fact that people have begun to reason things out for themselves. They judge matters differently from the Pope and base decisions on their own conscience rather than on his guidance. This can be proved in two ways.

1 Catholics dissent from Rome's teaching also on other questions of sexual ethics, but to varying degrees. To stay with the US statistics, two-thirds of Catholics condone remarriage without an annulment or a marriage without church sanction. But in the complex question of abortion, opinions are more divided.

Some 53% state one can be a good Catholic while practising abortion. The same percentage would agree to abortion being made legal in all circumstances, 33% only in rare circumstances, 41% believe abortion can often be a morally acceptable choice, 41% rarely, 13% never.[20]

In other words, people are thinking about the issues and attempting to decide them on their own merit. In all these matters of sexual ethics, however, including abortion, no more than 20% of Catholics hold that it is the church hierarchy that has the final say as to what is right and wrong.

2 The same is clear from extensive records of people's personal testimonies. They have *reasons* for rejecting the Church's official stance:

'I think that the Church's ways of thinking are absolutely ridiculous, especially that contraceptives are sin ... In the 1990s AIDS and unwanted pregnancy were very common. People being told that contraception is a sin are probably more likely to contract a disease.' (student)[21]

'*Humanae Vitae* is a beautiful document except for the few pages about artificial contraception that don't make sense. The rest is beautiful. They almost have it. The Church teaches beautiful things about sex and marriage and I use it so much in my life. And it is very useful when I try to explain sex to my children. But then they negate what they are saying by adding, "But we still believe that men and women should not practice artificial contraception." And I reply, "But you just spent twenty pages telling me why we should!"' (mother of two children)[22]

The sociologist Andrew Greeley maintains that since the encyclical *Humanae Vitae*, the Vatican has lost its credibility as a teacher of sexual ethics. 'Many have left the Church. No one takes it seriously on sexual matters anymore, not even its own members, not even devout ones.'[23] By its wooden and conservative views, Rome has undermined its own credibility.[24] But the development was unavoidable for other reasons too: people have learnt to think and decide for themselves.

But if Catholics make up their own minds on morals and doctrine, will we not end up with complete relativism and individualism? What about humility, docility and obedience? What about the teaching authority? Are we not heading for a chaos in which everyone 'does his own thing' or 'starts her own cosy cult', and this without regard to anyone else? Is this not an exaggerated liberty, a liberty that turns into sheer licence? Since the quest for greater autonomy arose in secular society, we should first turn to it for some fundamental considerations.

The Secular Struggle to Find Autonomy

The demand for a radical human autonomy reared its head in Europe as a basic alternative to Christianity. The Enlightenment attacked the conventions and superstitions of religion. 'Humanity is coming of age,' wrote Kant in 1784. 'Up till now the human race has depended on powers beyond itself. But human beings have reason. They must have the courage to think and choose for themselves. Dare to know! Have the guts to make use of your own understanding!'[25]

The new ideal was presented most forcefully by Friedrich Nietzsche (1844–1900), whom we will take as a useful starting point. Nietzsche began by reacting against the 'believer', the person brainwashed by priests, teachers and political leaders, the weakling who sacrifices his autonomy for the comfort and salvation promised by religion. Nietzsche chooses to be a 'free spirit' who follows his own reason and takes his own decisions. He compares this person to an audacious mountaineer. 'You are reaching the higher slopes. The wind blows fresher. Your step treads more surely and energetically. Your path, however, is lonelier and riskier than before.'[26]

Soon Nietzsche's thoughts rose to even more grandiose heights. Man should break the shackles imposed by clerics, moralists, poets and saints who have told him what is supposed to be good and evil, false or true. Man should rise free by becoming the Superhuman.[27]

> You have made your way from worm to man, and much in you is still worm. Once you were apes, and even now a human being is more of an ape than any ape ... What is human is

something that should be overcome. Behold, I teach you the Superhuman![28]

The most anxious ask today: 'How is humanity to be preserved?' But Zarathustra's first and only question is: 'How is humanity to be *overcome*?' The Superhuman is my concern, not my neighbour, nor the poorest, nor the greatest sufferer, nor the most virtuous ... At present petty folk have become your master: they preach submission and humility and charity and all the long list of petty virtues ... Overcome these masters of today, my brothers – these petty folk; *they* are the greatest peril to the Superhuman.[29]

I, Zarathustra, found people convinced they *knew* what is good and evil for human beings. They were asleep ... This sleep I broke when I taught that nobody yet knows what is good and evil – unless it be that he becomes a creator! A creator is he that creates a human being's goal and gives earth its meaning and its future: it is he that first makes good and evil to be.[30]

Nietzsche's Superhuman is the free and autonomous individual, who overcomes the limitations of the past by creating a new world for her or himself:

- in which life, the body, health and the joys of the flesh reign supreme;
- in which the passions are turned into virtues and joys;
- in which achievers are extolled: that is, the strong such as warriors and soldiers, rather than scholars and teachers;
- in which struggle is esteemed, and the will to power;
- in which the winners are rewarded without pity for the losers.

The danger of absolute human autonomy as exemplified in Nietzsche's thinking is clear. We only need to remember how the Nazis based much of their ruthless brutality on Nietzsche. The ideal of the Superhuman is also manifest in the arrogance of secular society that sanctions the rule of the winners, that drugs individuals with pleasure and entertainment, and that claims implicit ownership over nature, the earth and even the universe.

The generally accepted 'secular' ideal of human autonomy, however, is much healthier than the one proposed by Nietzsche or other extreme thinkers. In fact, it is in this secular ideal itself that we find some necessary corrections.

Among the characteristics of a mature personality listed by psychologists we find the following:

- the ability to judge situations and people accurately;
- feeling at home with oneself, with nature in general and with human nature;
- spontaneity and creativity;
- the aptitude to focus on authentic problems without being preoccupied with oneself;
- a good measure of detachment and independence;
- openness to learning new things, to wonder, awe and joy, to looking at the world around us with new eyes;
- basic feelings of identification, sympathy, and affection for others in spite of occasional anger or impatience;
- a democratic character structure which respects any human being just because he or she is a human individual;
- and, last but not least, the ability to take one's own considered and responsible decisions.[31]

This kind of analysis shows that concern for oneself needs to be balanced with concern for others. Nietzsche's Superhuman is, in fact, no longer human because he or she lacks a realistic view of his or her own dependence on others and is not really open to sympathy and affection for others. Nietzsche's Superhuman is nothing more than a spoilt and overgrown child who, by modern psychological standards, would be judged immature and psychotic.

The full realization of human autonomy implies not only a commitment to one's own freedom but also *acceptance*. It implies acceptance of what I am, my past, my origin, my place in the world and, crucially, the Other. The Other meets me in human faces, in people I cannot reduce to myself, who also are free and autonomous, and whom I cannot treat as objects in my control. The Other also meets me in nature, in the universe, in the laws of science, all of which I do not own but which give me life. Accepting the Other sets the environment in which my freedom and autonomy become possible.[32]

Psychology tells us that responsible decision-making is at the heart of being a fully developed person. The autonomous person observes reality, reflects on its implications, weighs up good and bad, and chooses a particular course of action. Both the ability to discern data accurately and the freedom to choose between various alternatives are essential in decision-making. A full human being is conscious and free.

In a way it is correct to state that we only become truly human to the extent that we make our own decisions. We build up our own personality through it. By nature we have a certain disposition or temperament. These do not form our character. Our 'character' develops as the result of the decisions we take in the course of our life.

Personal decision-making and human autonomy have, as never before, become the hallmarks of our society. Through science and technology we try to control and steer the world in which we live. In democratic processes we take responsibility for our own welfare. We select our food, our clothes and our entertainment from an incredibly rich spread of choices. We elect and reject the leaders who govern us. We are learning to sift critically the information presented to us through the media. We may not always use our freedoms wisely, but as members of a society that honours our freedoms we have changed.

But are true human freedom and autonomy compatible with our Christian calling?

The Roots of 'Christian' Autonomy

Catholics are reasserting their autonomy as is clear from the following responses to the www.womenpriests.org website.

'With all due respect to bishops and priests, and especially cardinals in the Vatican, how could they claim an authority which even God refuses to claim as our Creator? Did God not give each one of us intelligence, free willpower, creativity and responsibility? If God treats us as autonomous persons, why can't leaders in the Church?'

'Vatican II speaks of partnership, co-responsibility, involvement by all in the life of the Church. Almost nothing of this grand vision has been implemented. At present baptism relegates a man to the status of a B-class moron, useful to fill pews and collection boxes on a Sunday. And women are definitely C-class: no A-class can be recruited from them.'

'In every respect society is trying to overcome the limitations of the oppressive hierarchies of the past, whether this was in politics, business or class structures. I will not feel at home in a Church that hangs on to outdated cultural paternalisms.'

Is the secular ideal of the mature and autonomous personality in conflict with Christian faith? I believe it is not. What is more, I am sure that our Christian beliefs enhance and deepen true human autonomy.

Human autonomy springs from God's creative action in us. This should be properly understood. We do not just find traces of the Creator in God's created *works*. We also find God in the work God has left unfinished, in the freedom and autonomy he leaves to us. God has not just created the universe as a marvellous clockwork, a divine toy. He has created human beings as 'clockmakers'/'creators' in their own right: people who can think, plan and create. This is the fullest meaning of human beings having been created 'in God's own image'.

> If some of the creatures are not just part of nature but are themselves centres of freedom and creativity, then God's creation can no longer be considered as, from his point of view, a toy or even a work of art. It has become a potential partner with God, able to respond to him and to join with him in a continuing work of creation. Of course, since freedom is in itself neutral, the free creatures of the universe might turn against God. Man is God's risk. But even when one allows for the risk, how much richer is a universe that can freely respond through some of its members than one which can be no more than an object of contemplation, however infinite?[33]

The Renaissance theologian Pico della Mirandola (1463–94) describes human autonomy in a powerful image. God is a sculptor who carved all creatures. But God left the human being unfinished, as a block of marble with vast potential. God says to each human being: 'Other creatures have a limited nature confined by laws laid down by me. But because I have entrusted free intelligence to you, you are confined by no bounds and you will fix the limits of your nature for yourself . . . I appointed you your own guide. You are the moulder and maker of yourself; you may sculpt yourself into whatsoever shape you prefer.'[34] It is interesting to reflect that this comes close to Nietzsche's idea that a human being becomes autonomous by becoming 'a creator who creates his own goals and gives earth its meaning and its future'. Creative freedom is at the heart of human autonomy. It differentiates us from animals and is a breach from the rest of created nature, a mystery of 'God in us'.

Each Believer Carries the Intrinsic Principle of Love

In the course of history human beings became trapped in multiple kinds of slavery, but Jesus Christ restored our autonomy by liberating us from sin, from death and from 'law'. Here 'law' stands for all the trappings of organized religion. We live under grace and not under law (Rom. 6:14), which means: we are liberated from the domination of external religion.[35]

To understand the full implications of this, we should recall that traditional religions, including the Old Testament, rested on a distinction between the sacred and the profane. Everyday realities, such as houses, cattle, eating and sleeping, doing business, and so on, were ordinary or 'profane'. God was not really directly present in these realities. Other realities of our world, however, were considered to be filled with divine presence and to have become 'sacred' on that account. This is the origin of 'sacred' times (the Sabbath and feast days), 'sacred' places (mainly the Temple), 'sacred' objects (such as vessels used for worship), 'sacred' persons (priests) and 'sacred' actions. It was the Law that, through its 'sacred' rules and prescriptions, imposed the yoke of external religion.

When Christ came, he did not substitute new holy realities for the old ones. He radically abrogated the edifice of organized religion that separates us from God. This may seem startling to some who continue to think along Old Testament lines. They imagine the New Testament to be an updated version of the Old. They think our Churches have taken the place of the Temple at Jerusalem, that our Sunday replaces the Sabbath, that our paten and chalice continue the Temple furniture and that the New Testament priest is a polished version of the Old Testament one. They consider church laws as improved extensions of Old Testament legislation. They do not realize that something has radically *changed*.

Yes, we do have quasi-sacred realities in the Church: feast days, basilicas, a hierarchy of ministers, law books and regulations, rosaries and chasubles. These things re-entered Christianity as tools of an established religious community. But they are *only* instruments and helps. The basic reality remains that we have been given the freedom of the children of God (Rom. 8:21) – note: not children in the sense of dependents, but children as people who share the nature and autonomy of their parents. 'For freedom Christ has set you free. Stand firm then and do not submit again to any yoke of slavery!', Paul says (Gal. 5:1).

Traditional Catholics still think that the structures of the Church are the fundamental reality and that people somehow have to fit in. Just the opposite is true. The core reality is the Holy Spirit in each believer. The external structures are there to support their freedom and autonomy. Even the Son of God became human 'for the sake of us human beings and our salvation'. The Church that is the sacramental extension of Jesus Christ is totally dedicated to service, not to building up its own structural power.

Christians know they are free from any external law. The only law they acknowledge is the Holy Spirit in their hearts. 'If you are led by the Spirit, no law can touch you' (Gal. 5:18). When Christ taught that love of God and love of our neighbour is the highest commandment, he brought about a religious revolution. It is not the external laws that matter, whatever they are. It is love, the interior principle of responsible action, that supersedes any law (Luke 10:25–37.) This does not need to surprise us. For Jesus revealed that God is love, and that all morality can be summed up in a living up to the principle of love (1 John 4:7–12).

The Authority of the 'Law Written in Our Heart'

Paul states it emphatically: we cannot be saved by fulfilling external laws. We are saved by a new law that God has written in our heart: the law of the Spirit of life. This law is the love that has been poured into our hearts by the Spirit of God (Rom. 8:1–2, 5:5; Gal. 5:1–6). St Thomas Aquinas, who is traditionally seen as the norm of orthodoxy, explains it as follows:

> That which predominates after Christ's coming is the grace of the Holy Spirit which is given through faith in Christ.

Consequently, the New Law is chiefly the grace itself of the Holy Spirit, which is given to those who believe in Christ.[36]

To put it in the words of Cardinal Girolamo Seripando, who presided over the Council of Trent (1545–63): 'We have received the Spirit of God in our mind, to take the place of external law.'[37] External laws, which tell us what to do and what not to do, will not really change us. But God's Spirit can. God's Spirit gives us a new autonomy. It enables us to act responsibly and in harmony with selfless love, which is Christ's own, inner commandment (John 15:12). People who act like that are not under any law. They live by grace and not by the law (Gal. 5:18; Rom. 6:14). As Paul so aptly says: 'The letter [of external laws] kills, the Spirit [who works in our hearts] makes alive' (2 Cor. 3:6). Even the commandments found in the Gospel, in so far as they would be external 'laws', would fall under the letter that kills.[38]

The true source of Christian autonomy, therefore, is the Spirit in the heart of every believer. Jesus Christ came to bring us life and bring it abundantly (John 10:10). This abundance of life is unthinkable without the full development of our personality. We have been created 'in God's own image': that is, with some of God's own maturity and autonomy. When humankind had fallen into various kinds of slavery and bondage, Jesus redeemed us from these chains and raised us to a new dignity. Yes, in spite of being Christians we are still weak and need the support the Church can provide. But the principle of our autonomy lives in us. It is God himself/herself.

The Overflowing Measure

Precisely because God's love is the guiding principle in us, Christians should be prepared to *give*, rather than take. It is the theme of the sermon on the mount. Jesus declared that we must outdo others in tolerance and forbearance. We should turn the other cheek, give our cloak if someone takes our tunic, go an extra mile if we are forced to carry a pack (Matt. 5—7). 'Love your enemies. Do good to those who hate you. Bless those who curse you and pray for those who treat you badly ... If you love those who love you, what blessing is in it?' (Luke 6:27–28).

According to Jesus, there is no 'blessing' in just giving *quid pro quo*. If we truly are children of God who live under God's leadership, we will transcend a short-term view of things and decide to be patient, kind, forgiving, never mind how people respond. We will be loving on principle; not because others are patient, kind and forgiving to us, but because our goodness will eventually, in the long term, win the upper hand. There is blessing and reward in such an attitude, not only in the sense of us finding favour with God, but in our improving the overall situation itself. This is a higher logic. It is God's logic. It transcends the human law of mutuality.[39]

Paradoxically, it is by adopting this attitude and putting it into practice that we will realize our autonomy to the full. 'What will anyone gain by winning the whole world and losing his own self? Or what shall a person offer in exchange for his own self?' (Matt. 16:26). 'You must be "whole" as your heavenly Father is "whole"' (Matt. 5:48).

God's autonomy is generous. God does not abandon kindness even if people oppose God. God provides rain and sunshine to good and bad alike (Matt. 5:45). This unshakeable inner goodness of God derives from God's wholeness. The word Jesus used was *thamîm*. In translations it is often rendered by 'perfect' (via the Greek). But *thamîm* means 'whole'.[40] Jesus saw that we too should have this inner wholeness in us. 'If you greet only your relatives, what extra is it you are doing? Don't the pagans do the same? No, you must be whole as your Father in heaven is whole' (Matt. 5:47).

'What extra is it you are doing?' This sentence provides the answer to the question: How does the disciple differ from a pagan? What makes God's autonomy Christian? The truly Christian element adds the extraordinary gift, the extra tolerance, doing more than normal, daring to be different from the usual, offering the not so obvious.[41] However, this 'extra' should not be imposed by external law; it should be freely given. It enhances a person's freedom, character and autonomy only *if* and precisely *because* it is freely given.

By way of conclusion we can say that Christians have good reason to treasure their autonomy:

- by being free and mature individuals they share in the creative powers God entrusted to them;
- by relying on the Spirit in their heart they can enjoy the freedom of the children of God;
- by generously responding in love and dying to themselves, they can realize and 'fulfil' themselves in a manner that transcends limited, self-centred hopes and ambitions.

Implications for the Church

Church leaders should be happy that today's faithful are becoming more autonomous. Christian autonomy can easily be grafted on to secular human autonomy. It can gain from it and complement it. However, the present paternalistic structures and modes of practice in the Church clash with both secular and Christian autonomy.

It is not necessary here to detail all the reforms needed if the Church is to salvage its role as the sacrament of Christ's salvific presence. But some closing comments seem appropriate in the context of my topic.

From a management-theory point of view, the Church is a *voluntary* organization. Members are not controlled by physical constraint, economic profit or cultural necessity, but by internal motivation. This does not mean that members' wishes or opinions replace revelation or pastoral authority. It does mean that members will want to understand the reasons. They need to be *persuaded* of what is right or wrong, *convinced* of what is true or not true. Coercion will backfire, especially now that people are better educated and sure of themselves.

This is precisely what we have seen happening regarding compulsory celibacy for priests. Since the motivation has proved inadequate, priests have walked out in hundreds of thousands. And as to moral prescriptions, married couples too have voted with their feet. Sexual ethics need to make *sense* before the majority of people are willing to commit themselves to it. Surely, personal weakness and the secular environment also take their toll, but what we see now in the Church is that its lead is rejected by dedicated priests and practising Catholics.

The Church is an organization that exists to support the inner action of the Holy Spirit. It is internal and spiritual values that enjoy priority status. This applies in particular to truth and love. The organization will not function properly if its actions fail to safeguard these values. A case in point is the question of the ordination of women. The arguments of the Roman 'teaching authority' are not supported by theological research. They fail the test of truth.[42] Attempts by the Congregation for the Doctrine of Faith to regain the upper hand by ever more strident declarations, by imposing oaths of loyalty, and by harassing theologians have produced a silence of repression in the Church. They have not won over theological consensus. The attempts are doomed to fail.

The authority enjoyed by the Pope and the bishops does not operate in a vacuum. It needs to respect the cultural values of our time: openness, media scrutiny, participation of an informed membership in issues facing the Church, public opinion. Though the authority does not *derive* from the members but from God – and is not democratic in that sense – it needs to be collegial, credible and accountable in the way it is exercised. After all, its authority is a public service, justified only when exercised for the good of the Body of Christ. From being a power-conscious top-down, paternalistic practice, pastoral authority will need to become a people-focused, caring and empowering service.

Ordinary Catholics have to be rescued from the periphery and reinstated in the centre of the Church. With regard to doctrine, this implies giving due weight to the *sensus fidelium* as an important carrier of tradition. It requires an abolition of all restrictions imposed by Canon Law on the ministry of women. It calls for a true implementation of the coresponsibility called for by Vatican II, so that all believers share in the decisions affecting the life of the Church. It means a transfer of many external church activities, such as finance, administration and planning to non-clericalized ministries.

The bishops should be freed to exercise their crucial spiritual responsibilities. Bishops should not be officials of a sacred and powerful bureaucracy, but the living expression of Christ's love and guidance to their people. The election of men and women to the episcopacy should incorporate a prudent consultation among the faithful. Bishops should be given more local autonomy so that they can lead their dioceses as vicars of Christ, rather than vicars of the Roman Pontiff as they are perceived to be functioning now. The synods of bishops convened in Rome to discuss the world Church should allow the bishops to express their own views and contribute to real decision-making for the whole Church.

This is not the first time the Church has needed to undergo structural reforms, nor will it be the last. As on previous occasions, today's crisis offers the Church a precious opportunity to live up to its own avowed aims.

Notes

Chapter 1

1 Adrian B. Smith, *A Reason for Living and Hoping: A Christian Appreciation of the Emerging New Era of Consciousness*, London: St Paul's Publishing, 2002.

2 Alvin Toffler, *Future Shock*, USA: Amazon, Mass Market Publications, 2003.

3 Adrienne Rich, *The Dream of a Common Language: Poems 1974–1977*, New York and London: W. W. Norton, 1978.

4 Dorothea McEwan, Pat Pinsent, Ianthe Pratt and Veronica Seddon, eds., *Making Liturgy: Creating Rituals for Worship and Life*, London: Canterbury Press, 2001.

5 Peter Worden, *The Tablet*, 4 January 2003.

6 Natalie K. Watson, *Introducing Feminist Ecclesiology*, Sheffield: Sheffield Academic Press, 2003.

7 Alvin Toffler, Wisdom website, creative quotes, http://creativequotations.com/one/528.htm.

8 Carol Walker Bynum, *Jesus as Mother: Studies in the Spirituality of the High Middle Ages*, Berkeley, Los Angeles and London: University of California Press, 1984.

9 An area of land that encompassed modern-day Germany and parts of northern Italy.

10 The humiliation of Canossa, Emperor Henry IV of Germany and Pope Gregory VII, January 1077.

11 Paul Collins, *Papal Power: A Proposal for Change in Catholicism's Third Millennium*, London: Harper and Collins, Fount Paperbacks, 1997, p. 177. This book is a very good short historical overview of the development of papal primacy and infallibility, with suggestions for ways out of the present situation. Highly recommended reading for background to the whole question of high papalism.

12 This Council only implicitly asserted the power of a Church Council over the authority of the Pope. The clear assertion came later at the Council of Basel.

13 The three main points are: 1 The Council must be legitimately assembled. 2 It represents the Catholic Church. 3 It has immediate power from Christ.

14 For example, wearing the same clothes, including the veil for women, no matter what the climate; following the same timetable as the mother house in Europe, irrespective of local needs, etc.

15 *The Downside Review*, 'Abbot Butler and the Council', papers given at a symposium at Heythrop College, London, 12 October 2002, published by Downside Press, Bath, 2003.

16 See edition by Walter M. Abbott SJ, *The Documents of Vatican II*, London and Dublin: Geoffrey Chapman, 1966, p. 213.

17 For an interesting and very readable critique of both the strengths and weaknesses of the Council see Peter Hebblethwaite, *The Runaway Church*, London: Collins Paperback, 1978. Here Hebblethwaite points out that one of the major causes for the difficulties the Church faced in applying the various Decrees was not only that there were so many all at once, but also the documents were so worded that they simply 'set the contrasting positions alongside each other' (p. 103). Hence, future generations could interpret these documents according to their understanding of Church. See also John Allen, 'The Counter-Revolution', *The Tablet*, 7 December 2002, pp. 8–9.

18 Mary Daly, *Outercourse: The Be-Dazzling Voyage*, London: The Women's Press, 1993. This book is an account of her journey from a patriarchal church system, namely the RC Church, into an account of her time/space travels and ideas out of all forms of 'foot-binding' theologies. Mary Daly is one of the most radical philosophers in the developing feminist tradition. Even though her ideas are controversial to many, she has analysed the all-evading presence of patriarchy that has permeated all areas not only of female but also male life forms. Her work stands as a radical corrective to shoddy thought and the inability to grasp the underlying evil of our times.

19 A private talk given to CWO in March 1996, London.

20 Reports from the Fourth United Nations World Conference on Women, Beijing, 4–15 September 1995, *Report on the UK Delegation*, Sex Equality Branch 4, Caxton House, Tothill Street, London; *Your Story is My Story, Your Story is Our Story*, The Decade Festival, Harare, Zimbabwe, Ecumenical Decade: Churches in Solidarity with Women, Geneva: World Council of Churches, 1998.

21 Jonathan Raban, 'My Holy War', *The New Yorker*, 4 February 2002, p. 31.

Chapter 2

1 Mary Jo Weaver, *New Catholic Women: A Contemporary Challenge to Traditional Religious Authority*, San Francisco: Harper and Row, 1985. This is a well-documented historical book written in the 1980s as a good introduction into the developing insights of Catholic women and their Church. The author begins to show how Catholic women have to learn how to relate to their Church in a more critical way in order for these new valid insights to be made concrete in the life of the Church.

2 Rosemary Radford Ruether, *Introducing Redemption in Christian Theology*, Sheffield: Sheffield Academic Press, 1998. The author asserts for Paul it was initially the Jewish-Greco aspect of this formula that interested him most. Only when he entered into conflict with parties in the Christian Church of Corinth did he clarify his views that did not endorse this formula, at least on earth (pp. 20–5). The writers are aware that there is considerable controversy surrounding the views of St Paul and much has been wrongly attributed to him, but this is not the place for a full exegesis of scripture. This book by Ruether is a quick way to get a greater understanding of the Pauline controversy. What is clear is that the vision of this part of scripture has not been adhered to.

3 Mary Hunt, 'We Women Are Church', *Concilium*, London: SCM Press, 1993, p. 105.

4 *Ekklesia* in the Greek Bible, literally the assembly or meeting, is an eschatological term and realized only in heaven.

5 Raymond E. Brown, *The Churches the Apostles Left Behind*, New York: Paulist Press, 1984, and by the same author, *Biblical Exegesis and Church Doctrine*, London: Geoffrey Chapman, 1985.

6 Alfred Loisy (1857–1940) was a well-known scholar of the Modernist Movement of the early twentieth century. Although they were condemned by the Pope of the time, Pius X (1903–14) in the encyclical *Pascendi Dominici Gregis* (1907), all that these scholars called for was freedom of inquiry; a new historical approach to the development of theology and doctrine and to apply these to the Bible and church history, especially the early period of the Church.

7 Marcella Althaus-Reid, *Indecent Theology: Theological Perversions in Sex, Gender and Politics*, New York: Routledge, 2001, p. 77. The author writes from a South American–Argentinian perspective: 'Since my country is a Republic, it is difficult enough to explain the meaning

of the word "Kingdom" without first beginning a Greek lesson . . . "Kingdom of God" is a concept in conflict with itself, unstable and ambivalent and perhaps we should not try to stabilize it.'

8 The question of subjugated ways of knowing is being developed by June Boyce Tillman in her work as Professor of Applied Music at Winchester College. See June Boyce-Tillman, *Constructing Musical Healing*, London and Philadelphia: Jessica Kingsley, 2000.

9 Joseph A. Komonchak, Mary Collins and Dermot A. Lane, eds., *New Dictionary of Theology*, Dublin: Gill and Macmillan, 1987, p. 188.

10 From the 1960s a theological model of Church as Sacrament found leading advocates in Karl Rahner, Edward Schillebeeckx and Yves Congar, prominent academic teachers of theology. But it has remained primarily a model of theologians and never became generally popular.

11 The Church as Herald is primarily a Church of proclamation of the scriptures over interpersonal relations and mystical communion.

12 Avery Dulles, *Models of the Church*, New York: Doubleday, 1978.

13 A great deal of research has been undertaken on the development and widening of ministries. These include, E. Schillebeeckx, *Ministry*, London: SCM Press, 1981; Yves Congar, *Power, Poverty in the Church*, London: SCM Press, 1964; B. Cooke, *Ministry to Word and Sacrament*, Philadelphia: Fortis Press, 1976.

14 Dulles, *Models of the Church*, p. 56.

15 Natalie Watson, *Introducing Feminist Ecclesiology*, Sheffield: Sheffield Academic Press, 2003, p. 42.

16 Watson, *Introducing Feminist Ecclesiology*, pp. 44–7.

17 Madonna Kolbenschlag, *Women in the Church*, Washington: The Pastoral Press, 1987, p. 23.

18 Michael H. Crosby, *The Dysfunctional Church: Addiction and Codependency in the Family of Catholicism*, Notre Dame Indiana: Ave Maria Press, 1991.

19 Desmond Murphy, *A Return to Spirit: After the Mythic Church*, Dublin: Gill and Macmillan, 1997. An original and convincing analysis of the vast changes taking place in the Catholic Church as seen through the eyes of transpersonal psychology.

20 The 'remnant' is the term used by scripture scholars for the small groups of Jews who had no pre-conceptions of who the Messiah would be and whose minds were open to accepting the Messiah in whatever way he should come. Whereas the majority of Jews, Scribes and Pharisees believed in a political Messiah who would save them by the sword and give them a kingdom of their own.

21 Murphy, *Return to the Spirit*, p. 186.

22 Murphy, *Return to the Spirit*, p. 188.

23 Murphy, *Return to the Spirit*, p. 190.

24 Mary Daly, *Beyond God the Father*, Boston: Beacon Press, 1973, p. 64.

25 Mary Ann Rossi, 'The Legitimation of the Abuse of Women in Christianity', in *Feminist Theology*, no. 4, Sheffield: Sheffield Academic Press, 1993, 57–63.

26 Robin Morgan, ed., *Sisterhood is Global*, Harmondsworth: Penguin Books, 1984.

27 Canon 1024: Only a baptized man can validly receive sacred ordination.

28 Dale Spender, *Man Made Language*, London and New York: Routledge and Kegan Paul, 1980; Brian Wren, *What Language Shall I Borrow?*, London: SCM Press, 1989.

29 Susan Haskins, *Mary Magdalen: Myth and Metaphor*, London: Harper Collins, 1993; Carla Ricci, *Mary Magdalen and Many Others: Women who Followed Jesus*, Tunbridge Wells: Burns and Oates, 1994; Elisabeth Moltmann-Wendel, *The Women Around Jesus*, London: SCM Press, 1982; Lucy Winkett, 'Mary Magdalene, Apostle to the Apostles', an address delivered at the Go Tell! Celebration of Christian Women, July 2000, published by Churches Together in Britain and Ireland, London, 2000.

30 Aruna Gnanadason, ed., *No Longer Secret: The Church and Violence Against Women*, Geneva: WCC Publications, 1993, p. 67.

31 See Rosemary Radford Ruether, *Sexism and God-Talk: Toward a Feminist Theology*, Boston: Beacon Press, 1983 for a fuller understanding of the development of sexism as a 'norm'.

32 Dermot Lane, *Foundations for a Social Theology: Praxis, Process and Salvation*, Dublin: Gill and Macmillan, 1984.

33 Sandra Schneiders IHM, *Beyond Patching: Faith and Feminism in the Catholic Church*, New York: Paulist Press, 1991.

34 Gnanadason, ed., *No Longer Secret* and *Living Letters: A Report of Visits to the Churches during the Ecumenical Decade – Churches in Solidarity with Women*, Geneva: WCC Publications, 1997.

35 There is a rapidly developing literature on this topic, a topic too vast for the purposes of this book but central to any change towards a Church of partnership. See such books as Rosemary Radford Ruether, *Introducing Christian Redemption*, Sheffield: Sheffield Academic Press, 1998, especially for her argument 'Can a Male Saviour Save Women? Liberating Christology from Patriarchy', Chapter 6, p. 81; Julie Hopkins, *Towards a Feminist Christology*, The Netherlands: Kok Pharos, 1995; Elisabeth Schüssler Fiorenza, *Jesus: Miriam's Child, Sophia's Prophet: Critical Issues in Feminist Christology*, London: SCM Press,

1995; Susan Thistlethwaite, ed., *White Women's Christ and Black Women's Jesus: Feminist Christology and a Womanist Response*, Atlanta, GA: Scholars Press, 1989.
36 Althaus-Reid, *Indecent Theology*.

Chapter 3

1 Rosemary Radford Ruether, *Women-Church*, Boston MA: Beacon Press, 1995.
2 The latter is a controversial term used in metaphysical philosophy, meaning to speculate on the nature and essence of things.
3 See Ann Garry and Marilyn Pearsall, *Women, Knowledge and Reality: Explorations in Feminist Philosophy*, Boston MA: Unwin Hyman, 1989, p. 56.
4 Garry and Pearsall, *Women, Knowledge and Reality*, p. 56.
5 Garry and Pearsall, *Women, Knowledge and Reality*, p. 65.
6 Rosi Braidotti, *Metamorphoses Towards a Materialist Theory of Becoming*, Oxford: Polity Press in association with Blackwell Press, 2002, p. 67.
7 Catherine R. Stimpson, ed., *Women, History and Theory: The Essays of Joan Kelly*, Chicago and London: University of Chicago Press, 1984.
8 Christine de Pisan wrote a series of works. Her best known book is *The City of Women* (1404), where she wondered why women had not taken up their pens before to protest at the vile things written about them (Stimpson, *Women, History and Theory*, pp. 65–109). She studied most of her life and wrote fifteen volumes of works. But because she crossed the line between private and public she suffered many humiliations, braving whistles and shouts on the street as well as at the French court palace, where her husband was a royal secretary.
9 For a history of these many women see the very comprehensive treatment by Dale Spender, *Women of Ideas and What Men have Done to Them*, London: Pandora, 1988.
10 Olwen Hufton, *The Poor of Eighteenth Century France*, Oxford: Oxford University Press, 1974, Chapter 12, pp. 458–86.
11 Susan B. Anthony, *The Revolution*, 1868.
12 There is no explicit reference in this chapter to this form of feminism, which is understood best from the works of Simone de Beauvoir, *The Second Sex* being her most famous. Her work was greatly influenced by the philosophy of Jean Paul Sartre. Certain areas of her writings are quite controversial; she is accused of being an armchair academic philosopher, with a general mistrust of the female body. However, she had and has a large following and much can be said of her profound

feminism. She refused to accept that biology is destiny. In her words women have to transcend their bodies, i.e. transcend the limits of their innocence and cast off the weights that are impeding their progress. See also Rosemarie Tong, *Feminist Thought: A Comprehensive Introduction*, London: Routledge, 1992 for a fuller understanding of de Beauvoir's concept of woman as the 'Other', pp. 195–216.

13 Shulamith Firestone, *The Dialectic of Sex: The Case for Feminist Revolution*, New York: Bantam Books, 1970.

14 Hester Eisenstein, *Contemporary Feminist Thought*, London: Unwin Paperbacks, 1984, p. 16.

15 Adrienne Rich, *Of Woman Born: Motherhood as Experience and Institution*, New York: W. W. Norton, 1976.

16 Germaine Greer, *The Female Eunuch*, London: Harper Collins, 1999.

17 Tong, *Feminist Thought*, p. 137.

18 *The following books are very helpful for an introduction to French thought: Tong, Feminist Thought.* Chapter 8, 'Postmodern Feminist', pp. 217–33; Deborah Cameron, *Feminism and Linguistic Theory*, London: Macmillan Press, 1985; Jane Freedman, *Feminism*, Buckingham: Open University Press, 2001.

19 It is interesting to note that these French scholars do not call themselves feminist, although Luce Irigaray is not so uncomfortable with the term.

20 'Julia Kristeva believes that femininity is constructed by the mode of entry into the symbolic order ... She suggests that before the symbolic order there is a *semiotic* order linked to oral and anal drives which flow across the child. The "pulsions" of these drives are gathered in a *chora* (which means approximately a receptacle). Later, when the child takes up a position in the symbolic order as a result of the castration complex, the contents of the *chora* will be repressed, but its influence will nevertheless be discernible in linguistic discourse through rhythm, intonation, gaps, meaningless and general textual disruption. Indeed some discourses, like art, poetry and madness, draw on the semiotic rather than the symbolic aspects of language', Cameron, *Feminism and Linguistic Theory*, p. 126.

21 Cameron, *Feminism and Linguistic Theory*, pp. 125–7. Kristeva has criticized Irigaray and Cixous for trying to create a feminine language and female society outside masculine language and male society.

22 Irigaray uses the medical term 'speculum', a mirror in gynaecological usage, to help women discover the concept of difference through their bodies. Luce Irigaray, *Speculum: De l'autre femme*, Paris: Minuit, 1974, translated by Gillian C. Gill, *Speculum: Of the Other Woman*.

23 bell hooks, *Ain't I a Woman*, Boston MA: South End Press, 1981; bell hooks, *Feminist Theory from Margin to Centre*, Boston MA: South End Press, 1984; Audrey Lorde, *Sister Outsider: Essays and Speeches*, New York and Trumansberg: Crossing Press, 1984.

24 See Freedman, *Feminism*, Chapter 5, pp. 76–92 for a fuller understanding of the role that 'ethnicity and identity' play in any analysis of society.

25 Tong, *Feminist Thought*, p. 233.

26 Belenky Mary Field, Blythe McVicker Clinchy, Nancy Rule Goldberger and Jill Mattuck Tarule, *Women's Ways of Knowing: The Development of Self, Voice and Mind*, New York: Basic Books, 1986.

27 Carol Gilligan, *In A Different Voice: Psychological Theory and Women's Development*, Harvard: Harvard University Press, 1982.

28 Carol Gilligan believes that psychology has persistently and systematically misunderstood women – their motives, their moral commitments, the course of their psychological growth, and their special view of what is important in life, claiming that development theories have been built on observations of men's lives. Her research is based on the lives of twenty-nine women, ranging in age from fifteen to thirty-three, of diverse ethnic background and social class. She expanded her research by asking how people define moral problems and what experiences they construe as moral conflict in their lives.

29 For example, 'The Generalised and the Concrete Other', in S. Benhabib and D. Cornell, eds., *Feminism as Critique*, Minneapolis MN: Minneapolis University Press, 1988.

30 Janet L. Surrey, in *Work in Progress*, no. 82–02, Wellesley MA: Wellesley College, 1983, in the article entitled 'The Relational Self in Women: Clinical Implications'.

31 Jean Baker Miller, *Towards a New Psychology of Women*, London: Penguin Books, 1988; Nancy Chodorow, *The Reproduction of Mothering: Psychoanalysis and the Sociology of Gender*, Berkeley: University of California, 1978; Sandra Harding, in P. D. Asquith and R. N. Giere, eds., *The Norms of Social Enquiry and Masculine Experience*, vol. 2, East Lancing MI: Philosophy of Science Association, 1980.

32 Garry and Pearsall, *Women, Knowledge and Reality*, p. 60. It is notable that Caroline Whitbeck, in her article 'A Different Reality: Feminist Ontology', pp. 51–76, in Garry and Pearsall does not agree completely with the findings of Chodorow and Harding on the question that it is mothers who pass on dualistic thinking to their sons. Whitbeck claims that to believe that it is mothers who pass on a dualistic understanding of human nature misses the crucial distinction between seeing another as an opposite. People may, in fact, be much more determined

by their network of relationships and practices than by their mothers.

33 Rosi Braidotti, *Nomadic Subjects: Embodiment and Sexual Difference in Contemporary Feminist Theory*, New York: Columbia University Press, 1994.

34 Braidotti's book is an illuminating analysis of a different way of knowing, a different epistemology. The concept of the 'nomadic subject' and the cyclical multi-faceted ways of change are central to this book. Braidotti takes the philosophy of the French philosopher Gilles Deleuze and that of Luce Irigary and shows how one illuminates and critiques the work of the other. It is a radical and challenging book as are her other works, with Braidotti acknowledging that the roots of her feminism are in the French/continental tradition.

35 Braidotti, *Nomadic Subjects*, p. 174.

36 Braidotti in the 'Prologue' of *Nomadic Subjects*, p. 5 makes the following statement: 'I will also stress issues of embodiment ... I will refer to this as "radical immanence". This means I want to think through the body, not in flight away from it. This in turn implies confronting boundaries and limitations. In thinking about the body I refer to the notion of enfleshed materialism ... I have turned to the materialist roots of European philosophy, namely the French tradition that runs from the eighteenth century into Bachelard, Canguilhem, Foucault, Lacan, Irigaray and Deleuze. I call this the "materialism of the flesh" school that gives priority to issues of sexuality, desire and the erotic imaginary ... This continental tradition produces both an alternative vision of the subject and tools of analysis.'

37 Braidotti, *Nomadic Subjects*, p. 63.

38 *Nomadic Subjects*, p. 3.

39 *Nomadic Subjects*, p. 63.

40 Ursula King, 'Women in Dialogue: A New Vision of Ecumenism', *Heythrop Journal*, vol. XXVI, nos. 2 and 7, 1985; Constance F. Parvey, ed., *The Community of Women and Men in the Church: The Sheffield Report*, Geneva: World Council of Churches, 1983.

41 The first hesitant step was taken by Pope Leo XIII in 1893, who although seeing dangers in this developing criticism, recognized that the biblical authors had the scientific vocabulary and outlook of primitive times and so could not be easily invoked in the modern debate about science, reflecting the obvious implications for the whole creation/evolution debate that raged in the nineteenth century. The conflict and misunderstandings of the Modernist movement led to an atmosphere of retrenchment of further historical critique of the Bible. This struggle terminated in the issue of the papal bull *Pascendi*, 1907, which has long been a source of embarrassment to so many scholars.

The effect was a retrenchment in theological and biblical scholarship in the early part of the twentieth century. However, two developments occurred to free the Church from the impasse of these early years. The second enlightened phase began in 1944 when Pius XII published his encyclical *Divino Afflante Spiritu*, with its insistence that there are different literary forms in the Bible. And during Vatican II Pope Paul VI gave the Church's final stamp of approval to the development of understanding of the scriptures in 1964, when through the now established Biblical Commission the papacy approved historical criticism as a tool for research.

42 See the website of John Wijngaards, www.womenpriests.org, for a full account of the rapidly changing theological opinions on women's ordination and his book *The Ordination of Women in the Catholic Church: Unmasking a Cuckoo's Egg Tradition*, London: DLT, 2001.

43 See Raymond E. Brown, *Biblical Exegesis and Church Doctrine*, London: Geoffrey Chapman, 1985, p. 1, for a full understanding of the development of this historical/critical approach.

44 Elisabeth Schüssler Fiorenza, *In Memory of Her: A Feminist Reconstruction of Christian Origins*, New York: Crossroads, 1986.

45 Elisabeth Schüssler Fiorenza, *Bread Not Stone: The Challenge of Feminist Biblical Interpretation*, Boston: Beacon Press, 1984.

46 Fiorenza, *In Memory of Her*, p. xv.

47 Canon 762.

48 Women of all nationalities who spoke at the conference at the end of the Decade of Women at Harare, Zimbabwe, in November 1998, gave clear accounts of the multiple abuse of women by those who held positions in society and churches, among them the custom that young daughters are forced by their fathers to have sex with other men as a part of their culture and/or belief system.

Chapter 4

1 *Kyriarchy*. This term was coined by Elisabeth Schüssler Fiorenza from the Greek word *Kyros* (Lord). *Kyiarchy* is the rule of the emperor/master/lord/father/husband over his subordinates.

2 Gerda Lerner, *The Creation of Feminist Consciousness from the Middle Ages to 1870*, Oxford: Oxford University Press, 1993.

3 Compare the analysis from a South American perspective by Marcella Althaus-Reid, *Indecent Theology: Theological Perversions in Sex, Gender and Politics*, New York: Routledge, 2001. This book, '. . . unique in the field, well written and provocative . . . groundbreaking and wild', according to its blurb, is not for the fainthearted who cannot take

sexual imagery to illustrate the depth of patriarchal hold that has swept into all psyches.

4 Commissioned by BASIC, Brothers and Sisters in Christ, in Ireland, from the Polish artist Poldanski.

Chapter 5

1 Madonna Kolbenschlag, ed., *Women in the Church*, Washington DC: The Pastoral Press, 1987, Chapter 5, 'Women Preaching the Gospel' by Mary Catherine Hilkert. This is a book of talks given at the 1986 conference in Washington on 'Women in the Church', where over 2,500 women and men came together to learn and discuss a way forward on this topic, including Bishop Remi J. De Roo of the Canadian Church.

2 Janice Raymond, *A Passion for Friends: Towards a Philosophy of Female Affection*, London: The Women's Press, 1991, p. 98.

3 Walter M. Abbott SJ, ed., *The Documents of Vatican II*, London and Dublin: Geoffrey Chapman, 1966. *Gaudium et Spes*, no. 16. Italics by the authors.

4 Balasuriya was accused by Rome of denying the uniqueness of Christ by 'relativizing' the incarnation in the light of other non-Christian beliefs. See *Power vs. Conscience: The Excommunication of Fr Tissa Balasuriya OMI*, Hong Kong: Asian Human Rights Commission, 1997.

5 The First International Conference of Women's Ordination Worldwide (WOW), Dublin, Ireland, 29 June–1 July 2001.

6 The conference proceedings were published by Eamonn McCarthy, ed., *Women's Ordination Worldwide: First International Conference – Text and Context. A Celebration of Women's Call to a Renewed Priesthood in the Catholic Church*, Blackrock: Avoca Publishers, 2002. Tapes and a video are also available.

7 Aruna Gnanadason, *No Longer Secret: The Church and Violence Against Women*, Geneva: WCC Publications, 1993; *The Living Letters*, Geneva: WCC Publications, 1997.

8 McCarthy, ed., *Women's Ordination Worldwide*, chapter by Aruna Gnanadason, 'We Will Pour Our Ointment on the Feet of the Church: the Ecumenical Movement and the Ordination of Women', pp. 67–78.

9 McCarthy, ed., *Women's Ordination Worldwide*, Rose Hudson-Wilkin, 'Keynote Address', pp. 15–20.

10 McCarthy, ed., *Women's Ordination Worldwide*, Statement of Sister Christine Vladimiroff, pp. 83–4.

11 This passage is taken from the tape and video of the conference.

12 McCarthy, ed., *Women's Ordination Worldwide*, chapter by Joan Chittister, 'Discipleship for a Priestly People in a Priestless Period', pp. 21–9.

13 As quoted in *The Tablet*, 14 July 2001.

14 Rosemary Radford Ruether, 'A Voice for Women in the Church', in *New Women New Church: Women's Ordination Conference, A Voice for Women in the Church*, (newspaper of Women's Ordination Conference in the USA), Fairfax: WOC National Office, Fall 2001, p. 8.

15 Call to Action is made up of many groups in the USA who have been calling and working for change for over twenty years. It has a very large annual meeting attended by over 2,000 people. The quote is taken from 'Revolution in Boston', in Bill Thompson, ed., *Call to Action*, Chicago: CTA News, May 2002, p. 1, written in response to the paedophilia crisis in the USA.

16 McCarthy, ed., *Women's Ordination Worldwide*, p. 22.

Chapter 6

1 Marie Evans Bouclin has an MA in theology from the Université de Sherbrooke. She is a former nun and teacher who now works as a freelance translator in the areas of theology, ethics and education. She is a member of the executive committee of the Ethics Projects at the University of Sudbury, Ontario, and a member of the national work group for the Catholic Network for Women's Equality, whose mission is to promote the admission of women to ordained ministries within the Church in Canada. Marie is married and the mother of three grown children. She has been appointed Co-ordinator for WOW.

2 At the time of going to press the situation in her home parish was still unresolved. No further Masses are scheduled, a chaplain who is also a priest has not been found.

3 Anne Martin has been a professed member of a religious congregation for many years. She is an educator, who has taught and worked in a pastoral capacity in formal education in schools and colleges in England, Egypt and Chad, as well as informal education in Egypt. She first felt called to priesthood while working in an Egyptian village. She has since had training in theology and spirituality, and worked for a few years as pastoral assistant in a rural parish. She currently teaches in a men's prison and is a counsellor.

4 'Bishops in Crisis Talks Over Shortage of Priests', *The Times*, 25 May 2002, p. 1.

5 Andrea Johnson holds a bachelor's degree from St Mary's College,

Notre Dame, Indiana, and a master's degree in international relations and public diplomacy from the Fletcher School of Law and Diplomacy, Tufts University, Medford, Massachusetts. She has long served as a religious educator, and was for two years the Catholic parish minister in a priestless parish. For four years, she served as director of the Women's Ordination Conference, USA, and is a frequent speaker on the topic of women's ordination. She has been married for over thirty years, and has three grown-up children.

6 Judith McKloskey lives and ministers in Minnesota, USA. She was born in 1946, received a BS in Biology and an MS in Medical Library Science. Judith thrives on starting organizations and projects, and has directed library networks and church organizations. She serves as an occasional preacher in her parish. She often dances her prayer. One of her hobbies is finding and encouraging younger women who hear God's call to priesthood.

7 Mary Hunt, 'Priests, Priests Everywhere and not a Single One Ordained', in *Chrysalis: Women and Religion*, London: Movement for the Ordination of Women, November 1989, pp. 2–3.

8 Mary Ann Rossi received her PhD in Classics from Birkbeck College, University of London. She taught Classics and Women's Studies for twenty-five years at Lawrence University, Appleton, Wisconsin; the University of Wisconsin, Green Bay; Ball State University, Muncie, Indiana; and the City Literary Institute of London. She has lectured widely in the USA and Europe on women in religion and society, and, for the past decade, especially on the ordination of women in the early Church. Her articles and translations may be read on the website www.women-priests.org. The award-winning TV programme *Women's Ordination: the Hidden Tradition* is available from www.womensordination.com.

9 Mircea Eliade, ed., *Encyclopedia of Religion*, New York and London: Macmillan, 1987, vol. 4, p. 162.

10 *Ad Tuendam Fidem* is the name of the Apostolic Letter by John Paul II, 30 June 1998, by which certain norms were inserted into the *Code of Canon Law* and into the *Code of Canons of the Eastern Churches* to protect the faith of the Catholic Church against errors arising from certain members of the Christian faithful. Since it is the Pope's principal duty 'to confirm the brethren in the faith' (Luke 22:32), he considered it absolutely necessary to add to the existing texts of the *Code of Canon Law* and to the *Code of Canons of the Eastern Churches* new norms that expressly impose the obligation of upholding truths proposed in a definitive way by the Magisterium of the Church, and which also establish related canonical sanctions. One of the topics treated regarded the doctrine that priestly ordination is reserved only to men.

11 Judith Herrin, *The Formation of Christendom*, Princeton NJ: Princeton University Press, 1987, pp. 284–8.

12 Giorgio Otranto, 'Note sul sacerdozio femminile nell' antichita in margine a una testimonianza di Gelasio', in *Vetera Christianorum*, 19, 1982, pp. 431–60, transl. Mary Ann Rossi; 'Priesthood, Precedent and Prejudice: On Recovering the Women Priests of Early Christianity', *Journal of Feminist Studies in Religion*, vol. 7, no. 1, Spring 1991, pp. 73–94.

13 C. du Fresne, seigneur Du Cange, *Glossarium ad scriptores mediae et infimae latinitatis*, 4th ed. by Henschel, 7 vols., Paris, 1840–50. Vol. 7 includes a medieval French glossary; vol. 8, *Supplementum*: Dieffenbach, *Novum gloss. latino-germanicum mediae et inf. aetatis*, 1867; C. du Fresne, seigneur Du Cange, *Glossarium ad scriptores mediae et infimae latinitatis*, 5th ed., by Favre, 10 vols., Niort, 1883–87.

14 Otranto, 'Note sul sacerdozio femminile', p. 92.

15 Documents of the Church Fathers, translated by Mary Anne Rossi on the website www.womenpriests.org.

16 As happened on 1 May 2002 and reported in the Catholic press, *The Tablet*, 11 May 2002, p. 45.

17 Sue Williamson has a degree in Sociology from Glasgow University, in Psychology from the University of London and is currently studying theology at Oxford Brookes. She has worked as a teacher in high security prisons. She is a member of various reform groups in the Church.

18 Paolo Freiro, *Pedagogy of the Oppressed*, London: Penguin Books, 1972.

19 Article on Matthew Fox in the *National Catholic Reporter*, 31 May 2002.

20 Ruth Schäfer joined the Medical Missionaries of Mary in 1985, read Theology and Philosophy in Germany and Israel. From 1995–2000 she was employed by the Catholic theological faculty of the Ruhr University in Bochum and from 1995–98 was a lecturer in the Academy of the bishopric in Essen training pastoral workers. Her employment was cut short when she started to speak up for the ordination of women. At present she is writing her PhD on the Letter to the Galatians.

21 The colour purple has now been adopted far more widely than among RC circles in Britain. The Ecumenical Coalition of Women in Ministry and the Society for the Ministry of Women in the Church wear the purple stole in public for calling for equal opportunities in all Churches; for women bishops and rescinding the Act of Synod in the Anglican Church; for gender justice in the Methodist Church; for a free discussion of the ordination of women in the RC Church, as technically RC women are forbidden to even discuss the ordination of women;

lastly for the revival of the diaconate for women in the Orthodox Church.

22 The homily was delivered in Hattingen on 14 May 2000, translation by Dorothea McEwan. See also 'Als Ordensfrau bin ich gewohnt, über meine Berufung zu sprechen ... dieses Training härtet ab und zahlt sich aus', in Ida Raming *et al*, eds., *Zur Priesterin berufen: Gott sieht nicht auf das Geschlecht*, Thaur: Druck und Verlagshaus Thaur, 1998, pp. 225–32.

23 Petronella is a married mother of two sons. She was born into a devout Catholic family and lives in London. She is a Jungian therapist who has also worked for many years in the voluntary sector as a charity director. Her husband Barry is a musician and computer expert.

24 Adrian B. Smith, *A Reason for Living and Hoping: A Christian Appreciation of the Emerging New Era of Consciousness*, London: St Paul's Publishing, 2002, p. 56.

Chapter 7

1 Miriam Therese Winter, *Out of the Depths: The Story of Ludmila Javorova, Ordained Roman Catholic Priest*, New York: The Crossroad Publishing Company, 2001, p. 141.

2 Winter: *Out of the Depths*, p. 68.

3 Winter: *Out of the Depths*, p. 86.

4 These clandestine ordinations had a precedent in Canon Law: Pope Pius XI had given special faculties to bishops which allowed them to consecrate bishops and ordain priests for the survival of the Church, which was heavily persecuted in the Mexican revolution of the 1920s. These legal instruments were also used in Russia and Romania when secret consecrations took place as well as in Czechoslovakia. From 1967 onwards a number of men travelled to Görlitz to be ordained and returned to take up their priestly work.

5 Winter: *Out of the Depths*, p. 100.

6 Winter: *Out of the Depths*, p. 141.

7 Winter: *Out of the Depths*, p. 145.

8 Winter: *Out of the Depths*, p. 184. No date given, 'sometime around 1983' stated on p. 211.

9 Winter: *Out of the Depths*, p. 218.

10 Monica Furlong, *A Dangerous Delight: Women and Power in the Church*, London: SPCK, 1991, p. 95–6.

11 It took until 1992 for the General Synod to take the momentous step of allowing women to be ordained to the priesthood. While this was understood as a gender-inclusive measure, it did not change the

administrative set-up of the Church of England. It simply meant that new personnel could be channelled into old structures.

Chapter 8

1 'Aus erster Hand – Gedanken zur Ausbildung von Frauen für Weiheämter in der röminische-katholischen Kirche', in *JA*, September 2001. This article describes the training programme of women for the ordained ministry in the Church; 'Mit Mut und Zorn', in *Wir sind Priesterinnen. Aus aktuellem Anlass: Die Weihe von Frauen 2002*, Werner Ertel and Gisela Forster, eds., Düsseldorf: Patmos, 2002, pp. 14–19; numerous articles in newspapers, journals and radio and TV programmes.

2 Ida Raming *et al*, eds., *Zur Priesterin berufen: Gott sieht nicht auf das Geschlecht*, Thaur: Druck und Verlagshaus Thaur, 1998, transl. Mary Dittrich for the entry on the website www.womenpriests.org/called/lumetz.htm, p. 2.

3 The five topics were: 1 Building up a Church of partnership. 2 Full equality of women with men. 3 Free choice of lifestyle. 4 Positive attitude towards sexuality. 5 Proclaiming the good news instead of prohibitions.

4 Spirituality: priestly life, spiritual support. Sacramentology: theology, spirituality, importance, meaning, practical help and exercises. Liturgy: preparations, reflection. Function of leader: pastoral work for people of all ages, support in difficult situations, ecumenism, practical skills. Homiletics: introduction, language, practice. Psychology: conflicts, conflict resolution, culture of argument, team and leadership work. Creativity in all areas of pastoral work, sacraments for all senses. History of vocation and personal reflection.

5 Christine acknowledges a great debt to Peter Trummer's book '. . . dass alle eins sind . . .', in *Neue Zugänge zu Eucharistie und Abendmahl*, Düsseldorf: Patmos Verlag, 2001.

6 Veronica Dunne, Kirsten Goa, Carol Connick, Velma FitzGerald and Marie Bouclin, mail to members of the Steering Committee of WOW, 24 March 2002.

7 'Nun Raps Church on Female Priests', *The Universe*, 24 February 2002, p. 5.

8 John Hatfield, mail to members of CWO, 13 March 2002 and 14 March 2002.

9 Christine Mayr-Lumetzberger, mail to Dorothea McEwan, 14 March 2002.

10 From the opening paragraph of the 'Statement regarding the Ordination of Women in Austria', written by Iris Müller and Ida Raming,

handed out at the press conference following the ordinations on 29 June 2002, with slight adaptations in the translation into English by Dorothea McEwan.

11 In military hierarchies, courage in the face of seemingly unsurmountable difficulties is rewarded with the highest military order, in the RC Church it is simply forbidden.

12 Although the real name of 'Augustin Miller' was stated in the press, the bishop never confirmed the reports in the press and specifically asked that his identity be kept secret.

13 Statement dated 13 June 2002, issued by Iris Müller and Ida Raming.

14 Ertel and Forster, eds., *Wir sind Priesterinnen, p. 207.*

15 *Monitum,* 10 July 2002, Rome, signed by Cardinal Joseph Ratzinger and Tarcisio Bertone SDB, Archbishop of Vercelli, Secretary.

Chapter 9

1 Myra Poole, *Prayer, Protest, Power: The Spirituality of Julie Billiart Today,* Chapter 1, 'Women of Protest', London: Canterbury Press, 2001, pp. 9–35.

2 All information on Janice's actions in Washington from communication to the authors, dated 15 November 2001.

3 In November 2002, Janice began a three-month prison sentence for crossing the line at Fort Benning by co-leading a prayer group on to the base singing *Ubi Caritas.*

4 Quote from article in *Ms Magazine,* April/May 1999, pp. 36–9; Pamela Shaeffer, 'On the Edge of Prophecy', in *Uppity Woman,* published bimonthly by Liberty Media for Women, New York.

5 Full details of the outcome of the 'Shadow Synod' are on the website www.we-are-church.org.

6 *New Women New Church, Women's Ordination Conference, A Voice for Women in the Church,* Fairfax: WOC National Office, Fall 2001, p. 8.

7 Quote from press release, October 2001; see We Are Church website, www.we-are-church.org.

8 Communication to authors, 15 November 2001.

9 Mary E. Hunt received her doctorate from the Graduate Theological Union in Berkeley, California, the Masters in Divinity degree from the Jesuit School of Theology at Berkeley and the Masters in Theological Studies from Harvard Divinity School. She is a feminist theologian, who co-founded and co-directs the Women's Alliance for Theology, Ethics and Ritual. She is a prolific writer and member of

the editorial board of the *Journal of Feminist Studies in Religion*, *Journal of Religion and Abuse*, and adviser on women's issues of *Concilium*.

10 Diann Neu, once a member of a Religious Congregation, became a co-founder and co-director of WATER in the USA with Mary Hunt. Diann has a Doctorate in Ministry, a Masters in Divinity and a Masters in Sacred Theology from the Jesuit School of Theology at Berkeley, California. She also has a Masters in Social Work from the Catholic University of America in Washington DC and is licensed as a psychotherapist in Maryland, Washington DC.

11 See the following on this topic: Mary Hunt, *Fierce Tenderness: A Feminist Theology of Friendship*, New York: Crossroads, 1991; Janice Raymond, *A Passion for Friends: Towards a Philosophy of Female Affection*, London: The Women's Press, 1991; Elizabeth Stuart, *Just Good Friends: Towards a Lesbian and Gay Theology of Friendship*, London: Cassell, 1995.

12 Patricia Hunter, 'Women's Power – Women's Passion: And God Said "That's Good" ', in Emile Townes, ed., *A Troubling in My Soul: Womanist Perspectives on Evil and Suffering*, New York: Orbis Books, 1993, p. 194.

13 Hunt, *Fierce Tenderness*, Chapter 6, pp. 143–64.

14 Elisabeth Schüssler Fiorenza and Hermann Häring, eds., *Concilium*, (3), London: SCM Press, 1999. This thought permeates the chapter entitled 'We Women are Church: Roman Catholic Women Shaping Ministries and Theologies', pp. 102–13.

15 Fiorenza and Häring, eds., *Concilium*, p. 2.

16 Fiorenza and Häring, eds., *Concilium*, p. 3.

17 Some of her more recent works are Patricia Beattie Jung, Mary E. Hunt and Radhika Balakrishnan, eds., *We Women Are Church: Roman Catholic Women Shaping Ministries and Theologies*, New Jersey: Rutgers University Press, 2001; 'Catholic Lesbian Feminist Theology', in Patricia Beattie Jung, ed., *Sexual Diversity and Catholicism*, Collegeville MN: Liturgical Press, 2001.

18 This and other prayers and liturgies of Diann Neu are published in *Return Blessings: Ecofeminist Liturgies Renewing the Earth*, Washington DC: WATER, 2003 and *Women's Rites: Feminist Liturgies for Life's Journey*, Cleveland, OH: Pilgrim Press, 2002. The authors thank Diann for permitting a reprint of the prayer.

19 This is one of the most well-known phrases of Fiorenza and can be found interspersed in her work.

20 The following is a list of RC women's ordination groups around the world: USA: Women's Ordination Conference, WOC, 1976; Canada:

Catholic Network For Women's Equality (CNWE), 1981; Britain: Catholic Women's Ordination, CWO, and New Wine, 1993; Australia: Women of the New Covenant and Ordination of Catholic Women, 1993; New Zealand: Catholic Women: Knowing Our Place, 1994; Japan: Phoebe, 2000; South Africa: WOSA, incorporating Women's Ordination and We Are Church, 1996, the numerous Purple Stole groups which are the section of We Are Church that concentrates on women's ordination in Austria, Germany, Holland, France and elsewhere, as well as many individuals in different parts of the world linked to these groups by the worldwide organization Women's Ordination Worldwide, WOW.

21 In 1995 the referendum called 'Kirchenvolksbegehren' with five areas for church reform was signed by one and a half million people within the space of six weeks.

22 The First International Conference on Women's Ordination Worldwide that was held in Dublin, Ireland in 2001; see Chapter 5.

23 The Methodist Church in June 2001 officially adopted the purple stole in solidarity.

24 Their actions are a response to the suffering of many in the Church due to lack of freedom, justice and compassion. In the spirit of Vatican II they demand dialogue to bring about authentic renewal and substantial reform. They are taking steps to achieve these objectives immediately.

The delegates are in solidarity with Christians and organizations in the 'Second' and 'Third' World who fight for a Church engaged in the liberation of women and men.

The first pilgrimage, *'INCONTRO DEL POPOLO DI DIO'*, met in Rome on 11 October 1997, the 35th anniversary of the opening of Vatican II, which made promises to God's people which have not yet been kept. (This declaration was signed by We Are Church groups from the eleven countries.)

Manifesto of the International Movement We Are Church, proclaimed in Rome, 12 October 1997:

Here in Rome, 35 years ago, Pope John XXIII opened the Second Vatican Council. Catholics throughout the world have put great hope on this event: that might result in a more credible Church – free, collegial, poor and a servant.

We need a Church of love, where all are accepted equally.

We need a catholic [i.e. universal] Church, where each person is welcome with his/her life experiences, images of God and longing for community.

We need a Church that affirms God's creation, that acts in a reconciling manner and reflects the unconditional love of Jesus Christ for all humankind.

We need a Church committed to justice and peace, and which puts solidarity with the excluded of the world at the centre of its action.

In the certainty that God's Spirit leads her/his Church in new ways, millions of Christians have supported the Kirchenvolks-Begehren [i.e. Petition, Declaration, Referendum, etc.].

They acknowledged five major concerns:

The building of a Church of brothers and sisters that recognizes the equality of all the baptized, including the inclusion of the People of God in the election of bishops in their local churches.

Equal rights for men and women, including the admission of women to all Church ministries.

Free choice of either a celibate or married life for all those who dedicate themselves to the service of the Church.

A positive attitude toward sexuality, and a recognition of personal conscience in decision-making.

A message of joy and not condemnation, including dialogue, freedom of speech and thought. No anathemas and no exclusion as a means of solving problems, especially as this applies to theologians.

We stand here for all these people. We speak in their name and we declare that we will continue our journey within the Catholic Church.

We have a dream that the Third Millennium will begin with a truly ecumenical Council of all Christian Churches, which will regard each other as equals in their search for peace and friendship among themselves. This will be a Council marked by dialogue and respect for all religions – at the service of the world.

We support the call of the World Council of Churches in launching, in 2000, a process leading to a truly universal Council in the twenty-first century.

Chapter 10

1 Dorothea McEwan, Pat Pinsent, Ianthe Pratt and Veronica Seddon, eds., *Making Liturgy: Creating Rituals for Worship and Life*, London: Canterbury Press, 2001.

2 Brian Wren, *What Language Shall I Borrow?*, London: SCM Press, 1989.

3 Rosi Braidotti, *Metamorphoses Towards a Materialist Theory of Becoming*, Oxford: Polity Press in association with Blackwell Press, 2002, p. 41.

4 Eve Ensler, 'Introduction', *The Vagina Monologues*, London: Virago,

2001, pp. xvii–viii. She writes that in the 1970s she found an obscure history of religious architecture that assumed as fact '. . . the traditional design of most patriarchal buildings of worship imitates the female body. Thus, there is an outer and inner entrance, labia majora and labia minora; a central vagina aisle towards the altar; two curved ovarian structures on either side; and then in the sacred centre, the altar, the womb, where the miracle takes place – where the male gives birth.'

5 Constance F. Parvey, ed., *The Community of Women and Men in the Church: The Sheffield Report*, Geneva: World Council of Churches, 1983.

6 Parvey, ed., *Women and Men in the Church*, pp. 29–42.

7 Parvey, ed., *Women and Men in the Church*, p. 113.

8 Parvey, ed., *Women and Men in the Church*, p. 160.

9 Parvey, ed., *Women and Men in the Church*, p. 161.

10 Parvey, ed., *Women and Men in the Church*, p. 162.

11 A. Lewis, ed., *Motherhood of God*, Edinburgh: St Andrew's Press, 1984. This Church of Scotland report gives a very good introduction to female imagery of the divine and the question of language.

12 *Roman Catholic Catechism*, London: Chapman, 1994.

13 Braidotti, *Metamorphoses*, pp. 268–70.

14 Braidotti, *Metamorphoses*, p. 116.

Afterword

1 John Wijngaards, born 1935, is a Dutch theologian and scripture scholar, who worked in India as a Mill Hill missionary for fourteen years, after which he served as Vicar General of his congregation for six years. He has written twenty-one books and scores of articles. In 1998 he resigned from the active priestly ministry in protest against Rome's refusal to consider the ordination of women to the priesthood.

2 *Inter Insigniores*, 15 October 1976, accompanied by an official commentary; *L'Osservatore Romano*, 27 January 1977, and *Acta Apostolicae Sedis* 69, 1977, pp. 98–116.

3 *Ordinatio Sacerdotalis*, Apostolic Letter on Reserving Priestly Ordination to Men Alone, 22 May 1994; *Origins*, 24, 9 June 1994.

4 *Responsum ad Dubium*, 28 October 1995, concerning the teaching contained in *Ordinatio Sacerdotalis*; *L'Osservatore Romano*, 18 November 1995.

5 T. Angelico, *Taking Stock: Revisioning the Church on Higher Education*, Canberra: National Catholic Education Committee, 1997, p. 20.

6 One of the many responses I received to my website www.women-priests.org (as the other responses recorded in this Afterword).

7 The data have been analyzed by Anthony M. Abela, *Transmitting Values in European Malta*, Malta: Jesuit Publications, 1992; M. Abrams, D. Gerard and N. Timms, eds., *Values and Social Change in Britain*, London: Macmillan, 1985; S. Ashford and N. Timms, *What Europe Thinks: A Study of Western European Values*, Aldershot: Dartmouth, 1992; M. Fogarty, L. Ryan and J. Lee, *Irish Values and Attitudes: The Irish Report of the European Value Systems Study*, Dublin: Dominican Publications, 1984; N. Timms, *Family and Citizenship: Values in Contemporary Britain*, Aldershot: Dartmouth, 1992.

8 Ronald Inglehart has coined the terms 'materialists' and 'post-materialists', but as they are liable to be misunderstood especially in a theological context, I use the more expressive terms 'security seekers' and 'fulfilment seekers'. See Ronald Inglehart, 'The Rise of Postmaterialist Values and Changing Religious Orientations: Gender Roles and Sexual Norms', *International Journal of Public Opinion Research*, 1, 1989, pp. 45–74; Ronald Inglehart, *Culture Shift in Advanced Industrial Society*, Princeton: Princeton University Press, 1990.

9 John Wijngaards, 'God and Our New Selves: Church and Religion Between Secularism and Post-Modernity', *Religioni e Sette nel Mondo*, 4, 1998, pp. 172–93, here pp. 180–3.

10 E. Kennedy, *Tomorrow's Catholics, Yesterday's Church*, New York: Harper & Row, 1988. Kennedy calls them 'Culture I' and 'Culture II'.

11 The breakdown is roughly: 12% definitely external-authority culture, with 18% tending towards it; 35% definitely own-authority culture, with 34% tending towards it.

12 Pro Mundi Vita, *The Roman Catholic Church and Europe*, Bulletin 73, Brussels, 1976.

13 A. E. C. W. Spencer, 'Demography of Catholicism', *The Month*, 8, 1975, pp. 100–5; Pro Mundi Vita, *Aspects of the Roman Catholic Church in England*, Brussels, 1978; M. P. Hornsby-Smith and R. M. Lee, *Roman Catholic Opinion: A Study of Roman Catholics in England and Wales in the 1970s*, Southampton: University of Surrey, 1979; 'Have the British got Religion?', *Now*, 21 December 1979, pp. 22–31; J. H. Leslie, 'Religious Ideology in a North Midlands Parish', essay, University of Surrey, 1979.

14 W. Goddijn, H. Smets and G. Van Thillo, *Opnieuw: God in Nederland*, Amsterdam: De Tijd, 1979; W. Goddijn *et al.*, *Hebben de Kerken nog Toekomst? Commentaar op het Onderzoek Opnieuw: God in Nederland*, Ambo: Baarn 15; J. A. Coleman, *The Evolution of Dutch Catholicism 1958–1974*, Berkeley: University of California, 1978; Kaski, 'De RK Kerk in Nederland 1979/80', *121 Special*, 28 November

1980; J. Wijnen and Th. Koopmanschap, *Hoe Katholiek is Limburg?*, Roermond: De Lijster, 1981.

15 M. Mason, 'The Catholic Church Survey 1996', *Compass Theology Review*, December 1997, pp. 25–31; 'Differing Views on Morality', *The Catholic Leader*, no. 4499, 7 June 1997.

16 D. McLaughlin, *The Beliefs, Values and Practices of Catholic Student Teachers*, Brisbane: Australian Catholic University, 1999; see also D. McLauchlin, *Catholic School Lay Principals: Professional and Pastoral Issues*, Brisbane: Australian Catholic University, 1996.

17 W. V. D'Antonio, *Laity, American and Catholic: Transforming the Church*, Kansas City: Sheed and Ward, 1996; 'The American Catholic Laity', *National Catholic Reporter*, 29 October 1999.

18 'Pope Confirms Tough Birth Control Stance', *National Catholic Reporter*, 15 November 1988.

19 J. Eagan, *Restoration and Renewal: The Church in the Third Millennium*, Kansas City: Sheed and Ward, 1995, p. 346; see also J. Gremillion and J. Castelli, *The Emerging Parish: The Notre Dame Study of Catholic Life Since Vatican II*, San Francisco: Harper and Row, 1987.

20 A detailed Gallup Poll on this question was published in *Catholics Speak Out*, 5–17 May 1992.

21 T. Angelico, *Taking Stock*, p. 19.

22 J. Pieper, *The Catholic Woman: Difficult Choices in a Modern World*, Los Angeles: Lowell House, 1993, p. 74.

23 A. Greeley, *The Catholic Myth: The Behaviour and Belief of American Catholics*, New York: Touchstone, 1990, esp. pp. 90–105.

24 Even weekly Mass attenders say that church authorities are out of touch (49%; all Catholics: 60%). Among Catholics with a college education, only 28% find the teaching authority claimed by the Vatican of importance to the Church (all Catholics: 42%). See note 7 for European Values Studies.

25 E. Kant, 'Was ist Aufklärung?', *Sämmtliche Werke*, Leipzig 1867, vol. 4, p. 159 (freely translated).

26 F. Nietzsche, *Menschliches, Allzumenschliches*, vol. I (1886), Munich: Goldmann, 1962, p. 125 (author's translation), see also pp. 169, 205, 210, and passim.

27 In German: '*Übermensch*' = super human being; not '*Übermann*' = super man.

28 F. Nietzsche, *Zarathustra, Werke II*, Karl Schlechta, ed., Munich: Goldmann 1963, p. 279–80.

29 F. Nietzsche, *Thus Spake Zarathustra*, transl. A. Tille, London: Goldmann, 1933, pp. 253–4.

30 F. Nietzsche, *Thus Spake Zarathustra*, p. 176.

31 A. H. Maslow, *Motivation and Personality*, New York: Harper, 1954; M. Jahoda, *Current Concepts of Positive Mental Health*, New York: Basic Books, 1958; G. W. Allport, *Pattern and Growth in Personality*, London: Holt, Rinehart and Winston, 1963.

32 This has been well worked out by Emmanuel Levinas. See especially his 'Le Moi et la Totalité', *Revue de Métaphysique et de Morale*, 59, 1954, pp. 353–73; 'La Trace de l'Autre', *Tijdschrift voor Filosofie*, 25, 1963, pp. 605–23; *Difficile Liberté: Essais sur le Judaïsme*, Paris: Michel, 1963; *Het Menselijk Gelaat: Essays van Emmanuel Levinas*, Utrecht: Ambo, 1969.

33 J. Macquarrie, *In Search of Humanity: A Theological and Philosophical Approach*, London: SCM Press, 1982, pp. 23–4.

34 G. Pico della Mirandola, *Oration on the Dignity of Man*, Chicago: Regnery, 1960, p. 126.

35 S. Lyonnet, 'Liberty and Law', *The Bridge*, 4, 1962, pp. 229–51.

36 Thomas Aquinas, *Summa Theologica I–II*, q.106, a.1, c.; read also Thomas Aquinas, 'It was necessary for Christ to give us a law of the Spirit, who by producing love within us, could give us life', Commentary on 2 Corinthians, ch. 3, lect. 2.

37 H. Jedin, *Papal Legate at the Council of Trent*, London: Burns and Oates, 1974, p. 562.

38 'The letter that kills denotes any writing that is external to a human being, even the moral precepts such as are contained in the Gospel. Therefore the letter, even of the Gospel, would kill, unless there is the inward presence of the healing grace of faith', Thomas Aquinas, *Summa Theologica I–II*, q.106, a.2, c.; Augustine taught the same in *The Spirit and the Letter*, chs. 14, 17, 19, etc.

39 The American philosopher Ayn Rand has attacked Jesus' vision in her many publications. According to her, Christian charity degrades people because it treats others with patronizing condescension. Rather than speak of love and generosity, we should reaffirm every person's dignity. The only real love is self-love. When we do something for someone else, we do it because we receive an equivalent gift in return. That is the only sound basis for human relationships. A. Rand, 'The Virtue of Selfishness', in A. Rand, *For the New Intellectual*, New York: Signet, 1961. She expresses the same ideas in her novel, *The Fountainhead*, New York: Mayflower, 1962. While Rand is right in criticizing any form of patronizing charity, she overlooks the possibility of a generosity that enriches both the person who gives and who receives.

40 In the Old Testament it is applied to Noah, Abraham and the people of Israel; see Gen. 6:9; 17:1; Deut. 18:13.

41 D. Bonhöffer, *Navolging*, Amsterdam: Kampan, 1964, p. 135; see

also F. Boerwinkel, *Meer dan het gewone*, Baarn: Bosch and Keuning, 1977, esp. pp. 58–70.
42 The arguments are discussed extensively on www.women-priests.org.

Bibliography

Abbott SJ, Walter M., *The Documents of Vatican II*, London and Dublin: Geoffrey Chapman, 1966.

Abela, Anthony M., *Transmitting Values in European Malta*, Malta: Jesuit Publications, 1992.

Abrams, M., D. Gerard, and N. Timms, eds., *Values and Social Change in Britain*, London: Macmillan, 1985.

Allen, John, 'The Counter-Revolution', *The Tablet*, 7 December 2002, pp. 8–9.

Allport, G. W., *Pattern and Growth in Personality*, London: Holt, Rinehart and Winston, 1963.

Althaus-Reid, Marcella, *Indecent Theology: Theological Perversions in Sex, Gender and Politics*, New York: Routledge, 2001.

Angelico, T., *Taking Stock: Revisioning the Church on Higher Education*, Canberra: National Catholic Education Committee, 1997.

Ashford, S., and N. Timms, *What Europe Thinks: A Study of Western European Values*, Aldershot: Dartmouth, 1992.

Asian Human Rights Commission, *Power vs. Conscience: The Excommunication of Fr Tissa Balasuriya OMI*, Hong Kong: Asian Human Rights Commission, 1997.

Beauvoir, Simone de, *The Second Sex*, London: Picador, 1949.

Boerwinkel, F., *Meer dan het gewone*, Baarn: Bosch and Keuning, 1977.

Bonhöffer, D., *Navolging*, Amsterdam: Kampan, 1964.

Boyce-Tillman, June, *Constructing Musical Healing*, London and Philadelphia: Jessica Kingsley, 2000.

Braidotti, Rosi, *Nomadic Subjects: Embodiment and Sexual Difference in Contemporary Feminist Theory*, New York: Columbia University Press, 1994.

Braidotti, Rosi, *Metamorphoses Towards a Materialist Theory of Becoming*, Oxford: Polity Press in association with Blackwell Press, 2002.

Brown, Raymond E., *The Churches the Apostles Left Behind*, New York: Paulist Press, 1984.

Brown, Raymond E., *Biblical Exegesis and Church Doctrine*, London: Geoffrey Chapman, 1985.

Cameron, Deborah, *Feminism and Linguistic Theory*, London: Macmillan Press, 1985.

Chittister, Joan, 'Discipleship for a Priestly People in a Priestless Period', in McCarthy, ed., *Women's Ordination Worldwide*, pp. 21–9,

Chodorow, Nancy, *The Reproduction of Mothering: Psychoanalysis and the Sociology of Gender*, Berkeley: University of California, 1978.

Coleman, J. A., *The Evolution of Dutch Catholicism 1958–1974*, Berkeley: University of California, 1978.

Collins, Paul, *Papal Power: A Proposal For Change in Catholicism's Third Millennium*, London: Harper and Collins, Fount Paperbacks, 1997.

Congar, Yves, *Power, Poverty in the Church*, London: SCM Press, 1964.

Cooke, B., *Ministry to Word and Sacrament*, Philadelphia: Fortis Press, 1976.

Crosby, Michael H., *The Dysfunctional Church: Addiction and Co-dependency in the Family of Catholicism*, Notre Dame Indiana: Ave Maria Press, 1991.

Daly, Mary, *Beyond God the Father*, Boston: Beacon Press, 1973.

Daly, Mary, *Outercourse: The Be-Dazzling Voyage*, London: The Women's Press, 1993.

D'Antonio, W. V., *Laity, American and Catholic: Transforming the Church*, Kansas City: Sheed and Ward, 1996.

The Downside Review, 'Abbot Butler and the Council', papers given at a symposium at Heythrop College, London, 12 October 2002, Bath: Downside Press, 2003.

Dulles, Avery, *Models of the Church*, New York: Doubleday, 1978.

Eagan, J., *Restoration and Renewal: The Church in the Third Millennium*, Kansas City: Sheed and Ward, 1995.

Eisenstein, Hester, *Contemporary Feminist Thought*, London: Unwin Paperbacks, 1984.

Eliade, Mircea, ed., *Encyclopedia of Religion*, vol. 4, New York and London: Macmillan, 1987.

Ensler, Eve, *The Vagina Monologues*, London: Virago, 2001.

Ertel, Werner and Gisela Forster, eds., *Wir sind Priesterinnen. Aus aktuellem Anlass: Die Weihe von Frauen 2002*, Düsseldorf: Patmos, 2002.

Field, Belenky Mary, Blythe McVicker Clinchy, Nancy Rule Goldberger and Jill Mattuck Tarule, *Women's Ways of Knowing: The Development of Self, Voice and Mind*, New York: Basic Books, 1986.

Fiorenza, Elisabeth Schüssler, *Bread Not Stone: The Challenge of Feminist Biblical Interpretation*, Boston: Beacon Press, 1984.

Fiorenza, Elisabeth Schüssler, *In Memory of Her: A Feminist Reconstruction of Christian Origins*, New York: Crossroads, 1986.

Fiorenza, Elisabeth Schüssler, *Jesus: Miriam's Child, Sophia's Prophet: Critical Issues in Feminist Christology*, London: SCM Press, 1995.

Fiorenza, Elisabeth Schüssler and Hermann Häring, eds., *Concilium*, (3), London: SCM Press, 1999.

Firestone, Shulamith, *The Dialectic of Sex: The Case for Feminist Revolution*, New York: Bantam Books, 1970.

Fogarty, M., L. Ryan and J. Lee, *Irish Values and Attitudes: The Irish Report of the European Value Systems Study*, Dublin: Dominican Publications, 1984.

Freedman, Jane, *Feminism*, Buckingham: Open University Press, 2001.

Freire, Paolo, *Pedagogy of the Oppressed*, London: Penguin Books, 1972.

Fresne, C. du, seigneur Du Cange, *Glossarium ad scriptores mediae et infimae latinitatis*, 4th ed. by Henschel, 7 vols, Paris, 1840–50. Vol. 7 includes a medieval French glossary; vol. 8, *Supplementum*: Dieffenbach, *Novum gloss. latimo-germanicum mediae et inf. aetatis*, 1867; C. du Fresne, seigneur Du Cange, *Glossarium ad scriptores mediae et infimae latinitatis*, 5th ed. by Favre, 10 vols, Niort, 1883–87.

Furlong, Monica, *A Dangerous Delight: Women and Power in the Church*, London: SPCK, 1991.

Garry, Ann, and Marilyn Pearsall, *Women, Knowledge and Reality: Explorations in Feminist Philosophy*, Boston MA: Unwin Hyman, 1989.

Gilligan, Carol, *In A Different Voice: Psychological Theory and Women's Development*, Harvard: Harvard University Press, 1982.

Gilligan, Carol, 'The Generalised and the Concrete Other', in S.

Benhabib and D. Cornell, eds., *Feminism as Critique*, Minneapolis MN: Minneapolis University Press, 1988.

Gnanadason, Aruna, ed., *No Longer Secret: The Church and Violence Against Women*, Geneva: WCC Publications, 1993.

Gnanadason, Aruna, *Living Letters: A Report of Visits to the Churches during the Ecumenical Decade – Churches in Solidarity with Women*, Geneva: WCC Publications, 1997.

Gnanadason, Aruna, 'We Will Pour Our Ointment on the Feet of the Church: The Ecumenical Movement and the Ordination of Women', in McCarthy, *Women's Ordination Worldwide*, pp. 67–78.

Goddijn, W., H. Smets and G. Van Thillo, *Opnieuw: God in Nederland*, Amsterdam: De Tijd, 1979.

Goddijn, W., *et al.*, *Hebben de Kerken nog Toekomst? Commentaar op het Onderzoek Opnieuw: God in Nederland*, Ambo: Baarn 15.

Greeley, A., *The Catholic Myth: The Behaviour and Belief of American Catholics*, New York: Touchstone, 1990.

Greer, Germaine, *The Female Eunuch*, London: Harper and Collins, 1999.

Gremillion, J., and J. Castelli, *The Emerging Parish: The Notre Dame Study of Catholic Life Since Vatican II*, San Francisco: Harper and Row, 1987.

Harding, Sandra, in P. D. Asquith and R. N. Giere, eds., *The Norms of Social Enquiry and Masculine Experience*, vol. 2, East Lancing MI: Philosophy of Science Association, 1981.

Haskins, Susan, *Mary Magdalen: Myth and Metaphor*, London: Harper Collins, 1993.

Hebblethwaite, Peter, *The Runaway Church*, London: Collins Paperback, 1978.

Herrin, Judith, *The Formation of Christendom*, Princeton NJ: Princeton University Press, 1987.

Hilkert, Mary Catherine, 'Women Preaching the Gospel', in M. Kolbenschlag, *Women in the Church*.

hooks, bell, *Ain't I a Woman*, Boston MA: South End Press, 1981.

hooks, bell, *Feminist Theory from Margin to Centre*, Boston MA: South End Press, 1984.

Hopkins, Julie, *Towards a Feminist Christology*, The Netherlands: Kok Pharos, 1995.

Hornsby-Smith, M. P., and R. M. Lee, *Roman Catholic Opinion: A Study of Roman Catholics in England and Wales in the 1970s*, Southampton: University of Surrey, 1979.

Hornsby-Smith, M. P., and R. M. Lee, 'Have the British got Religion?', *Now*, 21 December 1979, pp. 22–31.

Hudson-Wilkin, Rose, 'Keynote Address', in McCarthy, ed., *Women's Ordination Worldwide*, pp. 15–20.

Hufton, Olwen, *The Poor of Eighteenth Century France*, Oxford: Oxford University Press, 1974.

Hunt, Mary, 'Priests, Priests Everywhere and not a Single One Ordained', *Chrysalis: Women and Religion*, London: Movement for the Ordination of Women, November 1989, pp. 2–3.

Hunt, Mary, *Fierce Tenderness: A Feminist Theology of Friendship*, New York: Crossroads, 1991.

Hunt, Mary, 'We Women Are Church', *Concilium*, (3), London: SCM Press, 1993, p. 105.

Hunter, Patricia, in Emile Townes, ed., *A Troubling in my Soul: Womanist Perspectives On Evil and Suffering*, New York: Orbis Books, 1993.

Inglehart, Ronald, 'The Rise of Postmaterialist Values and Changing Religious Orientations: Gender Roles and Sexual Norms', *International Journal of Public Opinion Research*, 1, 1989, pp. 45–74.

Inglehart, Ronald, *Culture Shift in Advanced Industrial Society*, Princeton: Princeton University Press, 1990.

Irigaray, Luce, *Speculum: De l'autre femme*, Paris: Minuit, 1974.

Jahoda, M., *Current Concepts of Positive Mental Health*, New York: Basic Books, 1958.

Jedin, H., *Papal Legate at the Council of Trent*, London: Burns and Oates, 1974.

Kant, E., 'Was ist Aufklärung?', *Sämmtliche Werke*, vol. 4, Leipzig, 1867.

Kaski, 'De RK Kerk in Nederland 1979/80', *121 Special*, 28 November 1980.

Kennedy, E., *Tomorrow's Catholics, Yesterday's Church*, New York: Harper & Row, 1988.

King, Ursula, 'Women in Dialogue: A New Vision of Ecumenism', *Heythrop Journal*, vol. XXVI, nos. 2 and 7, 1985.

Kolbenschlag, Madonna, ed., *Women in the Church*, Washington DC: The Pastoral Press, 1987.

Komonchak, Joseph A., Mary Collins and Dermot A. Lane, eds., *New Dictionary of Theology*, Dublin: Gill and Macmillan, 1987.

Lane, Dermot, *Foundations for a Social Theology: Praxis, Process and Salvation*, Dublin: Gill and Macmillan, 1984.

Levinas, Emmanuel, 'Le Moi et la Totalité', *Revue de Métaphysique et de Morale*, 59, 1954, pp. 353–73; 'La Trace de l'Autre', *Tijdschrift voor Filosofie*, 25, 1963, pp. 605–23; *Difficile Liberté: Essais sur le Judaïsme*, Paris: Michel, 1963; *Het Menselijk Gelaat: Essays van Emmanuel Levinas*, Utrecht: Ambo, 1969.

Lewis, A., ed., *Motherhood of God*, Edinburgh: St Andrew's Press, 1984.

Lorde, Audrey, *Sister Outsider: Essays and Speeches*, New York and Trumansberg: Crossing Press, 1984.

Lyonnet, S., 'Liberty and Law', *The Bridge*, 4, 1962, pp. 229–51.

Macquarrie, J., *In Search of Humanity: A Theological and Philosophical Approach*, London: SCM Press, 1982.

Maslow, A. H., *Motivation and Personality*, New York: Harper, 1954.

Mason, M., 'The Catholic Church Survey 1996', *Compass Theology Review*, December 1997, pp. 25–31; 'Differing Views on Morality', *The Catholic Leader*, no. 4499, 7 June 1997.

Mayr-Lumetzberger, Christine, 'Aus erster Hand – Gedanken zur Ausbildung von Frauen für Weiheämter in der römisch-katholischen Kirche', in *JA*, Haugsdorf, September 2001.

Mayr-Lumetzberger, 'Mit Mut und Zorn', in Ertland Forster, eds., *Wir sind Priesterinnen*.

McCarthy, Eamonn, ed., *Women's Ordination Worldwide: First International Conference – Text and Context: A Celebration of Women's Call to a Renewed Priesthood in the Catholic Church*, Blackrock: Avoca Publishers, 2002.

McEwan, Dorothea, Pat Pinsent, Ianthe Pratt and Veronica Seddon, eds., *Making Liturgy: Creating Rituals for Worship and Life*, London: Canterbury Press, 2001.

McLaughin, D., *Catholic School Lay Principals: Professional and Pastoral Issues*, Brisbane: Australian Catholic University, 1996.

McLaughlin, D., *The Beliefs, Values and Practices of Catholic Student Teachers*, Brisbane: Australian Catholic University, 1999.

Miller, Jean Baker, *Towards a New Psychology of Women*, London: Penguin Books, 1988.

Mitchell, Juliet, *Woman's Estate*, Harmondsworth: Penguin Books, 1973.

Moltmann-Wendel, Elisabeth, *The Women Around Jesus*, London: SCM Press, 1982.

Morgan, Robin, ed., *Sisterhood is Global*, Harmondsworth: Penguin Books, 1984.

Murphy, Desmond, *A Return to Spirit: After the Mythic Church*, Dublin: Gill and Macmillan, 1997.

National Catholic Reporter, 'The American Catholic Laity', 29 October 1999; 'Pope Confirms Tough Birth Control Stance', 15 November 1988.

Navarro-Valls, Joaquin, quoted in *The Tablet*, 14 July 2001.

Neu, Diann, 'Catholic Lesbian Feminist Theology', in Patricia Beattie Jung, ed., *Sexual Diversity and Catholicism*, Collegeville MN: Liturgical Press, 2001.

Neu, Diann, in *We Women Are Church: Roman Catholic Women Shaping Ministries and Theologies*, Patricia Beattie Jung, Mary E. Hunt, Radhika Balakrishnan, eds., New Jersey: Rutgers University Press, 2001.

Neu, Diann, *Women's Rites: Feminist Liturgies for Life's Journey*, Cleveland OH: Pilgrim Press, 2002.

Neu, Diann, *Return Blessings: Ecofeminist Liturgies Renewing the Earth*, Washington: WATER, 2003.

Nietzsche, F., *Menschliches, Allzumenschliches*, vol. I (1886), Munich: Goldmann, 1962.

Nietzsche, F., *Zarathustra, Werke II*, Karl Schlechta, ed., Munich: Goldmann, 1963.

Nietzsche, F., *Thus Spake Zarathustra*, transl. A. Tille, London: Goldmann, 1933.

Otranto, Giorgio, 'Note sul sacerdozio femminile nell' antichita in margine a una testimonianza di Gelasio', in *Vetera Christianorum*, 1982, pp. 431–60, transl. Mary Ann Rossi.

Otranto, Giorgio, 'Priesthood, Precedent and Prejudice: On Recovering the Women Priests of Early Christianity', *Journal of Feminist Studies in Religion* vol. 7, no. 1, Spring 1991, 73–94, 19.

Parvey, Constance F., ed., *The Community of Women and Men in the Church: The Sheffield Report*, Geneva: World Council of Churches, 1983.

Pico della Mirandola, G., *Oration on the Dignity of Man*, Chicago: Regnery, 1960.

Pieper, J., *The Catholic Woman: Difficult Choices in a Modern World*, Los Angeles: Lowell House, 1993.

de Pisan, Christine, *The City of Women*, 1404.

Poole, Myra, *Prayer, Protest, Power: The Spirituality of Julie Billiart Today*, London: Canterbury Press, 2001.

Pro Mundi Vita, *The Roman Catholic Church and Europe*, Brussels, 1976.

Pro Mundi Vita, *Aspects of the Roman Catholic Church in England*, Brussels, 1978.

Raban, Jonathan, 'My Holy War', *The New Yorker*, 4 February 2002, p. 31.

Raming, Ida *et al*, eds., *Zur Priesterin berufen: Gott sieht nicht auf das Geschlecht*, Thaur: Druck und Verlagshaus Thaur, 1998, transl. Mary Dittrich for the entry on the website www.womenpriests.org/called/lumetz.htm.

Rand, A., *The Fountainhead*, New York: Mayflower, 1962.

Raymond, Janice, *A Passion for Friends: Towards a Philosophy of Female Affection*, London: The Women's Press, 1991.

Ricci, Carla, *Mary Magdalen and Many Others: Women Who Followed Jesus*, Tunbridge Wells: Burns and Oates, 1994.

Rich, Adrienne, *Of Woman Born: Motherhood as Experience and Institution*, New York: W. W. Norton, 1976.

Rich, Adrienne, *The Dream of a Common Language: Poems 1974–1977*, New York and London: W. W. Norton, 1978.

Roman Catholic Catechism, London, Chapman, 1994.

Rossi, Mary Ann, 'The Legitimation of the Abuse of Women in Christianity', *Feminist Theology*, no. 4, Sheffield: Sheffield Academic Press, 1993, pp. 57–63.

Ruether, Rosemary Radford, *Sexism and God-Talk: Toward a Feminist Theology*, Boston MA: Beacon Press, 1983.

Ruether, Rosemary Radford, *Women-Church*, Boston MA: Beacon Press, 1995.

Ruether, Rosemary Radford, *Introducing Redemption in Christian Theology*, Sheffield: Sheffield Academic Press, 1998.

Ruether, Rosemary Radford, 'Reflections on Joan Chittister's Decision to Speak', in *New Women New Church: Women's Ordination Conference, A Voice for Women in the Church*, Fairfax: WOC National Office, Fall 2001.

Schäfer, Ruth, 'Als Ordensfrau bin ich gewohnt, über meine Berufung zu sprechen . . . dieses Training härtet ab und zahlt sich aus', in Ida Raming *et al*., eds., *Zur Priesterin berufen: Gott sieht nicht auf das Geschlecht*, pp. 225–32.

Shaeffer, Pamela, 'On the Edge of Prophecy', in *Uppity Woman*, published bimonthly by Liberty Media for Women, New York.

Schillebeeckx, E., *Ministry*, London: SCM Press, 1981.

Schneiders IHM, Sandra, *Beyond Patching: Faith and Feminism in the Catholic Church*, New York: Paulist Press, 1991.

Smith, Adrian B., *A Reason for Living and Hoping: A Christian Appreciation of the Emerging New Era of Consciousness*, London: St Paul's Publishing, 2002.

Spencer, A. E. C. W., 'Demography of Catholicism', *The Month*, 8, 1975, pp. 100–5.

Spender, Dale, *Man Made Language*, London and New York: Routledge and Kegan Paul, 1980.

Spender, Dale, *Women of Ideas and What Men Have Done to Them*, London: Pandora, 1988.

Stimpson, Catherine R., ed., *Women, History and Theory: The Essays of Joan Kelly*, Chicago and London: University of Chicago Press, 1984.

Stuart, Elizabeth, *Just Good Friends: Towards a Lesbian and Gay Theology of Friendship*, London: Cassell, 1995.

Surrey, Janet L., 'The Relational Self in Women: Clinical Implications', in *Work in Progress*, no. 82–02, Wellesley MA: Wellesley College, 1983.

Thistlethwaite, Susan, ed., *White Women's Christ and Black Women's Jesus: Feminist Christology and a Womanist Response*, Atlanta GA: Scholars Press, 1989.

Thompson, Bill, (ed.), 'Revolution in Boston', *Call to Action*, May 2002.

'Bishops in Crisis Talks Over Shortage of Priests', *The Times*, 25 May 2002, p. 1.

Timms, N., *Family and Citizenship: Values in Contemporary Britain*, Aldershot: Dartmouth, 1992.

Toffler, Alvin, *Future Shock*, USA: Amazon, Mass Market Publications, 2003.

Tong, Rosemarie, *Feminist Thought: A Comprehensive Introduction*, London: Routledge, 1992.

Trummer, Peter, '...dass alle eins sind...', in *Neue Zugänge zu Eucharistie und Abendmahl*, Düsseldorf: Patmos Verlag, 2001.

'Nun Raps Church on Female Priests', *The Universe*, 24 February 2002, p. 5.

Vladimiroff OB, Christine, 'Statement', in McCarthy, ed., *Women's Ordination Worldwide*, pp. 83–4.

Walker Bynum, Carol, *Jesus as Mother: Studies in the Spirituality of the High Middle Ages*, Berkeley, Los Angeles and London: University of California Press, 1984.

Watson, Natalie K., *Introducing Feminist Ecclesiology*, Sheffield: Sheffield Academic Press, 2003.

Weaver, Mary Jo, *New Catholic Women: A Contemporary Challenge to Traditional Religious Authority*, San Francisco: Harper and Row, 1985.

Whitbeck, Caroline, 'A Different Reality: Feminist Ontology', in Garry and Pearsall, *Women, Knowledge and Reality*, pp. 51–76.

Wijnen, J., and Th. Koopmanschap, *Hoe Katholiek is Limburg?*, Roermond: De Lijster, 1981.

Wijngaards, John, 'God and Our New Selves: Church and Religion Between Secularism and Post-Modernity', *Religioni e Sette nel Mondo*, 4, Bologna: Gris, 1998.

Wijngaards, John, *The Ordination of Women in the Catholic Church: Unmasking a Cuckoo's Egg Tradition*, London: DLT, 2001.

Winkett, Lucy, 'Mary Magdalene: Apostle to the Apostles', an address delivered at the Go Tell! Celebration of Christian Women, July 2000, London: Churches Together in Britain and Ireland, 2000.

Winter, Miriam Therese, *Out of the Depths: The Story of Ludmila Javorova, Ordained Roman Catholic Priest*, New York: Crossroads, 2001.

Worden, Peter, *The Tablet*, 4 January 2003.

Wren, Brian, *What Language Shall I Borrow?*, London: SCM Press, 1989.

Papal Documents

Ad Tuendam Fidem, 'To Defend the Faith', John Paul II, 30 June 1998.

Humanae Vitae, 'On Human Life', 25 July 1968.

Inter Insigniores, 'On Reserving Priestly Ordination to Men Alone', 15 October 1976, accompanied by an official commentary; *L'Osservatore Romano*, 27 January 1977, and *Acta Apostolicae Sedis* 69, 1977, pp. 98–116.

Instruction on the Ecclesial Vocation of the Theologian, 24 May 1990.

Mulieres Dignitatem: 'On the Dignity and Vocation of Women on the Occasion of the Marian Year'*, by Pope John Paul II, 6 October 1988.

Ordinatio Sacerdotalis, 'On Reserving Priestly Ordination to Men Alone', 22 May 1994, *Origins*, 24, 9 June 1994.

Responsum ad Dubium, 28 October 1995, concerning the teaching

contained in *Ordinatio Sacerdotalis*, Cardinal Ratzinger's commentary on Pope John Paul II's Apostolic Letter *L'Osservatore Romano*, 18 November 1995.
(Full texts available on www.womenpriests.org)